Dissecting the Mundane

International Perspectives on Memory-work

Edited by Adrienne E. Hyle, Margaret S. Ewing, Diane Montgomery, and Judith S. Kaufman

University Press of America,® Inc.

Lanham · Boulder · New York · Toronto · Plymouth, UK

University Press of America
4501 Forbes Boulevard
Suite 200
Lanham, Maryland 20706
UPA Acquisitions Department (301) 459-3366

Estover Road
Plymouth PL6 7PY
United Kingdom

Library of Congress Control Number: 2008931034
ISBN-13: 978-0-7618-4116-6 (paperback : alk. paper)
ISBN-10: 0-7618-4116-4 (paperback : alk. paper)
eISBN-13: 978-0-7618-4229-3
eISBN-10: 0-7618-4229-2

Table of Contents

Part Three   Dissecting the Mundane

Preface

At the time we began this project, we felt intellectually isolated to one degree or another. In search of an intellectual and emotional community of colleagues, Judy convened our group with the prospect of engaging in some radically different research. We were willing to take intellectual risks, cross disciplinary boundaries, and challenge our belief systems. We were also willing to eschew the immediate academic payoffs of publications presentations, and grants. We began this project in 1994. (Kaufman, Ewing, Montgomery, Hyle & Self, 2003, p. 1)

These words describe our coming together as a work group and they describe challenges taken on by every contributor to this volume. The work collected here stands as evidence for the years we all have dedicated to the method and it demonstrates the richness and variety of research produced using memory-work methods.

This method allows individuals opportunities to develop their own communities of like-minded intellectuals and reflective participants. Breadth of knowledge and openness to alternative and multiple knowledge bases are essential to develop the cross-disciplinary perspectives possible using the method. We have learned from our diverse collective and appreciate the greater diversity of perspectives unearthed by memory-work in comparison with other methods we use. We read broadly and think critically and openly across our memories.

The utility of the method is evident from the variety of ways in which it has been used, as illustrated in the work that is reported here. In addition to its use as a research method, many of us use it as a tool to enrich our teaching, which for some includes the preparation of teachers.

This method requires hard work. In fact, one of our book chapters is titled "The Hard Work of Remembering" (Ewing, Hyle, Kaufman, Montgomery & Self, 1999). Much of this work was face-to-face; some questions were best asked in person or only became evident when we were together. Writing collectively is one of the most difficult yet rewarding experiences associated with our implementation of the method. Wine, good food and lots of hospitality were required and offered freely. We've taken the group to New York and often met in each other's homes.

This is a social method. Being open and listening well are essential. Friendships and close working relationships have grown among us. We are now tenured, promoted, married or partnered. One moved; one retired; some are grandmothers, and all of us are older. Our memory-work collective has become an important part of our academic lives. Memory-work has helped us grow and understand our realities and those of others.

To the authors of the following chapters, we extend our gratitude for this opportunity to work with you and your work. To those of you just becoming interested in memory-work, we hope you have as good and productive an experience as we have had.

The Editors
Stillwater, Oklahoma
Hempstead, New York
January 25, 2008

References

Ewing, Margaret S., Hyle, Adrienne E., Kaufman, Judith S., Montgomery, Diane M. & Self, Patricia A. (1999). The hard work of remembering: Memory work as narrative research. In Joanne Addison & Sharon J. McGee (eds.), *Feminist empirical research: Emerging perspectives on qualitative and teacher research* (pp. 112-126). New York: Heinemann/Boyton Cook.

Kaufman, Judith S.; Ewing, Margaret S.; Montgomery, Diane M. Hyle, Adrienne E. & Self, Patricia A. (2003). *From girls in their elements to women in science: Rethinking socialization through memory-work.* New York: Peter Lang.

Part One

Introduction

Chapter 1

Philosophy and Overview of Memory-work

Judith S. Kaufman, Margaret S. Ewing, Diane Montgomery and Adrienne E. Hyle

We live, but why do we live? I think: to become more human: more capable of reading the world, more capable of playing it in all ways. This does not mean nicer or more humanistic. I would say: more faithful to what we are made from and what we can create. Helene Cixous and Mireille Calle-Gruber. (1997, p. 30)

The method of memory-work

Memory-work was developed by a group of German women who formed the *Frauenformen* collective in the late 1970s. They were an editorial group that formed within *Das Argument*, a Marxist journal originally launched in 1959, with the goal of bringing together their work in the Women's Movement with their work on the journal. Their reference point is Marxism, and their stated aim is to "inscribe feminism into the Marxist framework" (Haug[1], 1987, p. 23). Memory-work was developed for a writing and research project focused on women's socialization. The collective was dissatisfied with then current theories of socialization coming out of the disciplines of sociology and psychology. They felt that both disciplines neglected discussions of girls' socialization, and when they did include girls, they were treated as objects of various socializing agents acting on them and forcing them to take on particular roles. The question of how individuals appropriate certain ways of behaving or how they learn to develop one set of needs as opposed to another is neglected (Haug, 1987). As Haug notes, these theories never address the "existential afflictions and obstacles" (p. 24) faced by girls as they grow into womanhood. In *Female sexualization: A collective work of memory*, Frigga Haug describes the collective's attempts to analyze women's socialization by writing stories out of their own personal memories; "stories within which socialization comes to appear as a process of sexualization of the female body" (p. 13). The collective used the method termed "memory-work," derived from Haug's theory of socialization, "as a bridge to span the gap between 'theory' and 'experience'" (p. 14). They used personal memories related to love, marriage, happiness, and the desire for children to study various forms of feminine socialization. They also studied various parts of the female body such as legs or body hair and how they come to be sexualized.

Crawford, Kippax, Onyx, Gault and Benton (1992) were excited about the potential of memory-work after Haug spent some time at Macquarie University in Sydney, Australia. Using memory-work, they embarked on a study of the social construction of emotion and modified and refined the method over the four-year duration of the study. They were much more explicit than Haug in describing the method and researchers who use the method most often turn to Crawford et al.'s description. Relying on most of the injunctions developed by Haug's collective (1987), they describe at least three primary phases of memory-work. The first involves the writing and collection of memories according to a set of specific rules. Each member writes her earliest memory of a particular episode, action or event. The memory is written in the third person with as much detail as possible, including trivial and sensory components. At all times, interpretation, explanation or biography should be avoided (Crawford et al., 1992).

The second phase involves collective discussion and analysis of the memories. Each member expresses opinions and ideas about each memory in turn. All consider differences and commonalities or continuous elements across the memories. Autobiography and biography are avoided because they shift the focus from an analysis of social meanings to an analysis of the individual. This is important to keep in mind because the focus on social meaning sets memory-work apart from therapy. Nevertheless, memory-work can be therapeutic in the sense that as you begin to understand how you have been socialized, you can begin to free yourself from oppressive forms of socialization. Although, memory-work involves understanding the social construction of self, the meaning generated moves well beyond the individual. As Haug (1987) notes:

> Human beings produce their lives collectively. It is within the domain of collective production that individual experience becomes possible. If therefore a given experience is possible, it is also subject to universalization. What we perceive as "personal" ways of adapting to the social are also potentially generalizable modes of appropriation. (p. 44)

Schratz and Walker (1995) argue that memory work aims to "close the gaps between theory and experience in ways that are intended to change the nature of experience, not simply to accept it" (p. 41). Therapy is sometimes meant to help an individual change so she or he can cope or adjust to some set of social demands—the social is accepted as a given. In memory-work, the social is scrutinized and critiqued and the insights gained from understanding how members have appropriated social structures can be used to loosen the restraints of those structures. This is memory-work's connection with political and social action. Schratz and Walker (1995) point out that the tension in memory-work arises in the duality between, on the one hand, the role that memories play in socialization and social control and, on the other hand, the persistent potential those same memories have to undermine that control.

In addition to the activities already mentioned for the second phase of memory-work, members also identify clichés, generalizations, contradictions, cultural imperatives and metaphors, and discuss theories, popular conceptions, sayings and images about the topic. Finally, each member examines what is not written in the memories (but what might be expected), and rewrites her own memories given this review and analysis. Like Crawford et al. (1992) we did not find rewriting to be particularly productive. However, after we had finished generating memories and engaged in analysis and theorizing, we selected several memories for rewriting. The memories selected were ones that were particularly compelling and evocative for the collective.

The third phase involves reappraisal of the memories and analysis within the context of a broader range of theories. All the memories across different cue words (e.g., air, earth, and water) generated by the collective are compared and contrasted. Earlier theories are reevaluated in light of later theorizing and these revised theories are examined in light of particular theoretical positions and commonsense understandings. New understandings are recursively used to reappraise initial analyses of the memories. Referring back to the injunction to avoid autobiography, the rules facilitate writing a description of an event as opposed to an abstraction or summary of an event, something that is easier to accomplish in the third person. These rules challenge the urge to interpret and justify, resulting in the writing of a memory that is open to subsequent or concurrent analysis.

Philosophy of memory-work

Memory-work is an endeavor undertaken by a collective of individuals, or epistemologists, if you will, who are seeking to answer the question, "how do we come to know the world?" These individuals are not seeking an answer to this question in an ontological sense. They are not looking for essential ways of seeing, thinking and feeling. They are not looking for theoretical structures of the mind that may explain the way that we organize what we come to know. They are, as Helene Cixous observes in the passage which opens the chapter, trying to become better at reading the world and more capable of reading it for multiple meanings.

Memory-workers understand that the way we come to know and what we come to know is shaped by relationship and power. We come to know the world through interactions with others. What we know and how we know it are formed in the space where discourse and the contents of that discourse are shaped by the values of those who hold power in that community and culture. We are rarely aware of this process. As children, we generally do not step back and consider what we know and how we know it. Our caretakers put us in particular spaces, place objects within our reach, draw our attention with ideas and feelings and we participate and reproduce that which is valued. We become familiar with our spaces, come to know objects, and gradually, through increasing participation our ideas begin to meld into and shape the discourse that has shaped us. This is a process arising out of social interaction and thus shared or collective ways of being emerge as we participate in the discursive practices of our local communities and the dominant culture.

Because most of us live in communities that are subject to the influence of a dominant culture, we often participate in and are shaped by value systems that are defined by hierarchy, inequality, and injustice. A group that holds dominance in a culture maintains its power through marginalization, oppression, and by convincing the masses that it deserves its power while the "other" does not. These value systems seep into our communities and into our consciousness and shape the ways that we see the world. We are immersed in racism, sexism, and classism; in short, we are immersed in beliefs that serve the interests of those in power and function to maintain that power. If we have been part of any of the various movements that have attempted to counter these value systems, then we have done some personal as well as political work to unlearn, for example, racism. However, if we take seriously the idea that all of what we know results from our participation in community and the dominant culture, then all of our beliefs, all of what we know, is subject to critical scrutiny. Thus, in referring back to the question, "How do we come to know the world?" the memory-work collective scrutinizes the ways in which the discursive practices of a community influence the ways of being that we experience (Davies, 2000).

The questions of how we come to know and how the prevailing discursive practices shape us are approached by compiling evidence in the form of discrete memories; memories that stand alone and are cued by a single word or idea. The discrete memory is one that is usually not a part of the long and causal narratives that we might tell about our lives. The discrete memories produced through memory-work share many characteristics with stories or narratives of personal experience. Like stories or narratives, memories involve a sequence of events, a storyteller and an intended audience and like memories, narratives reflect events and experiences important to the teller. They reveal social, community, and institutional values and realities (Cole, 1991). They help us understand the meaning of everyday life. Just as narratives play a central role "in the formation of the self and in the construction, transmission, and transformations of cultures" (Witherell & Noddings, 1991, p. 3), so too, in our opinion, do memories.

Stories people tell about themselves, about others, and about events or experiences seen or heard reveal to the listener those cultural, social, and personal values and behaviors that are salient to the speaker's identification. This is so because people make choices about what is reportable in accord with their own views of the cultural models and values they hold to be inherent in their own psychological economies (Brunn, 1994).

The telling of stories, like the telling of our memories, as Clandinin and Connelly (1995) note, "is a way, perhaps the most basic way, humans make meaning of their experience.... Active construction and telling of a story is educative: the storyteller learns through the act of story telling.... The story is reshaped and, so too, is the meaning of the world to which the story refers" (pp. 2-3).

Despite the similarities, discrete memories retain a characteristic that sets them apart from the narrative forms of biography and autobiography. Carefully crafted stories about people are full of omissions and evasions. They are edited summaries of lives from the perspective of the present, often narratives of causality and logical sequences of events that resonate with our present views of events and ourselves (Evans, 1999). In contrast, the discrete memories generated through memory-work are intended to illuminate the moments of a life as opposed to causal strings and as such, these memories are much easier to unpack than tightly woven autobiographical summaries.

All of our memories, rambling causal narratives and short discrete memories, are archaeological artifacts, but it is easier to collectively dust off the discrete artifacts. Many of these discrete memories, in our own work and that of others (e.g., Davies, 2000), are memories of embodiment that conjoin mind and sensation; movement, smell, taste, feeling. These memories are no more true than biography or autobiography, but they point to experiences that are less shaped by the familiar discourse. They have the potential to reveal an alternative discourse, an alternative way of being. Ironically, these discrete memories are pointers to what we do not remember, the ways of being that are forgotten because they are not valued, and thus not a part of the discursive practices of our communities. They often present a contrast to the usual, to what we expect to remember, and it is in the contrast that we see the ways in which we have constructed ourselves. The process whereby we become the person we are may be studied because the complexities of our early experiences survive in these discrete memories. These are the effects of economic class, ethnicity, gender, sexual identity, physical limitations, experiences of inclusion and marginality, and values and ideology.

Given this distinction between discrete memories and autobiography, memories are still "reflections that return the past to the present" (Grumet, 1990, p. 322). To revisit a memory is to "see oneself seeing" (Grumet, 1990, p. 322), but through a new construction. We can never recall a memory as it was because we are no longer the same individuals whose experiences created the memory. Therefore, memories are constructions and reconstructions based upon who we were, are, and are becoming.

This notion of a memory simultaneously reflecting the past, present and future calls into question the idea that the past or, more particularly, our memories of the past, determine who we are in the present. For example, it is quite common to hear an individual say that "event X caused me to behave in this manner," or that "who I am now is inevitably based on the events of my past." Our memories are a record of our socialization, but they do not trace the inevitability of our present selves. When we remember or narrate a story of a particular event, the story of that event is only one of many stories that could be told about that particular moment in time. For example, in Kaufman, Ewing, Montgomery, Hyle and Self (2003) one of the researchers narrated a story of driving with her father to Boston on a hot summer day. Many, perhaps an infinite number, of stories could be told about that ride. She told a story about the play of her arm in the wind hanging out a car window because in the present she was searching for a memory about air. There is nothing inevitable or determinant in that memory, though it does contain evidence of the present and a link to the cue, air.

Given that multiple stories can be told about an event, questions concerning truth or accuracy can be posed regarding the use of discrete memories in memory-work. The memories are a lens through which individuals in a memory-work collective view how they felt and thought about the world around them as children, but what they see through that lens is subject to interpretation. We can never accurately record the moments of our lives because we are always constrained by particular ways of looking. Memory-work can only provide another way of looking, another lens for thinking about who we are and how we have been socialized.

The discrete memories retrieved through memory-work are determined by the questions asked by a collective, the context of listening to each other's memories, and the selves they believed and believe themselves to be. Memories reflect who we are now, but the past also influences the stories we tell. Experiences of sexual and physical abuse, in short any traumatic or compelling experience, can influence a life, and therefore influence the stories we tell. As Freeman (1993) wisely notes,

> We cannot think of this state of affairs in either-or terms but must instead embrace what I called a "both-and" perspective, in which we are willing to read the text of a life both backward and forward. Only then can we do justice to both the poetic figuration of the past and the humbling power of fate. (p. 226)

Memory-work also is concerned with the limits of language and the need to engage collectively when using the method. Haug's socialist-feminist collective analyzed their past experience with the aim of discerning their own participation in their subordination and oppression as women. They recognized, however, that they were constrained by the language of the patriarchy. As the collective noted, "we found ourselves speaking, thinking, and experiencing ourselves with the perception of men, without ever having discovered what our aims as *human beings* might be" (Haug, 1987, p. 36). Individually, it is difficult, if not impossible, to rethink and question ideas and ideologies that shape and become a part of our being; collectively, though, the task becomes possible. Each member, with her differing perception, has the potential to see what was previously unseen and to say what was previously unsaid. New ideas emerge from collective scrutiny of memories and from the continuing struggle to be more conscious of the use of language.

As is clear from the preceding discussion, memory-work is ultimately about transgression. It is about becoming conscious through interrogating and interrupting the hegemonic messages that have shaped our traditional ways of knowing the world. It is about loosening the strangle-hold of the dominant culture. Davies (2000) writes, memory-work is about "troubling the boundaries of the discourse," not erasing them and not doing away with them, but troubling them so we can begin to explore other ways of being, other discursive practices. "What I want to do is to free up the language from its... capacity to determine our modes of being" (Davies, 2000, p. 13). Gaining distance from the language of the dominant culture or at least being able to see the boundaries of this discourse through "troubling" them, making them apparent, is potentially transforming. Once you understand how you have been shaped by discursive processes, discerning what Kermode (1979) calls the secrecy of our lives, then other ways of being become possible. The ability to tell different stories, to see things differently means that our participation in the culture is transformed and as we transform our ways of being in the culture, then the potential for transforming the culture becomes very real. However, "the consciousness that results from this work must be practiced with vigilance. It is easy to fall into the old ways of seeing because we continue to live in a social world that constantly reinforces old boundaries and meanings" (Kaufman, Ewing, Hyle, Montgomery & Self, 2001, p. 140).

Validity of memory-work

We are prompted to ask why we should take our stories seriously—or ask why these stories are more acceptable than the previous stories we told. In short—can we justify these stories? In Kaufman et al. (2003), we investigated how we were socialized to think about the natural world. Memory-work helped us to weave a story that resurrects our interrelationship with the natural world, one of many stories we could have told based on the memories of the continuous moments of our lives. Together we became intimately aware through our memory-work that we tend to tell few rather than many stories and these often reveal and are constrained by the dominant values of the culture. The dominant values of the culture effectively function to select the moments that we take from the time stream to tell a coherent narrative of our lives. We are aware of these values in varying degrees, but many are very familiar; we take them for granted.

They have become invisible and sometimes oppressive influences in and around our lives. They shape what we see and know, and we participate in perpetuating their influence in the dominant culture. In this context, memory-work functions to make the invisible visible, to make the familiar strange.

Freeman (1993) suggests that we can judge or justify a narrative based on plausibility, and part of plausibility should be coherence—not in the sense of a tightly woven narrative, the kind that would set off alarms indicating cultural coherence, but in the sense that there is not blatant contradiction and "stupidity" (p. 165). Freeman also suggests that the narrative should be fitting or sensible. However, the criterion of plausibility should not constrain us so much that we simply reproduce the culture—rather we should "remain open to entirely new forms of interpretation" (p. 165). This is where the value of memory-work lies. Nevertheless, Freeman cautions that interpretation will never escape "the scope of our own idioms and habits of thought" (p. 165).

Freeman's exploration of memory is a solitary one. No others challenge him to break through the boundaries of the culture or the "idioms and habits of thought." The collective nature of memory-work however directly addresses this problem. The linking of self as subject and self as participant in the process of memory-work forges connections that allow us to challenge one another to move beyond the idioms, the boundaries of our encultured space. While we can-not claim that we have moved past these boundaries, we can confirm that we see them more clearly as a collective. New possibilities have opened up more read-ily for the collective than for us individually.

Current memory-work research: A critique

In the 20 years since Haug's 1987 publication, a great deal of research using memory-work has been conducted. Several questions and issues emerge in a review of this work. The first has to do with modifications and extensions of the method. Can researchers bend and break the rules of memory-work? Can we have more or less confidence in findings that emerge from a close adherence to the rules of the method? A related issue concerns the amount of time devoted to a study. One collective spent seven years researching a topic, another group came together for a week. What are the implications of time for analysis? In studies of short duration, one individual as opposed to a collective takes respon-sibility for analysis and authoring. Again, what are the implications and what are the issues we should consider? Another issue concerns the topic or focus of study. Researchers in the fields of marketing and tourism have used memory-work to understand the experiences of tourists and consumers. Is there a contra-diction between using a method intended to critique the dominant discourse in order to understand behavior and experiences intended to benefit those who profit from reproduction of the discourse? A final issue that emerges in the lar-ger body of research using memory-work has to do with the level of detail that researchers provide in writing up their studies. Rich description of the method and detailed explanation of procedure will help us reflect on the questions raised above.

Onyx and Small (2001) catalogue the extensive use of memory-work across a variety of disciplines since Haug's 1987 publication. They list 63 studies, 58 of which were conducted in Australia and New Zealand. They raise a number of issues and questions in relation to these studies, the first of which has to do with extensions and alterations of the method. Two, of what might be called, "traditional" uses of memory-work have been published since Haug. Traditional, because the researchers most closely adhered to the method as set out by Haug, even though each adapted the method to their specific needs. The first was Crawford et al.'s (1992) four-year study of the social construction of emotion. In their work, they modified and explicated a set of rules and procedures, which have become a template of sorts for subsequent researchers using memory-work. The second traditional study was Kaufman et al.'s (2003) examination of the self in relation to the natural world. In this study we attempted to use memory-work according to the injunctions and rules set out by Haug and Crawford et al., but also found it necessary to adapt and alter the method. What makes these two studies traditional or conservative is that in both the essential tenets and principles of memory-work are conserved. Both sets of researchers attempted to adhere as closely as possible to the method as laid out by Haug. Both studies were long term in that the researchers wrote, discussed and collectively analyzed the memories over four and seven years, respectively. Finally, all of the researchers took collective responsibility for writing and eventual publication.

Some of the questions Onyx and Small (2001) raise are whether the rules of memory-work are inviolable, and whether researchers must invest similar kinds of time and energy in discerning and challenging how we produce and are produced by the discourses of the dominant culture. Do the findings have more or less integrity because they result from use of the traditional approach? Are the researchers/participants more or less impacted by their extent of involvement? Onyx and Small point out that Haug herself was aware that there is no true method of memory-work. In reflecting on the collective's work, Haug (1987) wrote:

> The diversity of our methods, the numerous objections raised in the course of our work with the stories, and the varied nature of our attempts at resolution, seemed to suggest that there might well be no single, "true" method that is alone appropriate to this kind of work. What we need is imagination. We can, perhaps, say quite decisively that the very heterogeneity of everyday life demands similarly heterogeneous methods if it is to be understood. (p. 70)

With regard to the issue of time, Kaufman et al. (2003) had no earlier experience with the method and during the first few years we were scrutinizing the ways in which we were producing the memories and working with different ways of analyzing the memories. Additionally, we kept broadening the scope of the study. We decided to include not only early memories but adolescent and young adult memories. We also rewrote the memories that had generated lots of discussion and insight. By the time we were through, we had written over 75 memories. Additionally, as we began the process of preparing a book-length manuscript for publication, we found that we continued to interpret and analyze the memories. And because we wrote the book collectively, we edited and re-edited each other's work. We were in different parts of the country and relied on phone and Internet. We came together at least twice a year to edit and produce more writing. Crawford et al.'s (1992) project extended over four years and they also write about the labor involved in collective writing. On analysis, they write, "the process continues until the members feel that the topic or they are exhausted" (p. 50).

Memory-work is indeterminate and can continue ad infinitum, but must it extend over long periods of time? Davies and Dormer (1997) describe an exploration of silence using Davies extension of memory-work, which she calls collective biography. Seven women told their stories, listened, and wrote more stories over a two-week workshop. A first draft of a collective paper was produced and after the workshop, the draft was passed from one woman to another. Davies took responsibility for the final text that emerged as a journal article. They disrupted the borders of women's silence and ultimately gave voice to silence.

In a workshop with her postgraduate students, Davies (2000) describes a gathering that lasted for only a week on an island off the northeast coast of Australia. In the morning the participants worked on collective biography and the afternoons were devoted to activities around writing or embodiment. After telling their stories, the participants wrote them down and worked and reworked them trying to move beyond the clichés, the "before the naming, before the explanatory words that parcel it up as meaning" (p. 50). Davies, who took ultimate responsibility for the text that emerged from the workshop, concludes that through collective biography she and the participants were able to move beyond the constraints of traditional language and were able to "recover early moments of embodiment" (p. 61). They found the body in landscape, as landscape, and landscape as an extension of the body.

In this same volume on body/landscape relations, Davies (2000) describes a second project with four Japanese students studying in Australia. This project extended over a one-year period. They met once a week during an academic term and for a few additional months after Davies returned from a trip to Japan. Their goal was to tell and write stories that would uncover some of the discursive patterns used to describe body/landscape relations in Japanese culture. Davies notes that Japanese culture has a long history of connection between the landscape and body, but through extensive writing and listening, the students were able to step outside of some Japanese clichés and she was able to see underneath the "polished surface" (p. 109) of what it means to be Japanese.

In all of these projects, Davies brought the participants together around a focused topic and in the case of the short workshops, participants worked within delineated time constraints. The project with the Japanese students extended over a longer period because of the difference in culture (Davies had to gain familiarity with Japanese clichés) and because the students had to develop their own experience with writing the kinds of detailed memories needed for collective theorizing. Thus, experience with the method, time limits, pre-selected topics, and single as opposed to collective authoring account for whether a memory-work project is shorter or longer term. The question again is whether these issues have any impact on the findings. Time, in and of itself, does not seem to be a pivotal issue. That researchers have been able to carry out and complete memory-work projects on a short term basis makes the method more user-friendly and therefore may encourage broader use. Pre-selecting a topic could be problematic because it may undermine the collective nature of a group, but the topic will only draw those who have an interest. Koutroulis (1993, 1996) noted that she had selected menarche as a topic, but her collective rejected the idea and decided to write about significant moments in their experience of menstruation.

The question of single versus collective authoring clearly has an impact on the findings. The majority of memory-work research is single-authored. Haug took ultimate responsibility for authoring the work that came out of the collective. Koutroulis (1993, 1996) asks who ultimately takes responsibility for continued analysis and writing. She argued that while parts of the project were collective, she ultimately put in the most work and took ownership, for example, in writing this chapter on method. Ingleton (2003) raises the issue of the authority of the researcher in a memory-work collective when the data are used by the researcher for publication. At a conference on memory-work in Australia in 2000, a group of 11 researchers who had used memory-work met in two groups and wrote memories triggered by facilitating a memory-work group. Power issues around voice, group control, and integrity in analysis after the memory-work collective has disbanded emerged in discussion. Onyx and Small (2001) note that there are practical, theoretical, and ethical issues when a researcher uses the method for publication. If the researcher is working toward a doctorate, will participants modify their stories? Are the data impacted? Additionally, they ask if the process is truly collective, how can one person take ownership as a condition for gaining a degree, such as for a doctoral dissertation. In our case (Kaufman et al., 2003), analysis continued into the writing process, and the shape of our project was dramatically altered through our collective writing.

Another issue that arises in critiquing the memory-work studies of the last decade and a half concerns other significant modifications to the method. Haug called for imagination and a heterogeneity of approaches to deconstructing the dominant discourse. Perhaps the most imaginative and intriguing extension of memory-work is Davies (2002) use of collective biography, which allows her to move beyond the explicit rules of memory-work and adapt it to particular questions and collectives. Her interests are also broader than resistance to the dominant discourse.

The transgressive work that I do with others in undertaking collective biographies is oriented more discursively and collectively; learning to write and to tell stories of self against the grain of hegemonic discourse; making visible and therefore revisable the discourses through which we make meanings and selves; deconstructing the individual as existing independent of various collectives, of discourse, of history, of time and place. Our primary focus is not so much therapeutic, as it is on developing the process of collective biography as a means of learning to read/write embodied selves and to use that reading/writing to produce an empirical base through which we can explore various aspects of the processes of meaning making through which we become subjects and go on becoming subjects. (p. 3)

Other studies have merely borrowed the notion of generating memories, but do not engage with other participants in collective analysis. Widerberg (1998) uses experience stories, which she notes are based on the method of memory-work. She asked 100 undergraduates to describe in detail a situation in which they were made aware of their gender. She uses the stories as part of her teaching about gender and argues that they increase student involvement in reflecting and critiquing notions of gender. Reid-Walsh and Mitchell (2000) elicited memories of playing with Barbie dolls from students and colleagues. The researchers read the memories and subjected them to a process of working through which highlighted how the dominant discourse is appropriated in girls' play with Barbie dolls. Their point is that the memories can be subjected to the same kinds of political analysis engaged in by memory-workers. These studies are interesting in their use of memories as data and they add to a diverse literature on the impact of the dominant discourse, but do we become more conscious of the influence of the dominant discourse by reading about it or by experiencing that influence, remembering it, and then theorizing about our experience?

The focus or research topic is another issue that emerges in scrutinizing the variety of memory-work projects. Sometimes the topic appears to contradict the aim of memory-work, that is, uncovering and challenging the dominant discourse. A number of studies in areas such as consumer service encounters (Friend, 1997, 2000; Friend & Rummel, 1995; Friend & Thompson, 2000), leisure experiences (Friend, Grant & Gunson, 2000; Grant & Friend, 1997; McCormack, 1995, 1998), and tourist experiences (Small, 1999) raise the potential conflict.

To illustrate, Friend and Thompson (2000) describe the empowering effect of memory-work on a participant in their research group who describes memory-work as enhancing an awareness of her own agency in the context of shopping. It is unclear how the authors reconcile the contradiction between using a methodology intended to subvert the dominant discourse within a field devoted to understanding the behaviors of consumers in a capitalist culture. Friend and Rummel (1995) analyzed only one of the memories that emerged from two memory-work groups formed by the researchers to study consumer satisfaction and dissatisfaction in the purchase of clothing. Participants wrote memories triggered by "impulse buy, pressure purchase, and exhilaration" (p. 4). It is assumed that the researchers provided these triggers. The group analysis of "Susie's memory" of wanting to buy a dress that she discovered was damaged while trying it on explains Susie's emotions and an injustice she experiences with the store manager. The conclusions drawn by the authors may contribute to an understanding of customer dissatisfaction, but it is not apparent that Susie critically reflected on the dominant discourse surrounding consumption of retail goods. Again, the authors do not reflect on their contradictory use of memory-work to elucidate consumer behavior.

Small (1999) explored whether memory-work was appropriate for studying the gendered nature of tourist experiences among women. The author brought together four groups; a group of girls aged 12, women in their early 20's, 40's, and 65 and over. Where possible the groups wrote memories of being on holiday during the four age periods of 12, 20, 40, and 65. Issues of responsibility for others versus freedom emerged in group discussions. The researcher notes that like Kotroulis (1993, 1996, 2001) she took ownership of the data and subjected it to further analysis once the memory-work group had disbanded. The author concludes that the method is appropriate for studying tourism, but like the work in marketing research, the findings appear to be more beneficial for the researcher in understanding women's experience of being on holiday than for the groups themselves. Small does not provide enough detail to determine whether any of the participants in this study had the opportunity to theorize about their experiences or come to understand perhaps how the dominant discourse might shape their experience of being on holiday, e.g., why women are usually in the role of taking care of the kids on vacation.

A final issue concerns the level of detail that researchers provide when writing about their memory-work projects. The audience for and use of memory-work is growing and if the method is to continue to evolve, we need sufficient detail describing not only the findings, but the ways in which the method is used and how participants experience use of the method. For example, Boucher (1997) with five women who all held leadership positions used memory-work over a seven-month period to explore their cultural constructions of leadership. The ways in which women construct notions of leadership is very interesting; however, in this study the author provides little data. The memories the women generated are not described and there is no sense of how their theory of leadership is connected to their experience of leadership. Boucher describes the work as consciousness-raising and so the reader is left wondering whether memory-work was even necessary to the particular conclusions reached.

Pease (2000) describes a 15 month study with a group of 11 heterosexual profeminist white men who came together at the invitation of Pease in a consciousness-raising group to explore the politics and practices of profeminism. His article describes the use of memory-work during one session where six men were present. In this particular meeting, "the research group explored when they had wanted or needed a nurturing response from their fathers and did not get such a response" (p. 11). It is not clear from the article how Pease employed memory-work over the 15-month period, and how much preparation preceded the particular meeting described in the article. The memories are presented along with thick description of the analysis and theorizing of the memories. The participants concluded they were betrayed by their fathers and thus oppressed and understood that patriarchy of rule by fathers not only applied to women, but also the oppression of younger men by older men.

What was significant for Pease was that the memory-work participants were able to "identify with women's experiences of men" (p. 14). This is an interesting use of memory-work, but the lack of an adequate methodological description within the context of the study leaves too many questions unanswered. In a second study, Pease (2000) again reports on his 15-month study and this time notes that participants were asked to recall a memory in which "they were conscious of objectifying a women's body as a basis for sexual arousal" (p. 133). Pease concludes that the very act of recalling these memories subverts the reproduction of dominant masculinities. Again, the study presents fascinating findings but the dearth of information about the use and extension of the method within this particular research context prevents evaluation of the findings.

Organization of the book

Given the current scholarship on memory-work, we have invited a group of memory-work researchers to reflect on the work that they have done using memory-work. We asked them to reflect on how their use of the method has contributed to their respective disciplines. With respect to the method itself, the authors considered emerging issues. We asked them to describe the ways in which they have altered or appropriated the method, researcher voice and authority, and consistency between the aims of memory-work and their research.

Following this chapter Frigga Haug details her evolving method. In Part II, Stretching Memory-Work, first Susanne Gannon (Chapter Three) describes the process by which she gathers memory-work data through workshops, deconstructs those memories and then rearranges them into other discursive art forms. Bronwyn Davies recounts in the next chapter (Chapter Four) her work with collective biography, a strategy that moves beyond the explicit roles of memory-work and can be flexibly adapted to particular questions and collectives.

In Part III, Dissecting the Mundane, the different ways in which memory-work has been variously applied in specific domains are explored. Betty Johnston (Chapter Five) provides an account of a group of women using memory-work to unravel how mathematical identities are intricately woven into the fabric of our everyday lives. Glenda Koutroulis (Chapter Six) used memory-work as a sociological methodology in a study of women's experiences of menstruation. Karin Widerberg (Chapter Seven) explores memory-work as an individual and collective enterprise in both research and teaching. Bob Pease (Chapter Eight) explains the use of memory-work as one of three strategies to examine the practices of profeminist men in order to promote the process of change. Naomi Norquay (Chapter Nine) describes student's interrogations of their family immigration stories and their own social identities in relation to these stories as an instructional strategy for teaching social awareness. Judith Kaufman (Chapter Ten) uses memory-work to engage students in critically examining the assumptions about learning and teaching formed during their 12–year apprenticeship of observation (Lortie, 1975) in elementary and secondary schools. Mary FitzPatrick, Lorraine Friend and Carolyn Costley (Chapter Eleven) propose memory-work as an appropriate research strategy in the discipline of marketing.

Notes

1. Throughout this text we refer to the 1987 text by the collective as Haug (1987) but want the reader to know that the list of authors includes Frigga Haug, Sunne Andersen, Anke Bünz-Elfferding, Kornelia Hauser, Ursel Lang, Marion Laudan, Magret Lüdemann, Ute Meir, Barbara Nemitz, Erika Niehoff, Renate Prinz, Nora Rathzel, Martina Scheu, and Christine Thomas.

References

Boucher, Carlene. (1997). How women socially construct leadership in organizations: A study using memory work. *Gender, Work and Organization, 4*(3), 149-158.

Brunn, Michael. (1994, April). *Ethnohistories: Learning through the stories of life experiences.* Paper presented at the annual meeting of the American Educational Research Association, New Orleans (American Indian, Alaska Native Education SIG).

Cixous, Helene & Calle-Gruber, Mireille. (1997). *Rootprints: Memory and life writing.* (Trans. Eric Prenowitz.) London: Routledge.

Clandinin, D. Jean & Connelly, F. Michael. (1995, April). *Storying and restorying ourselves: Narrative and reflection.* Paper presented at the annual meeting of the American Educational Research Association, San Francisco.

Cole, Ardra L. (1991). Interviewing for life history: An ongoing negotiation. In Ivor F. Goodson & John Marshall Mangan (Eds.), *Qualitative educational research studies: Methodologies in transition, Occasional Papers, I* (pp. 185-208). London, ONT: Research Unit on Classroom Learning and Computer Use in Schools.

Connell, Robert W. (1987). *Gender and power: Society, the person and sexual politics.* Cambridge: Polity Press.

Crawford, June; Kippax, Susan; Onyx, Jenny; Gault, Una & Benton, Pam. (1992). *Emotion and gender: Constructing meaning from memory.* London: Sage.

Davies, Bronwyn. (1994). *Poststructuralist theory and classroom practice.* Geelong, AU: Deakin University Press.

Davies, Bronwyn. (2000). *(In)scribing body/landscape relations.* Walnut Creek, CA: Alta Mira Press.

Davies, Bronwyn. (2002). *The practices of collective biography.* Unpublished paper. Sydney, AU: University of Western Sydney.

Davies, Bronwyn.; Dormer, Suzy; Honan, Eileen; McAllister, Nicky; O'Reilly, Roisin; Rocco, Sharn & Walker, Allison. (1997). Ruptures in the skin of silence: A collective biography. *Hecate— A Women's Studies Interdisciplinary Journal, 23*(1), 62-79.

Davies, Bronwyn; Dormer, Suzy; Gannon, Susanne; Laws, Cath; Taguchi, Hillevi Lenz; McCann, Helen & Rocco, Sharn. (2001). Becoming schoolgirls: The ambivalent process of subjectification. *Gender and Education, 13*(2), 167-182.

Davies, Bronwyn & Gannon, Susanne. (2004,). Feminism/Poststructuralism. In Cathy Lewin & Bridget Somekh (Eds.), *Research methods in the social sciences.* London: Sage.

Evans, Mary. (1999). *Missing persons: The impossibility of auto/biography.* London: Routledge.

Freeman, Mark. (1993). *Rewriting the self: History, meaning, narrative.* London: Routledge.

Friend, Lorraine A. (1997a, July). *Analysing leisure experiences through memory-work.* Paper presented at the 3rd Conference of the Australian and New Zealand Association for Leisure Studies, University of Newcastle, Australia.

Friend, Lorraine A. (1997b, June). *Memory-work: Understanding consumer satisfaction and dissatisfaction of clothing retail service encounters.* New and Evolving paradigms: The Emerging Future of Marketing. Three American Marketing Association Special Conferences, Dublin, Ireland.

Friend, Lorraine A. (2000). Guilty or not guilty: Experiencing and understanding Sweetie's guilt as dissatisfaction. In J. Schroeder & C. C. Otnes (Eds.), *Proceedings of the fifth conference on gender, marketing and consumer behavior* (pp. 157-173). Urbana: The University of Illinois Press.

Friend, Lorraine A. & Rummel, Amy. (1995). Memory-work: An alternative approach to investigating consumer satisfaction and dissatisfaction of clothing retail encounters. *Journal of Consumer Satisfaction, Dissatisfaction and Complaining Behavior, 8,* 214-222.

Friend, Lorraine A.; Grant, Bevan C. & Gunson, L. (2000). Memories. *Australian Leisure Management, 20,* 24-25.

Friend, Lorraine A. & Thompson, Shonna M. (2000). Using memory-work to give a feminist voice to marketing research. In Miriam Catterall, Pauline Maclaran & Lorna Stevens (Eds.), *Marketing and feminism: Current issues and research* (pp. 94-111). New York: Routledge.

Gannon, Susanne. (2001). (Re)presenting the collective girl: A poetic approach to a methodological dilemma. *Qualitative Inquiry, 7*(6), 787-800.

Grant, Bevan C. & Friend, Lorraine. (1997, July). Analysing leisure experiences through "memory-work." Paper presented at the annual conference of Leisure, People, Places, and Spaces, Newcastle.

Grumet, Madeleine R. (1990). Retrospective: Autobiography and the analysis of educational experience. *Cambridge Journal of Education, 20*(3), 321-325.

Haraway, Donna. (1991). *Simians, cyborgs and women.* New York: Routledge.

Haug, Frigga. (1987). *Female sexualization: A collective work of memory.* (Erica Carter, trans.). Towbridge, Wiltshire, UK: Dotesios Ltd.

Ingleton, Christine. (2001, November). *Collectivity and analysis in memory-work.* Paper presented at the Australian Association for Research in Education, Fremantle.

Johnston, Betty. (1995). Mathematics: An abstracted discourse. In P. Rogers & G. Kaiser (Eds.), *Equity in mathematics education: Influences of feminism and culture* (pp. 226-234). London: Falmer Press.

Johnston, Betty. (1998, September). *Maths and gender: Given or made?* Paper presented at the Mathematics Education and Society Conference, Nottingham.

Johnston, Betty. (forthcoming) *Mess and order: Spotlight on time.* In selected papers from ICME-7, Kluwer Academic.

Kaufman, Judith S.; Ewing, Margaret S.; Hyle, Adrienne E.; Montgomery, Diane & Self, Patricia A. (2001). Women and nature: Using memory-work to rethink our relationship to the natural world. *Journal of Environmental Education Research, 7*(4), 359-377.

Kaufman, Judith S.; Ewing, Margaret S.; Montgomery, Diane M. Hyle, Adrienne E. & Self, Patricia A. (2003). *From girls in their elements to women in science: Rethinking socialization through memory-work.* New York: Peter Lang.

Kermode, Frank. (1979). *The genesis of secrecy.* Cambridge, MA: Harvard University Press.

Koutroulis, Glenda. (1993). Memory-work: A critique. In Brian S. Turner, Elizabeth Eckermann, Derek Colquhoun & Pat Crotty (Eds.), *Annual review of health social science: Methodological issues in health research* (pp. 76-96). Geelong, Australia: Centre for the Study of the Body and Society, Deakin University.

Koutroulis, Glenda. (1996). Memory-work: Process, practice and pitfalls. In Derek Colquhoun & Allan Kellehear (Eds.), *Health research in practice: Volume 2* (pp. 95-113). London: Chapman and Hall.

Koutroulis, Glenda. (2001). Soiled identity: Memory-work narratives of menstruation. *Health, 5*(2), 187-205.

McCormack, Coralie. (1995). Memories give meaning to women's leisure. In C. Simpson & B. Gidlow (Eds.), *Proceedings Australian and New Zealand association for leisure studies conference* (pp. 128–134). Lincoln, New Zealand: Australian and New Zealand Association for Leisure Studies & Department of Parks, Recreation and Tourism, Lincoln University.

McCormack, Coralie. (1998). Memories bridge the gap between theory and practice in women's leisure. *Annals of Leisure Research, 1,* 7-49.

Onyx, Jenny & Small, Jennie. (2001). Memory-work: The method. *Qualitative Inquiry, 7*(6), 773-789.

Pease, Bob. (2000). Beyond the father wound: Memory-work and the deconstruction of the father-son relationship. *Australian and New Zealand Journal of Family Therapy, 21*(1), 9-15.

Reid-Walsh, Jacqueline & Mitchell, Claudia. (2000). "Just a doll?:" "Liberating" accounts of Barbie-play. *The Review of Education/Cultural Studies, 22*(2), 175-190.

Schratz, Michael; Walker, Rob & Schratz-Hadwich, Barbara. (1995). Collective memory-work: The self as a re/source for re/search. In Michael Schratz and Rob Walker (Eds.), *Research as social change: New opportunities for qualitative research* (pp. 39-64). New York: Routledge.

Small, Jennie. (1999). Memory-work: A method for researching women's tourist experiences. *Tourism Management, 20*(1), 25-35.

Stephenson, Niamh & Kippax, Susan. (1999). Minding the gap: Subjectivity in research. In Wolfgang Maiers, Betty Bayer, Barbara Duarte Esgalhado, Rene Jorna & Ernst Schraube (Eds.), *Challenges to theoretical psychology* (pp. 183-191). York, UK: Captus Press.

Touraine, Alain. (1977). *The voice and the eye: An analysis of social movements.* Cambridge: Cambridge University Press.

Touraine, Alain. (1988). *Return of the actor.* Minneapolis: University of Minnesota Press.

Virno, Paulo. (1996). Do you remember counterrevolution? In Paolo Virno & Michael Hardt (Eds.), *Radical thought in Italy: A potential politics* (pp. 240-258). Minneapolis: Minnesota University Press.

Widerberg, Karin. (1998). Teaching gender through writing "experience stories." *Women's Studies International Forum, 21*(2), 193-198.

Witherell, Carol & Noddings, Nel. (Eds.). (1991). *Stories lives tell: Narrative and dialogue in education.* New York: Teachers College Press.

Chapter 2

Memory-work:
A Detailed Rendering of the Method
for Social Science Research

Frigga Haug

Even though different terms and different points of view are used, most of us deal with power, dominance, hegemony, inequality and the discursive practices of staging, secrecy, legitimization and reproduction. And many of us are interested in the subtle tools, used by the text on the one hand to lead the mind and obtain agreement, on the other hand to incite resistance and impeachment. (van Dijk, 1995, pp. 131-132)

When I began putting memory-work to use in my work, I had to prepare for questions about the exact steps, starting points and process, methodological comparison and justification, clarity and potential for generalization, and theoretical connections. I have learned a great deal in discussions of these questions, achieved greater clarity, and brought the preliminary nature of the individual methodological steps into the foreground. I have, however, refrained from actually documenting research steps in written form. The current research methodology seems in need of further improvement, arbitrary in individual steps, and one-sidedly limited to the linguistic problem. It has not matured enough to be publicized as a general guide.

However, I continually encounter great interest in this process wherever I present this work and I desire to have something in hand which people can use in their own groups. Thus, I will attempt here to document considerations for the research methodology. It has occurred to me after my original reflections that the interesting part of memory-work consists of two dimensions: the collaborative nature of the process and the theoretical foundation. The theoretical background is time and again rendered explicit and expanded on in the discussion of individual steps, a discussion that is something more than a methodological relationship with critical discourse analysis. I include theoretical argumentation in this process because of the freedom it provides, that is, freedom for individuals attempting to do memory-work to change the method for themselves, remaining within—or critically expanding—the theoretical framework of the process.

The method is designed and written as it applies to women's groups. The reason for my perspective of exclusivity is historical; memory-work was developed with and for the feminist movement. I am not certain if memory work is possible within the perimeters of traditional science, often seen as maleness. Apart from that concern about maleness, this method is recognized as feminist, but it has a general claim for recognition.

The research question

Memory-work is text work beyond conventional narrative analysis (Crawford, Kippax, Onyx, Gault & Benton, 1992). It is not only experience, but work with the experience, which is useful as a research method. The first step is developing a research question that opens up and delineates the field. The question should be of interest to everyone in the group. In fact, it should be a burning issue, so that the motivation to discuss creates a sense of commonality, a prerequisite for team work. This question can be established by the group or a topic may be announced for which interested female participants simply present themselves. Groups should be limited to no more than 12 to 15 women, so that all involved have the opportunity to be actively involved. If interest exceeds the group limit, additional groups may be formed according to size, so that everyone can actively participate. Using this strategy, I began doing memory-work about fear with more than 50 women.

Although differences among women have been emphasized in recent years to the point that females with mutual experiences have been disregarded, there is hardly any topic in everyday life that does not mutually touch every woman, independent of age, profession, or social class. For instance, consider the topic of fear. Granted, experiences of fear are individually different depending on cultural background, but all women can report memories of experiences of fear; most are painful and therefore important.

In the first session, the topic should be formed in lay terms. It is important not to pose the question in scientific or analytical terms since memories will not emerge when the appeal to them takes the form of language that is not in the vernacular. "A time when I was afraid" is common language to which everyone can relate. Setting the question in scientific terminology, "About the problematic gender-specific emotional inability to act" would elicit few memories. It becomes clear that although the meaning of the research question is assumed, that meaning must be acquired first through everyday language and personal experience.

The collective

Memory-work is a collective method that intends to intervene and such an intervention implies a demand for emancipation. Therefore, discussion of the method should begin with a paragraph on the collective. But to do so encounters the difficulty that all explanations assume the presentation of each step to be readily understandable. Thus, at each step the explanation will become clearer. At this stage I just offer some general statements.

Working with memory requires a collective, a group, because otherwise neither the ruling common sense as such, nor the critical counterpart, nor consensus in the argumentation, nor contrary experiences, nor the necessary fantasy could be mobilized. Though the method deals with the individual and presupposes an enfolded individual development, it goes beyond the isolated singular individual in the direction of an association of researchers. This renders the method both resistant and in opposition to the zeitgeist as well as looking to the future. It is obvious that the method found fruitful ground in the women's movement and we might therefore assume that the decline of the movement predicts the demise of such collective research. Actually my experiences with the method and its use do not bear this out. Maybe the groups organizing around the method do not last as long as before, when, for example, the project on anxiety worked together for more than four years. Maybe the hope that you can detect something really meaningful and useful about society and your own complicity has shifted to the short-lived idea that you can find an individual use of the method for yourself immediately. But certainly women are always gathering around a special issue and beginning to work on their experiences. This coming together most of the time is sufficient to collectively start more projects.

The remembered scene or memory

It is best to provide some time between asking the question and writing the remembered scene. This allows time to select an experience that is important for the author. In situations where this project is done in a weekend seminar or in which this is only the beginning of a longer-term project, it is best to let at least a night pass for this transition to occur. Time allows the author to process these thoughts while following her own habits and idiosyncrasies. Some people choose to write immediately, others late at night, and others prefer to get up early and write.

For writing about fear a few suggestions, which preferably will be theoretically justified, are in order. The whole process should be kept simple and open to examination so that it can be supported by everybody. The process should enable individuals to be active and avoid creating situations where omniscient experts give orders to an uninformed audience.

The suggestions might be as follows:

1. It is best to have participants use third-person narration. This forces the participants to explain themselves as not self-evident and, therefore, unknown persons. It allows the women to describe themselves in detail and to account for themselves; whereas, oftentimes with first-person narration too much is taken for granted, left out, or considered unimportant and embarrassing. We might call this choice of third-person narration historicizing or distancing the narrator. No rule is absolute, so should a person insist on writing in first person, this may be done. I can add at this point from my experience that people who are used to giving an account of themselves write more easily in the first person. However, I had a dispute with a woman that illustrates the contrary. She insisted on using the first person because she had just learned in the women's movement that women have to say "I" more often. This would make their stories stronger. After a very long time she came with four lines about an experience without any personal statement—except the defiant I.

2. Only the memory of an experience, an event, or a scene may be written. Sequences or biographical stories should be avoided. Extended descriptions allow the author to reconstruct herself, for example, as either fearful or non-fearful. The construction of oneself, which determines the format of any biographical note, shall be broken through because it is the development of the construct that we look for, not its final outcome.

3. A theoretical prerequisite for the work with memory is the assumption that we know much more about ourselves than we normally assume. Many things have been censored out of our self-image because we deem them not essential, too painful, or too chaotic. For instance, we may present ourselves as intrepid and daring and pass that off as an essential characteristic, or perhaps we remember ourselves as fearful and incapable of taking action in certain or all important situations. Inasmuch as our self-image is a part of our daily ability to act, it can also hinder expansion and continued learning. It tends to balance us to some degree. Removed from these assumptions is the challenge to write in as much detail as possible. That means the writer must not censor or leave out anything but, rather, note everything that exists in the remembered scene. Once the detailed writing begins, participants will notice that they remember more and that we do possess a past richer than we assumed. Self-reflection and remembering can be learned; it's a matter of practice.

4. For practical, research-related reasons, limiting the length of the written text of a memory is useful. The purpose is neither to find the whole truth nor to create a complete construction. Rather, it is to gain insights into the ways of constructing, into focal points, into common sense and its workings, and into the knowledge that we semi-consciously have about ourselves. We accept a certain sketchiness of our work. To avoid pushing a single session beyond two hours, it is advisable to limit description of the remembered scene to about one typewritten page, with one and a half spaces between lines. If time is not a consideration, this limitation may be unnecessary. In that case go ahead and gather a group working with a limit of around three to four typewritten pages and work until the written scenes or memories are finalized. Because the ways of constructing and the idiosyncrasies of individuals repeat themselves, it will soon be obvious that mutual tension will decrease, that some will leave the room, and that hunger, fatigue and requests for breaks will take the place of passionate interest.

Brainstorming: The collective as process

The seminar or research may begin with a brainstorming session about the topic before there are any written remembered scenes. Write the results for all to see on the chalkboard. To name "What I am afraid of" not as an experience but in quotes results in a wide array of responses, which surprise many and immerse all in the topic. This exercise will break the ice in that there will emerge a number of shared conditions of fear, but also strange circumstances that one may never have associated with fear. Both similarity and dissimilarity pull the group together, arouse curiosity and create agreement. The exercise creates a shared empathy into all kinds of situations even though individuals may not recognize them from their own experience. When dealing with the issue of fear, allowing for anything possible seems to demonstrate fear as overpowering and the individual as powerless.

Depending on the time frame and the purpose of the project, the group may continue with the theoretical work involved in this process. The group may attempt to learn something about the complexity of doing theoretical work from the common sense experience of creating categories from the list of fears. The group may order or categorize the different fears, for example, relational fears, fear of authorities, and fear of powerlessness. Other themes may emerge, within which fears of similar nature could be gathered. In doing so, it will become noticeable that each woman uses a system of categorization—similar to theories—which, without question or reflection, help her bring order to her everyday emotional chaos. At any rate, making this a topic of discussion promotes critical reflection.

Otherwise, brainstorming as a method is limited. But in the case of memory-work it serves the additional purpose of showing retrospectively that which was considered noteworthy before further reflection removes it from the category of something learned from our experiences. The superfluous nature of spontaneous namings conceals women as already finished products in the long-standing practice of connecting what is said to the anticipated cultural model, the non-pathological, cultural norm. Brainstorming is not free of ideological justification.

Organic intellectuals

It is easily recognized that memory-work, as a method, struggles with delegating the work as collectively as possible. At the same time, interventions by an experienced researcher are necessary. Each step must be thoroughly explained to every member of the group so that individuals may proceed to another group and share this information. Following the rules of collective debate, it should be possible to find mutual agreement. In his diligent study on collective learning, Miller (1986) maintained that collective argumentations which "conjointly try to answer a commonly identified contestable question" can and must do this in a communicative way via consensus (p. 25). This presupposes that participants really concentrate on the question and do not just devalue each other or elevate themselves.

When pursued in this way, the collective argument has the advantage that it reaches a higher level of new awareness than does the work of a single individual. In my experience this is always the case in memory-work.

Memory-work is applicable in a variety of situations. It is suitable for adult education outside the perimeter of the university, as it is for people beginning something new, or in social movements. Not all the necessary qualifications for the research process of memory-work have to be met by all members of the group, e.g., not every group member has to study big books on the topic in question. It is a good idea to be familiar with theories that surround the given research topic. Theories may help further knowledge, but may also serve as obstacles along the way insofar as they may rule the common sense discussion. For example, when dealing with the topic of fear, psychoanalytic and behavioral theories often are used in their vulgarized form. Such theories could be studied and critiqued during a research seminar using individual experiences. In a non-academic setting, or in a group with other necessities and interests, a selection of theory will have to be presented insofar as it is recognized as important in light of the gathered pool of experience. This necessitates research leaders for memory-work who are familiar with the theories that are associated with the topic and who at the same time will try to pass on as much knowledge as possible in order to be able to count on the critical imagination of each individual. Remember, the study of theory is not an inadvertent privilege of a university but rather is open to anybody.

I call the person leading memory work an organic intellectual. Coined originally by Gramsci[1], it denotes the figure within the group who assumes the intellectual tasks for the group. When doing memory work, there is no division of labor when it comes to writing the remembered experiences. Because the leader has had the same experiences, she should be free from the expert feeling and be able to participate in mutual discussion. This arrangement stirs up imagination while avoiding elitist judgment. No matter how much insight we think we possess, it is only when we have learned to see ourselves as children of these circumstances that we are equipped to work with others as we work about ourselves.

The selection

Depending on the group, a number of decisions have to be made. Suppose you are working with a group of 12 individuals. It is important that all the members of the group have completed the written scene (experience). All who have completed writing their experiences will be motivated to pay close attention to the details within the stories of others because they too have written about their experiences. This also enhances the tolerance for some stories, which may seem trite compared to worldly events. For instance, in a seminar with both male and female participants, I had difficulty getting the male participants to write about their experiences. We worked with the question, "How do we acquire moral judgments?" The men expressed the arrogant opinion that the texts they would create would be far superior in depth and quality and that they would not want to present them to such an unqualified audience. With this attitude the atmosphere was strained, and the analysis never became a reality.

The task that each person write down an experience conflicts with the necessity that initially in working with the whole group, only one or two of these scenes are chosen for discussion. The others are put aside. After the first, collective step, smaller groups of three or four members are formed, in which all works are processed. Nobody has written in vain. For the selection of the first scene, finding a volunteer is rarely a problem. Usually all women want their work to be chosen. Anonymity may be granted but is seldom an issue. The group makes this decision.

How do you choose a scene, though, that will serve as a pilot case to establish how the smaller group discussions should proceed? The criteria for selection should include richness in detail, inclusion of social/cultural background, and, of course, the interests of the group. Here again pragmatic decisions must be made. It is best that all group members take part in the selection process. Allow about an hour break for members to read the 12 scenes. After the scenes have been read, make a balanced majority decision. Admittedly, groups who have not done memory-work before will choose works based on things like tension, literary quality, presumed writer, or the mysteriousness rather than the general comprehensibility of a scene. You may also decide to have the team leader make the selection. This, however, takes away from the group feeling and is also stressful for the leader. This is especially true when one considers that the team leader will have to live through the actual work process afterwards, which requires explaining, analyzing, and additional sociological imagining and feeling for tensions in the group. Making the selections may take at least two hours.

A final consideration is the importance of legible text. Whenever possible, it is best to use typewritten text.

Introduction to some theoretical assumptions

Some of the theoretical assumptions of memory-work should be explained before working with the remembered scenes so that the members of the group are not necessarily at the mercy of the individual work steps. In particular, four theorems seem to be indispensable as known assumptions: the construction of one's own personality, the tendency to eliminate contradictions, the construction of meaning, and the politics of language.

Construction of one's own personality. Our personalities are not simply things we received, were born with, or were predetermined but, rather, are constructed by the self. This self-construction within pre-existing structures implies that a personality has a story, a past. We attach meaning to our personas and use this meaning, or understanding of our personality, to determine the steps we take in the near present and distant future. If we reconstruct and remember ourselves as failures, we will approach new activities timidly. On the other hand we may perceive ourselves as having been born under a lucky star; our memories are full of success stories. Accordingly, we act energetic and straightforward in the future and seize the present. A comprehensive list of our experiences would provide enough information for either construction. It is important we understand that we construct ourselves. That is to say, a personality has a history, and it is essential for both our present and our future to work with the past so that we may always be available for a change in perception. This construction is dictated by our desire to obtain the ability to act and remain able to act.

Tendency to eliminate contradictions. An important strategy in memory-work is the elimination of contradictions. We tend to disregard anything that does not fit in with the unified image that we present to ourselves and others. This mostly semi-conscious act of eliminating contradictions may become transparent in the written experiences as we document the details that do not fit. Deconstruction work is aimed primarily at drawing out these contradictions and breaking points in our experiences. It presents them in a new light and connects them to other developments, choices, or ways of life. The graveyard-like silence of sameness is thus disturbed in order to enable change. A sense of mental unrest is created. If we achieve this sense of mental unrest, we recognize that certain emotions are disquieting and destabilizing; the memory-work is in motion.

Construction of meaning. We attempt in our everyday life to give coherent meaning to ourselves. We create the kind of image of ourselves in which we believe. We try to convey this image in each and every communicative situation. The construction of meaning happens continuously. We speak of ourselves and expect that others receive the message as we wanted to send it out. The construction of meanings thus requires agreement by others. Meaning occurs in the first place through language, but also through gestures, appearance, and expression.

Politics of language. Working with language usage is of central importance in the discussion of an experience documented in written form. How does the writer use language to convey the meaning she is aiming at without raising much doubt? A prerequisite for this critical work is understanding that language is not simply a tool that we may use according to our liking. Rather, in the existing language, politics will speak through us and regulate our construction of meaning. Thus culturally a number of ready meanings lie around, so to speak; they push themselves on us when we write and dictate what we might not even have wanted to express. This happens when we less reflectively and more naively use language. Of course, the more we try not to stand out as personalities and wish to attribute normality to our experiences, the more we use these ready meanings.

The theoretical assumptions could be presented and made a subject for discussion in the first seminar session, and/or they could be read by the participants individually in preparation for the work. For that purpose, the following article, among others, seems useful: Haug (2000) Chapter 1, or in shorter version, Haug (1997), or Kippax (1997). There is secondary literature in all three.

Steps in the editing process

It is best to use a chalkboard or another device so that all participants can see the individual steps. Copies of the first remembered scene should be distributed to everyone and then read out loud. We first want the meaning the author wishes to convey. Most of us learned in school how to interpret text. What does the poet want to tell us? The method used in school is opposite to the method used in memory work; it takes things literally, tries to think and feel like the poet. We do not follow this method when doing memory-work, but it is critical in this first step.

We read the memories aloud to avoid a permanent temptation to put ourselves in the author's shoes rather than examine the meaning laid out by her. At this point it is important, however, to work toward a consensus about the author's meaning. This will open up a lively discussion. A number of different suggestions should arise, as each member of the group tries to understand the text. There are never any wrong answers. Each suggestion should build upon the others creating a thesis-like formulation of different statements, ultimately reaching a consensus. On one occasion, while doing a scene about fear in dark places, it was suggested that the author was afraid of animals in the dark. Another participant suggested that the author was afraid of trees and wind. All group members were immediately in agreement that the author was afraid of non-human nature. This was especially baffling in this case because most listeners first thought she was afraid of men.

Consensus about common sense. It is best to limit the initial discussion about the meaning or message to about 15 minutes. Everyone is still fresh and motivated to discuss endlessly, which will waste valuable time that will be needed later. In the first discussion many will still have on their academic masks. The group leader must be able to recognize a good breaking point and then summarize what has been said. It is not necessary to recite the whole dialogue, but rather sum up what was said. The message found within her writing not only conveys the author's intention, but also fosters the idea that we are working forward as a group towards our culturally shared self-understanding.

Adages or sayings are particularly suitable for expressing what somebody wants to say. They also give us the opportunity to reflect on those congealed common sense wisdom sayings and their functions. We may see that most often they are constructed in a way that their opposite is equally true. For instance: "Birds of a feather flock together," or "opposites attract," illustrate that we think-feel in such traditional patterns. The thesis statement is placed in the first row, which spans the chalkboard (see Table 2.1. Another version of the table can be found in Schratz &Walker, 1995). Try making the thesis statement as brief as possible so that it may be quickly written and so that it does not use up too much space.

The second row contains another dimension of common sense and was gathered in the discussion about the message. This row contains the everyday theory about the topic and its context in relation to the writer. Using the example from above, that would be: "Fear develops where civilization ends." This idea, which each participant has about the topic, is most often not a conscious and elaborate theory, but a supposition silently kept to herself. I call this common sense theory. It is a part of our everyday lives and necessary for daily orientation. Whenever we do not explicitly formulate it and put it in front of us, it unexpectedly, without questions, weaves its way into all discussions. It is almost always a surprise to the women since most of them never knew they harbored such theories or feelings. These theories are often replicas of simplified psychoanalytic theories that have woven their way into the fabric of everyday consciousness. They, too, will be exposed and confronted in the later part of our work.

Analyzing the elements of the language. The next step is simple and at the same time rigorous. We want to find out how the meaning that the author wanted to convey about her experience was expressed with language. The first task is to break from the realm of conveyed meaning, and distance ourselves for the work of deconstruction. This is not easily done because most individual experiences reported rely on empathy and comprehension and are successful in eliciting these in everyday communication. The consequence is the attempt to cultivate therapeutic discourses of sympathy and to relate connecting stories by way of "psychologizing." This stance and practice is not only theoretically unproductive, but it also stands in the way of insight. It invites group members to ally with opponents of understanding and active thinking and simply increases painful perceptions. It is absolutely necessary that distance be established in order to work with the text.

Table 2.1
Format for Record of Collective Editing Process
 (Individual cells, of course, may be expanded as needed.)

Statement of Author's Meaning:			
Common Sense Theory:			
Analysis of Elements of Language:			
List of Verbs As Activity	Linguistic Peculiarities	Emotion	Motivation
For Others Presented in Narrative:			
Activity	Emotion		Motivation
Vacuums		Contradictions	
Construction of "I:"			
Construction of Others:			
Thesis Statement Based on Deconstruction and Reconstruction:			

A method of distancing is posing questions to the text. Behind each question asked is a kind of theory about the subject. Try to keep the questions as simple as possible, and keep the implicit theory controllable at any time. The questions about the text are limited to language use—basic grammatical rules. Sentences contain a subject, a verb, an object, perhaps adjectives. They give information about the engaged person, her emotions, her activities, and other persons. With this notion, we split the text into its elements and place them in vertical columns. We are searching for the way and manner in which the writer constructs herself, that is, her personality, and how she thus creates meaning and coherence, as well as in what way other people are constructed in relation to her.

 1. The verb as activity. First write all verbs referring to the subject of the narrative. This simple act of collecting, which does not require more than about three years of formal education, reveals a number of surprises. Oftentimes the verbs are not found or are hardly detectable. All verbs are listed randomly, and a discussion begins about which verbs do, in fact, refer to the subject of the narrative. "It was cold for me." Is this a verb, an activity, which belongs to a person? Obviously, yes, and at the same time, no, because the subject of this sentence is an "It," an impersonal subject which determines the action. Furthermore, the verb is also an auxiliary verb.

2. *Linguistic peculiarities.* We create another column, which we call linguistic peculiarities. Here we list to what degree the narrative is written with impersonal subjects. This often reveals that the persona of the writer disappears almost completely, at least as an active agent, and instead is in the hands of other powers. It becomes noticeable that in such situations there is nothing she can do. One observes that there are experiences that are presented exclusively in such a way as if impersonal subjects will determine the plot. Consider, for example, "hunger grabbed me," "fog enveloped me," "the dark surprised me," "the sky exploded." These are phrases in which movement and activity appear compacted. None of the subjects, however, are people, and so the narrative subject herself does not act as an active agent. Another particularity is the use of negated verbs, for example, did not run, and the frequent weakening of activities through auxiliary verbs, such as, can, like, want. Both make the narrator less important for the narration. There are cases in which one to two active verbs are sufficient for the narrative subject and also those cases in which the same verb, such as, "said," is always used. These peculiarities will be discussed at a later point to see if it is merely the language deficit, using the same verb repeatedly, or whether it also demonstrates the hopelessness of the situation. Given the way the situation unfolded, there was nothing else to say.

In my experience the power of memory coupled with the desire to convey a certain message, for instance, that there was nothing one could do, is far stronger than the new knowledge that one makes politics with language, and vice versa. By the way, this step, which at first appears somewhat tedious, is usually deemed interesting by the whole group. During these discussions, many women realize for the first time how they actually use language when they narrate.

3. *Emotions.* The next column is reserved for emotions. We would expect that in a narrative about fear or about a touching movie, the scene would express a number of feelings through language. Additionally, with a group of women, the so-called sensitive gender, one would expect a number of strong emotions. It is always surprising though, that most narratives are written void of named emotions, as if emotions were not important. In most scenarios it seems as if the absence of feelings is necessary to make the observation appear reasonable. One might compare this to the reproduction of experiences of women when watching campy love stories in Haug and Hipfl (1995).

After two to three words are listed, this process is usually finished. A heated discussion often follows about whether or not certain hints, constellations, or even probabilities point toward feelings and emotions. The desire to read into, feel into, and interpret the text has been awakened anew. Because we study the language work of the author, that is, how she constructs herself through language, it is only the literal account, not an interpretation, that counts. I have grown restless from my long experience with memory-work. I want to get to know more about this curious insensibility in self-perception and self-projection, not having found yet any relevant literature or the time to initiate my own research project. The great pressure at the seminars to speak about fear and the number of love stories read weekly by women make pursuing such a project more and more important.

4. *Motivation.* The next column lists interests and desires. Only after some experience with memory-work did we begin to include this column. We discovered almost all narratives are constructed so that actions of both the narrator and other persons were basically incomprehensible. Creating confusion, such irrationality in language has the effect that the narrative subject again has no opportunity for active agency and appeals at best to the sympathy of her audience. Such a picture fits with the dominant ideology, therefore we should inquire about motive. Without having particularly radical theoretical premises, we assume that people act on the basis of motivation and that most will mention their motives in an event. The search for those motives, which is mostly in vain, sheds an interesting light on the self-perception and self-presentation of the narrator. The extensive absence of interests and desires is even noticeable when we do not insist on literally naming them in this column, but rather attempt to reconstruct the motivations from the narrations. Such reconstruction means analyzing and trying to understand instead of following the language used, which is a different method. It is also dangerous because it allows the members of the group to leave the surface of the words and open up a discussion on opinion and interpretation, which is hard to draw back to the actual narrative.

5. *The others.* The next columns, as needed, are reserved for the presentation of the other persons in the narrative. Most often other characters in the stories do not possess actions and feelings, nor do their desires and interests represent a plot that is cohesive to the structure of the story. These columns fill fast. This gives more time to discuss this characteristic in and of itself. A sharpened attention develops with the following questions. How do we refer to others in everyday life? What is it about others that we ignore? How much of their own lives do we grant them? And, most importantly, what is the meaning of this non-perception of others for the cohesion of a narrative in which others nevertheless appear?

6. *Vacuums and contradictions.* There are still two more columns, which may be filled during the discussion about individual linguistic elements or during the following discussion about the constructions of "I" and "Others." These elements do not refer to the literal text, but require inquiry into that which is not mentioned. One column asks for vacuums, that is, elements not mentioned in the written memory but necessary to the plausibility and agreement of the story. The

other asks for contradictions in the story. That these columns have become a part of the project implies that individuals, in order to remain agents, have to give their stories and their self-perception a sense of cohesiveness. They must eliminate contradictions that might possibly appear in this process, or simply ignore certain individual elements. For example, we came to know a story about the topic "waiting," which is important for women. Three women (grandmother, mother and daughter) regularly remained for hours in the garden, apparently without reason. The group pointed out that something was missing and the scene made no sense. Suddenly in a second version, a mentally handicapped father appeared. The three women were in the garden all the time because they walked around with him. You can imagine how different the story was now with this detail.

Elimination of contradictions is a well-known psychological process. We see this process in action in the narratives. To search for the silence or vacancies was a discovery in feminist research (first, in feminist theology, e.g., Fiorenza, 1983), which only now makes a connection to why scientific systems and theories seem to be right, even though women are not included. The search for silence or vacancies has by now become a recognized scientific method. In the narratives, we recognize that we use this technique in everyday life. Detecting these peculiarities, we are able to question the narrative without questioning the credibility of the writer. It becomes clear how artistically constructed a narrative of one's experience may be; how many additional possibilities for action and perception there are; and how differently one could have developed.

Construction of "I." The following steps are difficult and demand both analytical abilities and imagination. The former can be learned individually, while the latter requires the abilities of the group. We first examine the construction of the "I," the first-person narrator.

A line is drawn under the vertical columns. For the construction of the "I" we will need the whole width of the chalkboard and a different work process. As a guideline, it should be said that the basis for work is now exclusively the just finished chart, and we will not return to the text to make sure one knows the true opinion of the narrator. Transfer the chart to an overhead transparency or use another alternative surface. It is important that we have a new space in which to write, but we still must be able to see the old chart. Literal reports of authors are now completely rejected because the authors of the reports are tempted to note self-perception as a statement about personal construction, which means we are taken in by the writer. Thus, there will not be any writing about a scene, for instance, where the narrator says about herself, "I was a scared, fearful being." The writer constructs herself as scared and fearful. It is our task, however, to find out how she leaves that impression for us. In the present case, for example, it could be possible that we see the author mainly as active and able to act, not as scared and fearful. That means that the sentence "I was a scared and fearful being" perhaps intends to make us sympathetic toward the person. She probably earns sympathy because of her great though unsuccessful activity.

All statements about the construction are analytical, and require a parallel vocabulary of terms. Writing down these short sentences, I recall the work process with trepidation. It is easy to say that the work process at this stage should be analytical and use analytical concepts, but if you try to do this in a group, there are always some who become advocates of some "authentic" author who should be defended against the analysis. They start formulating sentences such as, "but she really loved her husband, mother, etc." Or, "she was afraid of them," e.g., with respect to the scenes about fear in the dark (recall this example in the Steps in the Editing Process section). When everybody was convinced that anxiety in the dark comes from men behind trees, etc. and the stories were all written without any male member of the species, it was hard to write down clear sentences, such as, "men were absent from the scenes." I have found that such difficulties give rise to a total unease that is both intellectual and emotional. It is unavoidable at this point not to be impatient because the tendency always is to try to go back to the text and rescue the "true" author, in opposition to the analytic method. This disposition, rather to feel and interpret, belongs to our daily orientation and probably is part of the usual literary analysis in a German or English class. This approach to thinking and its acquisition also should be a separate research project.

At first, the jump from a critical collection of textual elements to the invitation to formulate observations is a very big one. It is therefore beneficial to begin with a relatively easy observation. After noticing a column full of verbs, the first statement might be, "On first sight, the author constructs herself as a very active person." Now one approaches the multitude of activity words and checks their quality, for instance, "On second sight, however, the named activities all take place in the imagination;" or "the activities are mostly expressed in negative form as non-activities;" or they are "diminished through use of an auxiliary verb;" or they are "made vague through other additions." In my experience, it is easy to find the various qualities associated with the written activities, and oftentimes, there will be a lively discussion in the group. I have yet to experience a group that was not able to judge sharply and accurately, and able to note in brief sentences what was observed. Most of the time, there is additional amazement about how different the observations are from what was read spontaneously. The desire to make harsh judgments develops, maybe due to a kind of relief that one does not have to stick to the literal text anymore, maybe because one has the impression of moving forward, maybe also just to teach the writer a lesson.

It is necessary to avoid making a group member feel hurt or judged. Therefore, initially and again and again, it should be pointed out that it is not the writer who is the subject of investigation but the text. Also, indicate that the text itself does not contain the "truth" about the writer. Through our work with these texts, we come to understand the ways of construction, which reveal a mutual knowledge about self-representation and construction in our culture. Some individuals are very sensitive and not at all used to questioning themselves. In some groups, something like a climate for unmasking emerges. Generally, however, this step is enjoyable and encourages the participants to work more and gainfully on themselves. At this point, during the discussion of the noted activities, it is beneficial to consult the Linguistic Peculiarities column. It often results in better explanations of strange phenomena. This is the case, for instance, when on first sight, the writer constructs and presents herself as incredibly active, but in the bigger picture she gives the impression that she is unable to do anything. This effect is reached among others through the usage of many impersonal subjects, which take over the direction in the text.

The Emotion column will often elicit, "The writer constructs herself as being without emotions." Dealing with this finding is mostly unambiguous on the level of observation. No emotions or very few emotions are named although the threshold to feelings is approached, as in "she had a feeling." The writing style does not allow any other conclusion than that emotions do not play a role for the narrator in her experiencing, or that they are not worth mentioning. Most of the time, however, this observation meets with forceful protest from both the writer and the rest of the group. Evidently, it is important for self-presentation and self-perception to have emotions. Since the mutual observation cannot simply be interpreted away but a feeling of uneasiness remains, it is beneficial to pose further questions about the fate of emotions and to stimulate further discussion and research about this topic.

The group leader should make provocative and contradictory statements to arouse further research on the subject. For example, "Evidently, women, this supposedly so emotional gender, are unable to express feelings," or, "Something happens to the emotions and feelings of women in our society; they wilt, become not allowed or unnamed," could be said. What does it mean when activities that we know are accompanied, steered, blocked, or perpetuated by feelings are reported without mention of the feelings, but we still deem what we have written out as a carefully laid out, valid experience? Maybe, this is the beginning of a new research project. From my experience, the following statement always holds true. In documented experiences by women, feelings occur highly peripherally, even when the documents concern the experience of antagonistic feelings. In addition the feelings have to be regarded by the group as mostly superficial, measured on the scale of humanly possible passions. You can respond to the arguments within the group with a short break. Everybody has to write down which feelings are evident and, accordingly, what language cues they use to determine the feeling in the scene.

Surprise about the language construction along the way makes looking at the column Motivation seem like a mere confirmation. Usually this column is empty, as if women lived and acted without motivation. Similar to the question of feelings, this observation also stimulates further research. Concerning the construction of the narrator, the sentence emerges, "She constructs herself as devoid of interests." Perhaps in looking at the impersonal subjects or in looking ahead toward the construction of others, it may become evident if the woman constructs herself as powerless, faint, or left in the hands of strange powers, for example.

Construction of the "others." After the difficult task of tracing the construction of "I," construction of the others is quickly detected most of the time. First of all, are there any others? It is clear that the way others are perceived and documented is also a part of the I-construction and it also needs to be handled this way. For example, in a long remembered scene that took place in a big demonstration in a major city, other persons were not ever mentioned, or at best, mentioned as part of the scenery. The writer thus constructs herself as lonely, as a single protester, alone. Sometimes, however, there are other persons, such as, the mother, the father, boyfriend, girlfriend. In attempting to find out something about their constructions, one almost always realizes that the authors did not make an effort to bring reasonably alive fellow human beings into the experience. Perhaps one or another activity is described, but rarely feelings, wishes, or interests. The other persons often function as a service to the credible presentation of the narrator, but they do not have their own lives. They are not people with whom some mutual activity would be done, solved, or lived.

On an abstract level each participant knows that she neither lives by herself nor that she can do much by herself. Since especially in such a memory-work group a collective attempt is made to live a part of feminist culture, the self-perception of an individual woman as living on an island like Robinson Crusoe and having to tackle everything by herself is articulated by all as a scandal, which necessitates individual efforts toward resolution.

At the same time, the group should discuss the issue of tracing back any events to the inner part of a person, the fading out of others, and the social circumstances as contributing to a self-perception that is culturally supported in our individualistic society. The development of our own culture becomes an urgent task, which relates to individual development and freedom.

Shifting the problem. In this last and most difficult editing step, especially when this work is being done for the first time, we search for the message or meaning created by the deconstruction of the narrative and latent praxis connections. This is different from, and even in contrast to, the initially agreed upon message that was discussed, and which the author was trying to convey through her story. It is recommended, therefore, not to look quickly to the first lines of the Initial Thesis Statement and also not to go back into the narrative. Rather, formulate a new message in the form of a thesis statement from the constructions of "I" and Others, and from the columns about Vacuums and Contradictions. The reconstructed thesis does not correspond to the author's intended meaning. She has nevertheless written it down, and it shows the semi-conscious awareness of the connection she is living. Oftentimes, it is discovered that alone one cannot do anything, or, where one does not listen to advice one is lost, or, similar sentences, which sound like pebbles smoothed on truth. They are that which is not said but wanted to be said.

Finally, one can compare this last thesis statement, a reconstruction based on deconstruction, with the initial thesis statement deduced in consensus. One often will be surprised how poor and also how ideological the earlier intended message was, compared to the new meaning elicited after the deconstruction process. This does not mean that one is true and the other invalid. Both messages are from the author. The circumstances that produced the one at the cost of the other show how strange our dealings are with ourselves, and how we struggle with ambiguity and knowledge in everyday life.

Insecurity and therapy

Time and again questions are posed: "Is memory-work a careless endeavor because it makes participants highly uncertain? And is its process so similar to that of psychoanalysis that memory-work could be used for therapeutic purposes?" To avoid extensive discourse on such a broad, complex fundamental as differing personalities in our society, I will limit myself to a few sentences, which shall be elaborated at another time.

The fear that one may become uncertain about herself by reflecting and working on the self is justified. However, without any uncertainty, there is no development. The desire to be able to live without uncertainty is naive.

Memory-work is not intended to provide therapy for suffering persons. This is not cynically meant, but the formulation is derived from the opinion that therapy uses expert knowledge to help people who cannot help themselves. If increases in self-recognition, knowledge about socialization processes, competence about language and meaning, and critique of theory are fundamental and prerequisites for the growing ability to act, memory-work aims at such an outcome.

The second version

To assist with the writing of a second version, it is best if the author is present when her written scene is being analyzed, and if possible, assists with the deconstruction. There should be an explicit ban, however, on the author heading into more explanation and teaching of others every time she feels that the others get off track. Similarly, she should not expand her explanation when she does not like something said, when she wanted to say something completely different, when she expressed herself in the wrong way, etc. After all that has been said before, when she persists, it is clear that she will only attempt to present her message in a more articulate way and thus block the analysis. One can smuggle in a lot of meaning in oral communication because nobody afterwards can put a finger on individual words.

Even though women who stand on their rights as authors often hinder the process so that you want to cut off their comments, you should still take the growing concerns of the author into account. If you have enough time, it is a great advantage to obtain a second written version of the edited scene. The writer can rewrite all of the parts where she felt she was misunderstood, did not express herself clearly enough, or where she remembers now that things were different. She should be instructed to fill in the vacant spots that were found and make statements about the obvious contradictions. For the continuing editing process it is useful to note the parts that were left standing in another typeface in order to clearly mark the changes. The writer soon realizes from her undertaken corrections that the whole scene does not fit anymore, and she will rewrite more and more. The group will be surprised to see that the opposite of what was initially written has sometimes appeared. In summary, the leveling of contradictions, the artful vacancies, all of these attempts to make the narrative cohesive now all of a sudden appear fragile. The new story is a lesson to everyone—the writer herself and the editors—and it adds new proof of the value of strategies for the harmonization of memory. Most of the time it is the persona of the "victim" who suddenly appears in an unfavorable light in the rewritten memory.

For example, once, after a first memory of a family in which mother and daughter were subjects to a jerky father, we received a second version in which father and daughter saw themselves confronted with a noisy, good-for-nothing, indifferent mother. She chased the father out of the house, destroyed a wonderful father-daughter relationship, and put all the responsibility on the daughter. These discrepancies between the first and the second versions lead to suspicion that the scene was not becoming "truer" but that we were getting closer to the author's manner of construction. In this instance the case consisted of an absolute enemy-friend perception in which the author herself was always a victim merely of different personas.

In another case, a story about a bad, lusting, physical education teacher was rewritten into one which depicted how the fanciful wishes of a whole class brought individuals in harsh competition with each other, an arrangement that motivated best performances in order to secure the favor of the teacher. In each case, the writing and editing of a second version of the experience strengthens the insight about the constructive nature of our memory. At the same time it creates insecurity about whether something like a true or real memory exists at all, and it shows that it is worthwhile to continue with more care.

About the politics of language

To make an insecurity productive, if it is worthwhile at all to use such a burdensome procedure as memory-work for everyday life and its knowledge, a repeat discussion about language and its usage is helpful. We so far have given the impression that strategically we use certain linguistic means in order to achieve the desired meaning and effect. We will now turn to the linguistic expression in whose captivity we find ourselves.

Michel Foucault made the statement that language is a field of conflict, where the dominant culture wins its hegemony. While speaking and expressing our feelings and our will, dominant normality is speaking. There is no way out. We follow this thought a short way and assume that in patriarchal cultures such "foreign" speaking or the absence of women's "own" language most likely applies. But following such a view would consequently sentence us to eternal deconstruction, and there would be no basis for winning our own home. For memory-work this leads to the question, where do sense and meaning, which are constituted in the story, come from? Also you have to ask yourself the importance of the other parts of the story.

We can agree that every author of an everyday situation first has to try to write in the dominant language. She must write with appropriate feelings, sensibly and logically ordered and, at first glance, without contradiction, a story completed with beginning, climax and end so that we can understand her. By using the dominant language we get to know the dominant cultural pattern. Using such language conveys experience. The proclaimed experience is therefore a political process, which is made automatically. In telling the story you confirm that you went through this process. But nobody other than the describing subjects is able to see this process as development and not as an experience of a class goal. We assume that we can find in the experience evidence of semiconscious things, departures and contradictions. Often this is revealed in the stories as inappropriate words, senseless pieces, reasonless silence, or contradictory statements. These are also experiences, but stand in conflict with the dominant meaning of the experience gained.

We compare the single experience against the potential of a single person in the world. It seems possible to assume that every single person has the need to escape from the conditions in which she is acting and to reach competence, autonomy, and codetermination in every important question. This condition has a political and critical-of-domination dimension as well as a methodical dimension. Each woman in the research group can examine her own texts, how she makes compromises, how she falls in line or submits so that she does not lose her ability to act in contradictory structures. The way of life, attitude and pattern of processing conflict become readable as a solution that was functional, but seems today as if you have never been older than four years old. At the same time, you wish for the complete ability to act, comprehensive solutions, and the ability to create a living culture of contradiction instead of a culture of inequality. This is a position where you can work for the possibility of a freer life and which therefore may become a vision, a possibility to make happen something you wanted or divined. This search is collective. The language is found in the process and the material is lying around in the described experiences as undiscovered knowledge. The process is always unfinished.

The end

Memory-work is an emancipating learning project. So there is no summary of the results from this guide. It started with the naive desire to obtain quite quickly and comprehensively a collection of socialization experiences of women, which, maybe worldwide, would bring back the forgotten women to the social sciences. The difficulty was not the lack of passion or the lack of people who wanted to participate. The difficulty and also the results were the topic itself. It became more and more obvious that things went the same way with us as they did with Gulliver and his trip to the Lilliputians. We were tied up at every single hair and woven into the social power connection. The first easy task became the enormous task to break away from so many ties. It became clear that our task was not to develop knowledge to spread. We found out that memory-work is a process, which is itself a way and a goal. At the same time, it is a departure and impulse for change, which has to include the condition of our actions and beings.

Notes

1. Antonio Gramsci has developed a theory of the intellectuals in his Prison Notebooks. His main idea is that the intellectual is not a professional but fulfills a function that anyone could perform if she is trained. Every class and every movement has its own intellectuals who formulate the interests of this group and serve it. These intellectuals, who are independent whether they serve the ruling class or the workers or the women in our group, being members of the group, are called organic intellectuals. The concept is as clear and practicable as the term is difficult and unusual.

References

Crawford, June; Kippax, Susan; Onyx, Jenny; Gault, Una & Benton, Pam, (1992). *Emotion and gender: Constructing meaning from memory*. Newbury Park, CA: Sage.

Fairclough, Norman. (1995). *Critical discourse analysis: The critical study of language*. London: Polity Press.

Fiorenza, Elisabeth Schussler. (1983). In memory of her: A feminist theological reconstruction of Christian origins. New York: Crossroad.

Haug, Frigga (Ed.). (2000). Sexualization of the female body. London: Verso, 2nd edition.

Haug, Frigga & Brigitte Hipfl (Hg.). (1995). *Suendiger genuss? Filmerfahrungen von Frauen*. Hamburg: Argument-Verlag.

Haug, Frigga. (1997). The Hoechst Chemical Company and boredom with the economy. In R. Hennessy & Chrys Ingraham (Eds.), *Materialist feminism: A reader in class, difference, and women's lives* (pp. 129-140). New York & London: Routledge.

Kippax, Susan. (1997). Erinnerungsarbeit. In W. F. Haug (Hg.), *Historisch-Kritisches Woerterbuch des Marxismus, Bd. 3* (pp. 734-739). Hamburg: Argument-Verlag.

Miller, Max. (1986). *Kollektive lernprozesse: Studien zur grundlegung einer soziologischen lerntheorie*. Frankfurt: Suhrkamp.

Schratz, Michael; Walker, Rob & Schratz-Hadwich, Barbara. (1995). Collective memory-work. The self as a re/source for re/search. In Michael Schratz & Rob Walker, *Research as social change: New opportunities for qualitative research* (pp. 39-64). London:Routledge.

Tischer, Stefan; Wodak, Ruth; Meyer, Michael & Vetter, Eva. (1998). *Methoden der textanalyse: Leitfaden und ueberblick*. Wiesbaden & Opladen: Westdeutscher Verlag.

van Dijk, Teun A. (1995). Editor's foreword to Critical Discourse Analysis. *Discourse and Society, 4/2*, 131-132.

Part Two

Stretching Memory-work

Chapter 3

Practicing Collective Biography

Bronwyn Davies

Collective biography is a research strategy that is inspired by Frigga Haug's (1987) memory-work. Like Haug and her colleagues, the collective biography groups I have been part of have worked with memories to generate new insights into the processes through which we are subjected. Similarly, the memories are generated by a group of scholars working together on a particular topic. In *Female sexualization: A collective work of memory* (1987), Haug and her colleagues worked on the topic of the body. My own collective biography groups have analyzed our embodiment in academic workplaces, but also topics such as becoming schoolgirls, reading fiction, the feminist subject, reflexivity, and power (Davies & Gannon, 2006)[1]. One of the reasons we have chosen to name our process differently from Haug and her colleagues is that our emphasis is different in several significant ways.

The term collective biography is chosen to highlight the possibility of opening up a different relation between the individual and the collective, both theoretically and in practice. The individual identity is no longer so clearly separate(d) from others as it is in humanist theories. A new meaning of empathy is generated in which there is, as expressed in the Reggio Emilia schooling context: "a closeness that creates bonds, that enables each group member to recognize the other and to recognize him/herself in the other" (Ceppi & Zini, 1998, p. 19).

Collective biography focuses on the movement from individual biographies as these are drawn on in the memory stories, to a different relation among those individuals and their stories. That different relation is opened up through the particular mode of telling and listening to each other's stories, and through the collaborative work of analyzing the topic at hand in relation to the corpus of stories that have been written in the workshop. In each of these processes, the focus shifts from the individual to the processes of subjectification in which all subjects are necessarily caught up. Memory-work is a vital tool in this process of deconstructing the binary individual/collective. The specific task of collective biography workshops is to use memory-work to produce new insights into the social and discursive processes through which individuals are, from one moment to the next, constituting themselves and being constituted.

Female sexualization had a foot both in the poststructural camp and a foot in the radical feminist camp. At the time of its publication, both camps, who were more often in opposition to each other, found much of value in that book. In order to accomplish the unusual feat of appealing to opposing theoretical positions the poststructural elements of their theorizing were downplayed. In the English translation, these appear primarily in the translator's introduction (Carter, 1987). It is nevertheless problematic to hold these two approaches together. In radical feminist methodologies, "experience" is read as the fundamental building block of resistance; it reveals the way the world "really" is, and should not be. In poststructural methodologies, stories of experience are no longer read as having a veridical relationship with a real world that exists independent of our engagement with it. In this approach, the analytic gaze shifts from the individual's experience of the world, to the discursive means through which that experience is made meaningful. The interest is no longer in expressions "of an individual's being or consciousness" (Scott, 1992, p. 27) or in discursive strategies through which meanings might be fixed and limited.

From a poststructural perspective, what is seeable, hearable, even thinkable, shifts with the interactional space the researcher inhabits, with the time and the purpose in telling, and with the discursive possibilities available (or brought to the surface of speech) at the time of each telling (Davies, 2003). In contrast, realist paradigms such as radical feminism, maintain/insist that there are truths about the real world that can be uncovered from/through data that is "collected" and that these truths should inform/foreground collective policy and action (Gannon & Davies, 2007; Davies & Davies, 2007). Although the realism and humanism of the radical feminist subject appears and reappears in poststructural work (Davies, Browne, Gannon, Hopkins, McCann & Wihlborg, 2006), it is a difficult balancing act that Haug accomplished in holding them together in the same conceptual space. Our choice, in developing collective biography as a research strategy, to be named differently from memory-work has been to move outside these tensions and to place both feet more squarely in the conceptual space of poststructural theory.

In generating memories in collective biography workshops, then, we do not take memory to be "reliable" in the sense of providing an unquestionable facticity, nor do we take what initially surfaces as being truer, or more valid, than the texts that are worked and reworked in this approach. In a sense it is the very *unreliability* of memory that enables this close discursive work, since it denaturalizes the subject and her experiences by making the discursive work visible, and makes it possible to look in detail at how individuals become subjects of power/knowledge. In collective biography workshops the talk around memories, the listening to the detail of other's memories, is a technology for enabling the participants to produce, through attention to the embodied sense of being in the remembered moment, a truth in relation to what cannot actually be recovered—the moment as it was lived. The truth of the memory stories is not a naturalistic or realist "Truth," but a truth that is more akin to an artist's truth. It is a truth that takes risks, that breaks with the repetitive, citational practices through which the story might more usually have been told. It evokes that still moment of recognition in the listener or reader, in which it is possible to say, "Ah, yes, so that's how it is. I too can recognize myself here." It is a truth that is worked on, through a technology of telling, listening and writing, and it is a truth that does not set out to re-present a static pre-existing reality.

The subject and power

In a Foucauldian analysis, power resides not so much in those who are seen in common-sense terms to "hold it," but in the collective, detailed workings of everyone's everyday lives. Individuals discipline themselves and each other to become recognizable within the terms of those discourses practiced in common (Davies, 2003). They become appropriate and appropriated subjects (Davies, 2000a) whose practices serve to establish and maintain multiple relations of power to produce and reproduce the subjection of themselves and each other (Foucault, 1994). It is in the very act of becoming a recognizable subject that one gains a purchase on power/knowledge, and power/knowledge gains a purchase on that subject. And as Foucault points out, that purchase on the subject is greatest when the power is least visible, that is, when it has been "normalised" and so made to appear as unquestionably the way the world is and thus should be.

The strategies of surveillance that operate socially, and that we take up as our own, must thus be made visible. In discussing panopticism and the power of the gaze, Foucault analyzes the ways in which we become subject to our own controlling gaze, becoming both controller and controlled:

> He who is subjected to a field of visibility, and who knows it, assumes responsibility for the constraints of power; he makes them play spontaneously upon himself; he inscribes in himself the power relation in which he simultaneously plays both roles; he becomes the principle of his own subjection. (Foucault, 1979, pp. 202-3)

In this way, the power that weighs on us and subjects us becomes invisible; its touch is often so light that we do not know it is there. What collective biography does is make this force/movement/action/process of turning on oneself visible—the mechanisms of power at work in oneself and on oneself become available for inspection. The identity accomplished in that taking on of power over oneself may no longer be, in that new awareness, the precious, naturalized, essentialized object to be maintained at all costs. It becomes instead an observable way of being taken up both by oneself and by others, a way of being that identifies one, makes one a recognizable subject, and makes one, at the same time obedient to the powers of government.

Foucault (1994, p. 331) identifies three types of struggle against the powers through which lives are shaped:

> . . . against forms of domination (ethnic, social and religious); against forms of exploitation that separate individuals from what they produce; or against that which ties the individual to himself and submits him to others in this way (struggles against subjection [*assujettissement*], against forms of subjectivity and submission).

Although each of these struggles is bound to the others, the emphasis of radical feminism, and of Haug's memory-work, is on the first (although Foucault has omitted to add gender in his list). Haug and her collective used memory-work as a strategy for resisting the dominance of Marxist theory in which the actual lived experience of women was written out of theory as irrelevant. They set out to generate theory that began with their experience as women. They used memory stories to build theory differently, not as Marxism was built, on the (implicit) experiences of men, but explicitly on the experiences of women.

As a strategy of resistance, collective biography places its emphasis on the third type of struggle, without ignoring the first two, of course, since they are inevitably bound up with each other. It is in this type of resistance that Foucault sees the necessity of work in the present:

> Maybe the most certain of all philosophical problems is the problem of the present time, and of what we are in this very moment.
> Maybe the target nowadays is not to discover what we are but to refuse what we are. We have to imagine and to build up what we could be to get rid of this kind of political "double-bind," which is the simultaneous individualization and totalization of modern power structures.
> The conclusion would be that the political, ethical, social, philosophical problem of our days is not to try to liberate the individual from the state, and from the state's institutions, but to liberate us both from the state and from the type of individualization linked to the state. (1994, p. 336)

But how are those of us writing in the Social Sciences to take up this challenge? Collective biography opens up one possible strategy among many others for analyzing the individualizing and totalizing strategies that work on us and through us in our own everyday lives.

Collective biography seeks to make power visible, both in the way it is taken up in individual lives, and as it works on each individual. The analysis of each memory, and of the corpus of memories, allows us to ask, with Foucault, "What's going on just now? What's happening to us? What is this world, this period, this precise moment in which we are living?" (1994, p. 335). Its strategies open up the possibility of different ways of seeing and thinking and in doing so they gesture toward a Deleuzian engagement with difference. That engagement involves a reconfiguring of the relations between the author, the subject/object of writing, the text, and the reader. First, it invites us to discard the self-conscious "I," the one who "knows." Second, it invites us to abandon representation, in which one re-presents the same, a repetition of the original. Each act, instead is specifically itself—it is this—not that. Third, it invites us to experience/experiment with language and with ourselves, each in order to enable us to think beyond what is already thinkable—what is already there to be thought (Deleuze, 1994).

In my book with Susanne Gannon, *Doing collective biography* (2006), we coined the term mo(ve)ment in order to evoke the doubled action involved in our collective story-telling and writing, of dwelling in and on particular *moments* of being, and of *movement* toward, or openness to, new possibilities both of seeing and of being. In telling, listening, questioning, writing, reading and rewriting our stories, a shift takes place. The memories are no longer told and heard as just autobiographical (that is, the assemblage of already known stories that mark one person off from the next, that pin down the essential self), but as opening up for, and in each other, knowledges of being that previously belonged only to the other as that other's marks of identity. In working collectively with memories we have each imagined, and thus lived intimately within our own bodies, the places and modes of being that previously marked only the specificity of each in her difference from the other. Through a particular attention to listening, the possibility of movement is opened up. Each subject's specificity in its very particularity, in its sensory detail, becomes the collectively imagined detail through which we know ourselves as human, even as more human.

In a conversation about her writing and of what it is she means when she thinks about individual human subjects in her writing, Helene Cixous says to Marie Calle-Gruber, "We live, but why do we live? I think: to become more human: more capable of reading the world, more capable of playing it in all ways. This does not mean nicer or more humanistic. I would say: more faithful to what we are made from and to what we can create" (Cixous, in Cixous & Calle-Gruber, 1997, p. 30). What we hope for from collective biography as a research strategy, is that it enables us as researchers, as writers, to become more faithful to the matter of ourselves (both material, embodied matter and things that matter to us), more able to read the ongoing processes of becoming selves, and more faithful to what we can create, the open field of possibilities that lie beyond the already known, already experienced, already located as the things that matter.

Collective biography thus potentially addresses the Foucauldian question of the present moment and the Deleuzian question of how we might move beyond that present moment. It is in this sense transgressive and potentially transformative. It makes visible, and therefore revisable, the discourses through which we make meanings and selves. It powerfully deconstructs the idea of the individual as one who exists independent of various collectives, of discourse, of history, of time and of place (Davies, 2000a). It is a means of learning to read/write embodied social selves. It uses that reading/writing to produce a textual base through which to explore various aspects of the processes of meaning-making through which human beings become subjects and go on becoming subjects.

In collective biography the remembered moments detail discursive habits that are peeled away, not to find the "real" embodied self hidden beneath, but in order to see the movement, the flow, the working of "organisms, forces, energies, materials, desires, thoughts, etc" (Foucault, 1980a, p. 97). Through a very intense, focussed gaze on the particularity of our own memories, collective biography searches for an understanding of the social, of the way individual subjectivities are created and maintained through specific kinds of discursive practices, within particular historical moments, in particular contexts, that in turn afford particular interactions and patterns of meaning making. It verges on the paradoxical to require a detailed and loving attention to individual selves, and their memories, in order to arrive at new understandings that deconstruct those individual selves. It is a double movement of immersion and letting go, of both remembering and forgetting.

Methodic practices of collective biography

While remaining open to changing the strategies of using memories, depending on the topic, the particular group, the place, the available time, and so on, there is a describable pattern that has emerged in the collective biography workshops that can serve as a guide for further workshops. It is possible to run a collective biography workshop for half a day or a day, as part of an introductory workshop on the method, or as an integral part of a teaching program. For the purposes of research, however, I would recommend a small group, no more than six or seven, who meet for 3—5 days, working into the selected topic through reading, discussion, story telling, listening and writing, and, finally, analysis of those stories. The strategies of collective biography have evolved, and go on evolving as each group makes its way through the work with memories, and through the analysis and writing up of the particular topic. The particularities of a number of different workshops are elaborated in Davies and Gannon (2006). The brief summary that follows here is a thumbnail sketch of strategies we have come to adopt in most of our workshops.

Selecting the group to work on the project. Haug initially drew together participants for her projects through her networks in socialist women's organizations and the journal *Das Argument* and selected participants who were committed to meeting regularly and working on the project over two years (1987, pp. 21-22). The shifting membership of each of the collective biography projects included in Davies and Gannon (2006) began with whichever of my students could get away from their work for the week-long bi-annual workshops that I ran for my PhD students. The membership of each workshop grew to include guests from among local colleagues and guests visiting from other universities and other countries. Participation was always voluntary, and assumed some degree of familiarity with collective biography (either through reading or their previous engagement in it).

Selecting the topic. Before each workshop begins, a topic for investigation is negotiated, usually arising from my reading of students' work. I then circulate readings around that topic, and based on that reading I develop, as group leader, trigger questions that will spark off memories relevant to the topic. For example in the workshop on power, the questions were about first memories of power as multiple lines of force, adding one's own line of force to one's own submission to another; conducting the self as appropriately submissive, desiring to submit to another; and becoming a line of force, desiring not to submit, refusing submission. The trigger questions are circulated prior to the workshop to give people time to ponder their own memories as they read the circulated papers, but are also open for re-negotiation during the workshop itself once it begins. If the collective biography is run as a part of a methodology or other course, the topic of mutual interest is negotiated at the workshop itself. Topics that may prove too confronting or traumatic should be avoided, especially with the groups who are only meeting for a short period of time.

Structuring the workshop. Two to three hours are devoted to each memory question, including the telling, writing and reading back of the chosen memories. This means that no more than two sets of memories can be generated each day. It is a good idea to spend time enabling the participants to build up some knowledge of each other, if that has not already been established, since a sense of openness and trust is important. Reviewing the topic, the process and the overall aim is also useful at the outset. Apart from the sessions dealing with the memory questions, it is helpful to allow several hours on the last day to plan the collaborative process of analyzing and writing up the topic if this is part of the agreed process.

Remembering and listening. Each memory that is told in response to the trigger question inevitably leads to the generation of new memories. Sometimes these memories are of moments that had until then been completely forgotten. Often those who arrive with "no memories" are amazed at how quickly stories begin to come to them once the storying begins. In this sense each memory is threaded on to the last. Each person is invited to tell at least one story. The process of listening is vital. Each participant is asked to listen to the stories of the others, in such a way that each can imagine being in, and living, that moment. They are invited to ask as many questions as they need to ask in order to be able to engage in that act of imagination. Very often the questioning is probing through the surface of clichés such as, for example, "I felt really scared." "How did it feel when you were scared?" is not a very helpful question. The art of questioning begins, rather, with an attempt to read one's own body, as listener, in its bringing of the story to life in imagination. The question, in reading one's own body, might be "In that moment of feeling really scared, did you feel goose-bumps on your scalp?" Such a question that comes from the imagined goose-bumps of the questioner enables the story teller to say, "Yes, exactly, it was as if the top of my head was cold" or "No, not like that, more like a creepy feeling going from the top of my spine down to my tail bone." The probing does more than allow the story-teller to remember and tell a more detailed, embodied story. It allows the listeners to enter into a story that they might not otherwise have been able to imagine, and to know how that moment was for the person who lived it. Instead of hearing the story as evidence of how the story-teller is different from others, it becomes a remembered moment that each person in the group has imagined and lived. In this way the topic in hand is brain-stormed and body-stormed; actively excavating what was buried, each participant amazing themselves with what they find in their own and others' memories. This collective remembering is difficult, provocative, challenging, funny, sad, and pleasurable, evoking laughter and sometimes tears.

Memory writing. After this memory-telling and listening, the group separates, each person into a quiet space, to write one or two of their own memories. In this process of writing the focus is primarily on the embodied memory, but also on the writing itself. Participants are instructed to avoid clichés and explanations and to focus on one crucial moment, rather than a long and complex sequence of events. The focus on the moment and the body helps in resisting the effects of narrative structures that are inclined towards linearity, causality and closure. As a rule of thumb the memory should take place in one or two minutes, though this rule is often broken. If the explanations seem crucial to comprehending the moment they can be written as separate to the memory, a little in the way the Japanese poet Basho wrote explanatory notes as background to many of his poems. Twenty to 30 minutes is sufficient for the writing.

Reading and listening to stories. The written stories are then read to the group, each member of the group again listening carefully to the words, again with the explicit intention of entering into the experience as it is told in the memory, and also noting any specific points in the story where it loses the reader who is not able to imagine what it was to be there. When the story is discussed, and the reactions of the listeners expressed, sometimes details that were there in the telling, and that have been dropped out in the written form, are brought back in, and in the discussion of the points where the text lost the readers, there are usually explanations or clichés located for later weeding out. This is a collective process of bringing the story to the point where all the participants "know it" in their bodies, and have, in effect, been there. Stories are usually re-written in light of the discussions that follow. That rewriting generally takes place at night and the new day begins with a reading of any rewritten stories being brought back from the previous day's work. Again, attentive, embodied listening is brought by the listeners to the stories that are read.

What collective biography might accomplish

Through the telling of and listening to the spoken and written stories, and through the questions and answers, spaces are opened up in which the stories become not merely autobiographical, but are the means to make visible the discursive processes in which each has been caught up in the very process of becoming subjects. The stories no longer primarily signify individuals' identities, but in their similarities and differences each participant becomes visible as a constituted and constitutive being. The stories are not serving to construct a pre (or post or apart and outside of) discursive self, but to make visible some of the invisible threads within which all subjects are entangled, and to make visible and open for interrogation the discourses in which they have constituted others and have themselves been constituted as particular kinds of subjects—as girls, or boys, as students or teachers, as moral or immoral beings, and so on. The constitutive force of categories, for example, is thus made visible. We catch ourselves in remembered acts of turning on ourselves, seeing how we take up forms of power and strategies of surveillance on others, on ourselves. We attend to the ambivalent processes of subjection. We develop and refine our capacity to reflexively turn our gaze on ourselves in remembered moments of turning, of constituting ourselves and being constituted.

The writing of memory stories does not seek merely to document what was said in the first telling of the memory (as if that telling captured some kind of authentic truth about the story-teller's individuality), but to tell the memory in such a way that it is vividly imaginable by others, such that those others can extend their own imaginable experience of being in the world through knowing the particularity of another. In this sense, working with memory stories does not work with discourse-as-usual, or with the gathering of the sedimented practices of telling that are taken to "reveal" the world that the teller inhabits. Memory-work attempts to go beyond the clichéd practices of everyday life, by attuning the telling and writing of stories to the embodied detail of the memory. The telling and writing of the memory stories attends to language itself as it is in the present and as it worked in the past to constitute the embodied self, but it also struggles to find a new way of working with language that begins with the cells of the body, the senses of the body, as they were in the remembered moment—to re-live the moment as far as possible, and to open it up for re-living by those who are listening to it, and interrogating it. This imaginability comes not out of the repetition of predictable or familiar storylines, nor out of the retrieval of pristine "authentic" memories, but out of the collective detailed attention to embodied detail in the collective memories that brings a new and unexpected view of "what happened" to light. This does not involve any kind of deliberate fictionalizing or fabricating of the memory, but, ironically, goes in a different direction—seeking to evoke the remembered moment through attention to touch or sight or smell or taste, or through the particular attention to the muscles and flesh of the body in the particular moment being told. Often, additional details of the memory arise during the telling of others' stories, and during the discussions. These new details are not only remembered because they are the same as the detail in those other stories, but also because the details in another's story draw attention to gaps and silences in one's own story. Sometimes the additional details do not become available until the writing, or later rewriting, is taking place, as each participant struggles, alone, to put herself again in the body of the child or woman experiencing that moment. While they write out of what they can recall, rather than "what might have been," it is also true that they are, in remembering and in writing, engaged in a constitutive act in which the remembered subject is re-created on the page and in the imagination of the others and themselves. Although collective biography writing attempts to avoid words that the remembered child would not have known, memory is not a veridical act that reproduces the original, it is necessarily always constituted from a particular time, place, discursive frame and present self of the writer. The ethical and aesthetic practices of collective biography begin to dissolve a binary that sets "true" representation against good fiction.

In *Female sexualization* (1987) the body is recognized as the central site of female subjectification to the social. The female body is the site of Haug and her collective's investigation, as it is in our own and other work with memories. (This is not to say that male bodies cannot be similarly used in collective biography—see for example Davies, 1994). Although the body is recognized as the site of production for memories, the idea of "embodied writing" is rarely directly addressed in the memory-work literature. Feminist writers have written about embodied writing and memory in other contexts. Virginia Woolf, for example, saw memory as a physically embodied practice rather than an intellectual practice. Writing memories, she wrote, "[I was] hardly aware of myself, but only of the sensation. I am only the container of the feeling of ecstasy, of the feeling of rapture." She gained access to embodied memories not from the "direct gaze" of the intellect but "by side glances and hints, in the effects of sound, light, smell, touch" (cited in Benstock, 1991, p. 1053). Basic to the collective memory project is the attempt to reclaim embodied memory, to mine the hints and glances and to uncover the things that one does not remember in the first full, direct gaze. It could be claimed that any good writing, that is, writing that is evocative, detailed and multidimensional, is embodied in this way. But collective biographers engage in embodied writing not just to produce good writing, but to access the body's knowledge. Focussing on the corporeality of subjectivity, Grosz (1994, p. vii) suggests that:

> (A)ll the effects of subjectivity . . . can be adequately explained using the subject's corporeality as a framework. . . . All the effects of depth and interiority can be explained in terms of the inscriptions and transformations of the subject's corporeal surface. Bodies have all the explanatory power of minds.

The memories that are excavated and analyzed in collective biography provide the data for tracing such inscriptions and transformations as they manifest on and in bodies. Learning to write from the body is to learn to align the words we write as closely as possible to the remembered embodied moment, such that in reading the words on the page, the reader also knows in her or his own body, as though to relive it, that particular moment.

What collective biography has not so far accomplished is attention to the particular nature of the historical "moment" that Foucault is interested in. Although there are two papers on the effects of neoliberalism at work in Davies and Gannon (2006) this aspect of Foucault's project needs to be carried more strongly forward in future work.

An example of memory-work from a collective biography workshop

The story that I've selected for this paper is from the workshop on power (Davies, Flemmen, Gannon, Laws & Watson, 2002) and was written in response to the trigger question on first memories of power as a multiple line of force, adding one's own line of force to one's own submission to another. The story is of a father-daughter relationship when the girl was six years old:

> The long drive to the beach over the mountains took them over winding dusty mountain roads, through rivers with no bridges and through numerous shut gates. Four kids in the back. Two adults in the front. The kids took it in turns to open the gates. The older kids. The father was irritated by their slowness and incompetence. The tension in his back and the smell of dust and cigarettes always made her feel sick. Now, at six, she was old enough to take her turn at opening the gates. She feels sick in anticipation. She'd rehearsed the detail in her imagination. She'd watched where the others had got it wrong, swinging the gate the wrong way or letting it swing open and then get stuck on a rut in the road, not wide enough open for the car to get through. Or they fumbled with the gate lock, or dawdled back to the car. She knew they were not good enough because she could feel the rising tide of her father's irritation. Now it was her turn. She opened the car door, jumped out of the car and closed the door all in one smooth movement. She ran to the gate, looking to see which way it swung open. Tiptoe, lift the metal ring up over the post, smoothly, evenly, so it doesn't get stuck, pass it through the small hole in the gate. Turn it the right way so it will fit through. Lift the gate so it doesn't get stuck on the ruts, run out

with it all the way so it's fully open. Lift it again the moment the car passes through, swing it back, hold it steady with your foot while small hands thread the metal ring through the gate, pulling it tight. Panic. It won't fit over the post. Adjust the gate, hold it, pull again, wriggle and twist, get it over the post. It goes over. Quick rush of air out of her lungs. All done in a few seconds. Run, jump back in the car. He's not irritated. Good. She got it right. No one says anything.

No words are exchanged in this memory. There is no evident imposition of knowledge on the girl. Yet the girl works hard to embody the skills she sees as appropriate for her to have. The rationalities that give sense to the episode are, from the adult point of view, that as children get older they develop new competencies; not all children are equally competent; open comparisons between children should not be made; children must be given the opportunity to practice new skills. From the girl's point of view, there is pleasure in the acquisition of new competencies: power "induces pleasure, forms knowledge, produces discourse" (Foucault, 1980b, p. 119). But the urgency of her performance suggests another rationality: that approval (identity?) comes to those who are visibly competent. In this she exemplifies Butler's observation that: "Subjection exploits the desire for existence, where existence is always conferred from elsewhere; it marks a primary vulnerability to the Other in order to be" (Butler, 1997, pp. 20-21). The multilinear ensemble draws together, with pleasure and vulnerability, power and knowledge, working together to produce the subject. The girl works to become an appropriately subjected being in order that she can have existence (a particular form of existence that she desires) conferred on her by her father. Even if his conferral is in silence. The power exercised by the father need not be read as an assault in this instance, since it is taken up by the girl, actively, as a force that she will bend to her own will—the will to become recognizably competent. As Foucault observes:

> Power would be a fragile thing if its only function were to repress, if it worked only through the mode of censorship, exclusion, blockage and repression . . . . If, on the contrary, power is strong this is because . . . it produces effects at the level of desire—and also at the level of knowledge. Far from preventing knowledge, power produces it. (Foucault, 1980c, p. 59)

The knowledge produced by the girl's exertion of power on her own body, is the bodily knowledge of how to open the gate, and also the knowledge that she can do it, perhaps better than her older, more laid back siblings. She anticipates a particular kind of existence being conferred on her by "Others." The line of force she reads from the father (and related to rationalities that suggest she should at this age develop these skills), are taken up by her as power that she exerts on her own body in acquiring new skills, and perhaps a new recognition of who she might be able to be.

Deleuze suggests we might distinguish between active and reactive effects. The girl's action upon her own body might be read as reactive, by definition—in that she reacts to what she reads on her father's body. It is also her observation that her older siblings are less concerned to react to their father's will. She is able, in a sense, to use their non-reaction to her own benefit, to carve out a small arena in which she might be recognized, comparatively, as having competence, and thus as recognizably existing. In this sense the active and reactive lines of force become one another, they merge in a movement in which she takes up as her own the line of action out of which, and through which, she is subjected and becomes an active agent. To reactively engage power is not, Deleuze points out, to be passive, but to be caught up in an "irreducible encounter" between action and reaction:

> To incite, provoke and produce . . . constitute active affects, while to be incited or provoked, to be induced to produce, to have a "useful" effect, constitutes reactive affects. The latter are not simply the "repercussion" or "passive side" of the former but are rather "the irreducible encounter" between the two. (Deleuze, 1988, p. 71)

The girl's action can also be understood in terms of the "conduct of conduct" as she carefully attends to her behaviors, actions and comportment (Foucault, 1994, p. 341; Dean, 1999, p. 10). She experiences herself as behaving autonomously, conducting her own conduct, whilst at the same time both parents sit watching her through the car window, an audience who might judge whether she gets it right or not. The metaphor of "conduct" is compatible with her "rehearsal" of the act in her mind. She conducts her own performance, and calculates how to get it right. She forms an idea in her mind of the perfect action and organizes her body to perform it. She judges whether it is good enough, not only against her imagined image, but through the audience reaction. Her father is not in a negative state, so she reads herself as having conducted her own conduct in a successful performance. She has not only not dis-pleased her parents, but she has conducted herself in a way that gives her a pleasurable sense of her own competence and agency.

Ethically reflexive practice in the current neoliberal moment

Dominant, normative discourses lend us an habituated sense that we know what is going on, and position us, sometimes, as those with authority to assert the correctness of our views. In contrast, through collective biography, we offer an ethical reflexivity that enables us not simply to reiterate habituated knowledges, but to see, feel, touch, and hear our own and others' ongoing vulnerability to those normative discourses and practices. In acknowledging our mutual vulnerability to those normative discourses, and in making ourselves open and vulnerable to each other's stories, we can begin to work towards an ethically responsible understanding of the part we play in granting or withholding recognition of the other.

Of such ethically responsible recognition, Butler (2004) says:

> Consider that the struggle for recognition in the Hegelian sense requires that each partner in the exchange recognize not only that the other needs and deserves recognition, but also that each, in a different way, is compelled by the same need, the same requirement. This means that we are not separate identities in the struggle for recognition but are already involved in reciprocal exchange, an exchange that dislocates us from our positions, our subject-positions, and allows us to see that community itself requires the recognition that we are all, in different ways, striving for recognition. (pp. 43-44)

In the collective biography workshops participants develop their capacities for paying attention to each moment of story-telling and listening in such a way that they are each fully present to the other, and at the same time vulnerable to the other, and vulnerable to their own incomplete knowledge of themselves. This form of attention enables recognition of the other, not as a fictionalized and completed subject who in her or his completeness is necessarily foreign, but a recognition that responds to our mutual vulnerability to normative discourses and to each other.

The full knowledge of self that is implicated in humanist ideals of ethical practice is put aside in favour of an awareness of the emergent process of mutual formation. The recognition of the unfamiliar in oneself opens up a new approach to the other, one that does not mark off absolute boundaries between oneself and the other, between oneself as the known and the other as the unknown. In this model of reflexivity the recognition of the limits of self-knowledge and self-understanding opens up a different understanding of what it might mean to know the other and to act responsibly towards the other. As Butler (2004) says:

> I find that my very formation implicates the other in me, that my own foreignness to myself is, paradoxically, the source of my ethical connection with others. I am not fully known to myself, because part of what I am is the enigmatic traces of others. In this sense, I cannot know myself perfectly or know my "difference" from others in an irreducible way. . . . I am wounded, and I find that the wound testifies to the fact that I am impressionable, given over to the Other in ways that I cannot fully predict or control. I cannot think the question of responsibility alone, in isolation from the Other; if I do, I have taken myself out of the relational bind that frames the problem of responsibility from the start. (p. 46)

This particular take on responsibility is almost opposite to the *responsibilization* currently espoused in the neoliberal forms of government that dominate the globalized world (Davies & Bansel, 2005; Rose, 1999). "Responsibilisation" in neoliberal forms of government requires each individual to accept responsibility for self but to shed any responsibility for others—except to participate in acts of surveillance and control. Neoliberalism heightens individuality and competitiveness seeking to shape each of us as a flexible economic unit to be of use in a market economy. Neoliberalism's (usually implicit) intentions have been to make democratic citizens both more governable and more able to service capital (Crozier, Huntington & Watanuki, 1975).

Neoliberalism as a form of governmentality works by convincing students and workers that there is no choice at a systemic level. Instead, their power lies in their individual choices to become appropriate and successful within that (inevitable) system. Such a system is extraordinarily difficult to reflexively examine and may dismantle resistance to itself through discourses of inevitability (of globalism, of the dominance of information technology, of free markets) and of necessity (for individual and national survival). But as Saul (2005) points out, such discourses of inevitability and necessity signal a kind of fundamentalism that should be resisted.

The ethical reflexivity that informs the practices of collective biography is in profound contrast to the end-driven, market model of the individual. The social, psychic and intellectual work can better be described as an emergent practice (Somerville, 2005). Although collective biographies can be carried out with an end-product in mind (a paper, a book), and can be carefully planned in advance, these organizational practices operate in tandem with an openness to the unknown, and to the dynamic unfolding process through which a group of individuals work together to enable new insights to emerge from their collective work. Responsibility, in this model, lies inside social relations and inside a responsibility to and for oneself in relation to the other—not oneself as a known entity, but oneself in process, unfolding or folding up, being done or undone, in relation to the other, again and again.

Returning, then, to the concept of ethical reflexivity, one of the main contributions of collective biography has been to investigate the ways in which subjects are locked into normative patterns and to explore how the work we do might decompose some aspects of that normative power. Bodily and mental habits serve to lock subjects into familiar patterns of behavior and thought. These habituated practices may be within the realm of conscious awareness or they may be unreflected on. The modes of thought, or rationalities, through which those habits and habitual ways of being are understood are frequently tied to ideas of "real" or essential selves, and are perceived as unchangeable. In the social domain such practices are monitored and managed through forms of government, including self-government, that reward and punish particular ways of being. These forms of government and the behaviors that they perpetuate and police are historically (and culturally) specific, but are generally experienced as the only way things could be within one's own culture. Collective biography develops the practice of viewing language as a complex practice through which reality is discursively constituted and understood. The collective work of talking, writing, reading and questioning makes visible the patterns and habitual ways of thinking and speaking our selves into the world that we are immersed in, including those to which we might be passionately attached. Through this collective work we begin to see the extent to which these practices and ways of thinking and being are both habituated and discursively constituted. In this process they are dislodged from the natural (and inevitable) world and opened up for critical scrutiny and revision. That kind of reflexive work can be difficult and uncomfortable; but as the prized possession of one's essential self slips out of one's (tenuous) grasp, another power emerges. Whereas poststructuralism has been perceived as antithetical to the possibility of radical social action, through our collective biographies we have experienced a freedom from the weighty sense of inevitability and with it a strong sense of agency, though one that is always "radically conditioned" (Butler, 1997, p. 15).

As a framework for interrogating everyday lived experience, collective biography thus dislodges the familiar, making bodily and mental habits visible *as habits*, reflexively opening them up to scrutiny. It affords a mode of thought that shows those bodily and mental habits to be historically specific and discursively constituted. The gaze is turned on particular forms of discourse through which such ways of thinking and being could have come to be seen by subjects as normal and desirable. In this dual movement, of letting go of the accomplishment of the unified essential self, and the making visible of the ways discourses work on us and shape us up as appropriate(d) subjects, we understand more acutely our vulnerability to normative discourses, and our vulnerability to each other. In this dual movement we can, as well, begin to recognize the "enigmatic traces of others" (Butler, 2004, p. 46) in ourselves, and in doing so accept our partial foreignness to ourselves. Having done so, we can greet each other with recognition of our common location in discourse—of our shared, enigmatic traces—And our mutual vulnerability to the need for recognition. We can also shrug off, now and then, the sense of inevitability of the way things are and move toward the kind of democratic engagement that welcomes multiplicity and difference and remains open to that which is yet to unfold.

Present social and moral orders are not inevitable. They do not grant viable lives to everyone. So-called democratic countries are currently caught in their own fundamentalism, their own rhetoric of inevitability, their own inability to see otherwise. The practices of collective biography enable us to examine the ways we become caught in those apparent inevitabilities and they enable us to carry forward the project of imagining alternatives. They do so through a set of practices in which we afford each other a profound recognition in the shared moments of being that are encapsulated in our stories, through a practice of making visible the common threads of being that come from the power of normative discourses to shape the way things are, and through a shared commitment to the belief that the world can be otherwise.

Notes

1. Participants in the various collective biographies that I have initiated and that are gathered together in the book edited by Susanne Gannon and me (2006), include Jenny Browne, Phoenix de Carteret, Suzi Dormer, Anne Britt Flemmen, Eileen Honan, Lekkie Hopkins, Cath Laws, Hillevi Lenz Taguchi, Helen McCann, Babette Müller-Rockstroh, Margaret Somerville, Eva Bendix Petersen, Danielle Stewart, Sharn Rocco, Barbara Watson, and Monne Wihlborg.

References

Benstock, Shari. (1991). Authorizing the autobiographical. In Robyn R. Warhol & Diane Price Herndl (Eds.), *Feminisms: An anthology of literary theory and criticism* (pp. 1040-1057). New Brunswick, NJ: Rutgers University Press.

Butler, Judith. (1997). *The psychic life of power: Theories in subjection.* Stanford, CA: Stanford University Press.

Butler, Judith. (2004). *Precarious life: The powers of mourning and violence.* London: Verso.

Carter, Erica. (1987). Translator's Foreword. In Frigga Haug, Kornelia Hauser & Nora Rathzel (Erica Carter, Trans.). *Female sexualization: A collective work of memory* (pp. 11-20). London: Verso.

Ceppi, Giulio & Zini, Michele (Eds.). (1998). *Children, spaces, relations. Metaproject for an environment for young children.* Milan: Domus Academy Research Centre.

Cixous, Helene & Calle-Gruber, Mireille. (1997). *Rootprints: Memory and life writing.* London: Routledge.

Crozier, Michael; Huntington, Samuel P. & Watanuki, Joji. (1975). *The crisis of democracy. Report on the governability of democracies.* New York: New York University Press.

Davies, Bronwyn. (1994). *Poststructuralist theory and classroom practice.* Geelong, AU: Deakin University Press.

Davies, Bronwyn. (2003). *Frogs and snails and feminist tales: Preschool children and gender* (Second edition). Hampton, NJ: Hampton Press.

Davies, Bronwyn. (2000a). *(In)scribing body/landscape relations.* Walnut Creek, CA: Alta Mira Press.

Davies, Bronwyn. (2000b). *A body of writing: 1990-1999.* Walnut Creek, CA: Alta Mira Press.

Davies, Bronwyn & Bansel, Peter. (2005). The time of their lives? Academic workers in neoliberal time(s). *Health Sociology Review, 14*(1), 47-58.

Davies, Bronwyn; Browne, Jenny; Gannon, Susanne; Hopkins, Lekkie; McCann, Helen & Wihlborg, Monne. (2006). Constituting "the subject" in poststructuralist discourse. *Feminism and Psychology, 16*(1), 87-103.

Davies, Bronwyn & Davies, Cristyn. (2007). Having or being had by experience. *Qualitative Inquiry.*

Davies, Bronwyn; Flemmen, Anne Britt; Gannon, Susanne; Laws, Cath & Watson, Barbara. (2002). Working on the ground. A collective biography of feminine subjectivities: Mapping the traces of power and knowledge. *Social Semiotics, 12*(3), 291-313.

Davies, Bronwyn & Gannon, Susanne. (2006). *Doing collective biography.* Maidenhead, UK: Open University Press, McGraw-Hill Education.

Dean, Mitchell M. (1999). *Governmentality: Power and rule in modern society.* Sage: London.

Deleuze, Gilles. (1994). *Difference and repetition.* (P. Patton, Trans.; first published 1968, France.) New York: Columbia University Press.

Deleuze, Gilles. (1988). *Foucault.* (Sean Hand, Trans.). London: The Athlone Press.Foucault, Michel. (1979). *Discipline and punish: The birth of the prison.* (Alan Sheridan, Trans.). New York: Vintage.

Foucault, Michel. (1980a). Two lectures. In Colin Gordon (Ed.), *Power/ Knowledge: Selected interviews and other writings 1972-77 by Michel Foucault* (Colin Gordon, Leo Marshall, John Mepham & Kate Soper, trans.; pp. 78-108). Brighton, UK: The Harvester Press.

Foucault, Michel. (1980b). Truth and power. In Colin Gordon (Ed.), *Power/ Knowledge: Selected interviews and other writings 1972-77 by Michel Foucault* (Colin Gordon, Leo Marshall, John Mepham & Kate Soper, trans; pp. (109-133). Brighton, UK: The Harvester Press, 109-133.

Foucault, Michel. (1980c). Body/Power. In Colin Gordon (Ed.), *Power/Knowledge: Selected interviews and other writings 1972-77 by Michel Foucault* (Colin Gordon, Leo Marshall, John Mepham & Kate Soper, Trans.; pp. 56-62). Brighton, UK: The Harvester Press, 56-62.

Foucault, Michel. (1994). The subject and power. In James D. Faubion (Ed.), *Michel Foucault and power: Essential works of Foucault* (pp. 326-348). London: Penguin.

Gannon, Susanne & Davies, Bronwyn. (2007). Postmodern poststructural and critical perspectives. In S. Nagy Hesse-Biber (Ed.), *Handbook of feminist research: Theory and praxis* (pp. 71-106). Thousand Oaks, CA: SAGE.

Grosz, Elizabeth. (1994). *Volatile bodies: Toward a corporeal feminism.* Sydney: Allen and Unwin.

Haug, Frigga (Ed.). (1987). *Female sexualization: A collective work of memory* (Erica Carter, Trans.). London: Verso Press.

Rose, Nikolas. (1999). *Powers of freedom: Reframing political thought.* Cambridge, UK: Cambridge University Press.

Saul, John Ralston. (2005). *The collapse of globalism and the reinvention of the world.* London: Viking.

Scott, Joan W. (1992). Experience. In Judith Butler & Joan W. Scott (Eds.), *Feminists theorize the political* (pp. 22-40). New York: Routledge.

Somerville, Margaret. (2005, May). *Postmodern emergent methodologies.* Paper presented to the First International Congress of Qualitative Inquiry, Champaign-Urbana, IL.

Chapter 4

Messing with Memories: Feminist Poststructuralism and Memory-work

Susanne Gannon

Once we start talking
Stories spill out
Lap over each other
Wash us into other stories
We give our gifts,
memories,
to each other[1]

Memory-work, as I have taken it up, attends to unravelling the ways in which discourses have become sedimented and inscribed into our bodies and everyday practices. In my research into women's subjectivities and lived experience, I have worked with a feminist poststructural paradigm that disrupts the subjects, memories, truths and texts produced in and through memory-work (Davies & Gannon, 2004; 2007). My interest in textual aesthetics and ethics has led me to produce "transgressive" texts by messing with memories to produce new texts (Gannon, 2001; 2004a, 2004b, 2004c, 2006a). The forms of data representation that I have adopted for some of my memory-work—poetry and theater—are not conventionally valued in social science research, though it may be argued that they are more accessible to audiences beyond the academy.

Background and context

As a member first of the Magnetic Island collective (Davies & Gannon, 2006) and now of the Narrative, Discourse and Pedagogy group (Linnell, Bansel, Ellwood & Gannon, forthcoming), I have worked with Bronwyn Davies and others in a mode we prefer to call "collective biography." Our topics have included gendered subjectification at school and at work, power/knowledge, embodiment, reflexivity, fiction and femininity (Davies & Gannon, 2006), and speaking and listening (Linnell et al., forthcoming) and we have generally later published co-authored scholarly texts based on our work together. In these workshops, undertaken within established research groups with academic peers and colleagues, we have investigated theoretical concepts through the lens of everyday life, in order to enrich our understandings of both. I have also convened collective memory groups in other locations and on other topics with other sorts of groups. Our topics have foregrounded women's bodies, in particular in a series of workshops on "breasts" held in Germany (Gannon & Müller-Rockstroh, 2004a, 2004b; 2005). Another series of workshops explored collectively generated provocations such as "isolation" (Gannon, 2001), "boundaries" (Gannon, 2004a), the "views of others," and "mistakes," which is the subject of the latter part of this paper. Some of these memories have been used more or less conventionally as data texts in diverse disciplinary locations—in the guise of philosophy (Gannon & Müller-Rockstroh, 2004a), sociology (Gannon & Müller-Rockstroh, 2004b; 2005), and pedagogy (Gannon, 2004a)—but I have also taken the texts further in my work on transgressive writing practices by using them as raw data and shaping them into other texts for other purposes, locations and audiences. This transgressive text work, particularly that of rewriting memories as poetry, is the subject of this chapter.

In taking up collective memory-work within a feminist poststructuralist framework, my gaze shifts from "truth" towards the effects of discursive regimes that constitute the subjectivities that we take to represent our particular individual "selves" at particular points in time and place. The focus thus shifts away from the individual and her memories, and away from the group's collective set of memories, to the discourses which make the events in those memories possible and the rationalities that make them reason-able and imagine-able. In working further with these memory texts—in "messing" with them to produce new texts in different forms—I have continued this discursive interrogation.

In the collective memory-workshops that I have convened, groups of women have generated sets of memories around selected topics and begun together, in the embodied space of the workshops, to collectively disentangle the discourses circulating within the texts we have produced. This deconstructive work enabled us to begin to recognize our collusion in the circulation of hegemonic values, norms and desires as we (have) take(n) them up in our own bodies, psyches and ways of being in the world. Yet the "collusion" we identified was not conscious, nor as individualistic or pathological as psychological frames for understanding social behavior might suggest. In taking up memory-work as our method, we have foregrounded the social rather than the psychological and place the body at the center of deconstruction. Thus we recognize that (our) bodies are connected to other bodies: they exist and acquire meaning in social spaces. The poetic texts shaped from the memories in these workshops emphasize the sociality of subjectivity. The responses and behaviors of the girls we recalled were shaped by the others we love and live with, and were limited by the discursive possibilities that structured those relationships in those times and places. Our opportunities to resist, or to behave otherwise, were constrained by what we experienced individually as a lack of agency. In a feminist poststructural framework, we understand that possibilities for agency do not arise as we step outside of discourse, for we are always already discursively inscribed (Gannon & Davies, 2006). Rather, agency – necessarily tentative, fleeting, contingent – is glimpsed as we shift and multiply the discursive frames through which we understand the memories. Agency arrives in transitory moments that we might figure as "mo(ve)ments" and within which we might take up new possibilities for understanding, and acting, otherwise (Davies & Gannon, 2006, p. 7). In the collective context we aim to trace the formation of our own subjectivities, so that we might see the movement, the flow, the working of "organisms, forces, energies, materials, desires, thoughts, etc." (Foucault, 1980, p. 97) on us and in us, and how they might be otherwise.

The further work I have done in shaping poetic texts from memories has kept them in play beyond the workshop, emphasizing mo(ve)ments of intention, desire and agency inscribed in the girl subjects we remembered and which other women might recognize in their own embodied memories.

Messing with data texts is characteristic of the interpretive shift in social research of which Denzin (1997, 2003) and others have written. Social research has always assumed that "experience is the 'great original,'" assuring readers "that there is both a 'there' and 'beings' who are there" (Britzman, 2000, p. 28). Yet collective memory-work problematizes the transparency of experience, and of research practices where subjects simply recount their experiences to researchers. In memory-work we do not go looking for any "sacred originary" but for traces and unreliable fragments as they are written in our bodies. Memory writing is not a veridical act that reproduces the original experience as it was lived but is necessarily always constituted from a particular time and place and discursive frame. The double spaces it utilizes—the memories of then and there, and the present of here and now and us together—create an intense awareness of the performativity of texts. Collective memory-work can be understood as a sort of "performance ethnography," representing knowledge as "partial, plural, incomplete, and contingent" rather than valorizing "analytical distance or detachment" (Denzin, 2003, p. 8). In such work the description of everyday life that characterizes ethnographic research is realized through a textual aesthetic that acknowledges that "a theory of the social is always a theory of writing" (Denzin, 1997, p. xii). The messed with texts that I have subsequently produced write further across the binaries of self/other and individual/social, as they weave particular and separate stories into a single text. This work is influenced by Richardson's rigorous crafting of poetic texts from interview transcripts in order to crystallize and heighten the discursive affects of her data (Richardson, 1997).

Feminist poststructuralist research disrupts "foundational ontologies, methodologies, and epistemologies" (St. Pierre & Pillow, 2000, p. 2). The intent of such research is to deconstruct dominant discourses through close work with data, and, in addition, to use data itself as a generative space for producing multiple readings that might subvert and fracture hegemonic discourses so that, in these fissures, we might catch sight of possibilities for agency. Disrespectful ways of working with data become possible. In contrast to positivist epistemologies, in poststructuralism "language as it is presented in texts produced as data is not respected as if it did reveal 'the real' but may be deconstructed and broken open to show *the ways in which the real is constructed"* (Davies & Gannon, 2004, p. 319).

Deconstructive work begins inside the workshop space, as participants collectively work their way in to the memory texts that are generated. The texts, the written memories, become data fragments for discursive analysis, separated from the individual producers who at one time lived those events. Haug's recommendation (1987) that memory-workers take up third person grammatical voice is one strategy for dislocating memory stories from the individual producers into a collective story space; another is that memories should aim to recall particular moments in vivid sensual detail, rather than to produce narratives underpinned by psychological explanations that stress causality and linearity. These strategies can also help to dislocate the memories from the individual and any residual investment in the particular self that she is accustomed to producing.

In an additional turn, the memory stories generated in a workshop might be understood as discursive fragments, or data, that contribute to a collective pool—a "sea of stories" (Rushdie, 1991). In that sense, the collection of data around a topic might go on over a longer period and might include different participants. For example, the three workshops on "breasts" convened by myself and Babette Müller-Rockstroh in Germany had participants who came to all three workshops and others who came to only one. Different workshops focused on "getting breasts," "nurturing breasts" and "dangerous breasts," but our collective knowledge of the complexity of discourses around breasts was extended and enriched across the three workshops. In another series of workshops within which the topic of "mistakes" arose, participants remained the same across six weeks of workshops while our collective understandings about the discourses of gender in our lives and their constitutive force (Butler, 1990) continued to build as the sea of stories around diverse but interrelated topics became deeper and wider.

After the workshops, which are often experienced as powerful and transformative spaces, have finished, participants tend to disperse and often any further work with those texts is left to one or two participants, positioned as the researcher(s). Although I have participated in groups who continued to work collectively with the texts (Davies & Gannon, 2006; Linell, Bansel, Ellwood &

Gannon, forthcoming), more often than not, as noted in the introduction to this volume, the collective work ceases at this point. This was the case with the workshops I discuss in the final section of this chapter. My broader interests in experimental writing practices in social science has led me to work with other methodologies including autoethnography (Gannon, 2006b), poetry (Gannon, 2001, 2004a, 2004c), multiple narratives (Gannon, 2002) and theatre (Gannon, 2004b, 2006a). The further text work that I have done with collective memory texts, after the workshops have been finished, has in a sense been part of this broader project. It has also been deeply informed by the notion of collective knowledge.

In terms of the politics of collective memory-work, it has come to be insufficient for me that the work be contained within academic spaces, and that the individual stories stand alone in the texts of this work. Pushing the work into broader contexts, outside journals and theses and conferences, into the wider world, is also compatible with feminist perspectives on non-hierarchical knowledge production, as well as broader issues of access and equity. The analytical and imaginative work done in memory-workshops can migrate and mutate into other texts for other audiences, thus adding to the pool of discourses in circulation amongst women in social spaces outside the original group. Multiple passes may be made through the data for different audiences and different purposes.

Messing with memory texts

The work completed in Germany on breasts as sites of inscription led me to write a play called "The Breast Project" that had a season with a professional theatre company in Australia (Gannon, 2006a). My sisters, my mother, my friends, as well as many women who are strangers to me, and some who had contributed memories, were able to see the text unfold embodied before them—as both a distillation and an expansion of the original memory-work (Gannon, 2004b). The storyline of women from different parts of the world telling "breast stories" was one thread in the complex weave of the final text but the subtext of the play and the three characters I invented for the core narrative of the play were informed by the original memory workshops and by the subsequent analytical writing that Babette Müller-Rockstroh and I did around those memories. During the development of the play, other women as actors and dramaturges enriched the text with their own embodied knowledge, and the conversation about breasts continued into the theatre. The collectively generated stories that began within the space of the memory workshops thus became texts "that get away, that escape . . . (t)hat can't be closed, that leave us behind, that can't be finished" (Cixoux, 1998, p. 44). In response to the invitation that closes the opening chapter of this book, this textwork might be considered an appropriation or subversion of memory-work methodology, yet I have taken it up—with the permission of the women who participated—as a further opportunity to make the research matter, to send it into new collective spaces and to make it work harder in the world.

In messing with the memory texts as I have in the playscript and other transgressive textwork, I have abandoned the quest for any sort of recognizable social scientific validity; rather I seek in these texts a sort of voluptuous validity, where a female imaginary might create a "disruptive excess" (Lather, 1994, p. 46). In the poetry I have constructed from memory-work projects, I have "crystallized" (Richardson, 1997) multiple memories into a single text and collapsed the separate speaking/writing subjects of these texts into a single collective subject who speaks as "she" (Gannon, 2001, 2004a). In so doing I have abandoned any lingering fascination with the "authenticity of voice" and the "romance of the speaking subject" (Lather, 2007, p. 136). Poststructuralist approaches problematize both the author and memory as a source of truth (Barthes, 1977; 1989), and writing as a technology of the self (Foucault, 1997). Indeed, poststructuralism's legacy can be seen as the "evacuation of any ground upon which one could speak the self" (Probyn, 1993, p. 14). In most memory-work texts, the stories are presented as intact and inviolable—each person's memory is discrete and separated from the other memories—spaced and shaped so that they cannot be conflated. They are presented as (if) they tell separate and different stories of "selving," though the analytical texts that wrap around them talk of collective experience. In my text work I leap across this tension and shape the data texts themselves into a single text that both writes and represents collectivity. These texts can then go into the world to do different sorts of analytical and emotional work. For example, one poem became data for a discussion, in the journal *Sex education,* of the complex and ambivalent discursive positions available for adolescent girls as they cross the "boundaries" of childhood and adulthood through becoming sexual, and how these might impact on the effectiveness and the pedagogy of sex education programs in high schools (Gannon, 2004a). The paper provides no grand narratives and no replicable research moments but it does provide close and multiple readings of a complex context. It forms a textual intervention into a field where research tends to be framed by public health discourses, takes little account of girls as active subjects, and continues to be marked by what Fine calls "the missing discourse of desire" (1988).

The "Boundaries" poem and the one that follows on "Mistakes" were from the same series of workshops I convened as a writing workshop with women I had met in other writing workshops in our town. We were all passionate about writing, and understood the transformative possibilities of writing in (and of) our lives, but I was the only one of us who was interested in reframing writing within an academic context. We adopted collective memory-work methodology with guidance from Haug (1987) and Davies (1994) and generated topics from week to week collectively, picking up a thread that emerged from talking and writing each week to pursue in the following week. The poem below is crafted from the multiple texts we produced in one of those weeks, and examines—as many of our texts did—aspects of our collective experiences of growing up as girls into hegemonic heterosexuality. The topic—"she never makes the same mistake twice"—which was a line from one of our previous texts—provoked memories of passive, vulnerable girls and women. Although each memory was

separately told and we attended systematically and initially to each story in turn
as a separate text, we found strong resonances amongst our stories. It was the
stories that resonated with all of us that work best as compelling and aestheti-
cally convincing texts. In the work of Haug (1987) the participants wrote and
rewrote their memories until they reflected the group analysis but in memory
groups such as mine, convened in the first instance as a women's writing group
and made up of people keen to discuss the texts extensively but expecting to
work on a new topic each week, rewriting was not feasible. In a sense, the rewriting practice that I adopted, beginning with the texts but informed by the tape
recorded discussions of them, was a "messing" that equated with the rewriting
phase of Haug's process. Although Haug and her colleagues insisted on third
person voice in their writing, the women in this group chose to write as each of
them preferred, in whichever voice gave them best access to the sensory detail
of the remembered experience. In messing with the texts after the workshop, I
made the voice and tense consistent and organized them into chronological order
by age. Thus the "messing" work, created a textual "collective girl" from our
disparate but related experiences. Where the collective girl who speaks as "I" in
this poem does act, her actions are often directed at self harm and humiliation.
These were the sorts of "mistakes" we thought to set behind us, the moments
that we did not want to experience again but that we recognized in the irony of
our topic. In the stories, and the further work we did with them in the workshop
space, we recognized the moments where we acted despite our constraints, and
despite our intentions. They documented movements that were dangerous as
well as those that were ultimately redemptive, and are part of our present senses
of our selves as strong and resilient women.

Mistakes

Late afternoon—
a tin can, lid hanging open, out of reach in the sink;
I stand/ wobbling on a chair dragged from the kitchen table;
I know sharp/ hot/ spiky things are dangerous
I pick it up—
ragged edge, snags of metal bent up, jagged;
look out the window to the yew tree
(where the song-thrush has her nest
I stole an egg from her
and keep it on a bed of cotton wool in the cupboard)

I roll the ragged edge of the tin can lid,
very gently,
up and down the inner side of my arm.
up and down,
up and down,
no pain;
thin streams of blood,
blood mixing with potato peelings

my mother comes,
you silly billy,
washing blood away, bandaging
hugging

...

My mother is out
with her new lover.
I'm home alone;
the house is dark spooky,
full of bad memories.

I sit on the sofa thinking what if,
what if a burglar broke in,
what if I have to defend myself,
what if I have to use this ordinary knife,
this supper-eating knife,
as a weapon?
How sharp is it?
What pressure would it need?

I push the blade into my left thumb
It doesn't break the skin
I press the blade harder into flesh
I know it will cut
I can't stop
I press harder
keep pressing
Skin splits
hurts like hell
Blood all over everywhere
(if I bleed to death they'll all be sorry)

...

I love my mami
but live with my grandparents
want a white picket fence
mother/ father/ sister/ dog all living together.
a real family.
I want to be a proper daughter
I move in with mami for high school

first day
red satin skirt, black six inch platforms
You look like a hooker
I swish through in red satin
I swish through to my room
the stinging burn of the belt on my back

How dare you walk away when I'm talking to you! Condenada!
I stay silent
the belt on my flesh
swish swish
welts rising
swish swish
against my silence
skin splitting
swish swish
eyes burning
voice bursting
I hate you! I hate you! I hate you!

...

Be my summer girlfriend?
My insides flip-flop
Palms sweat
I stand in front of him in choir
he plays with cascades of hair
half touches
accidental contact
he rearranges a barrette
undoes a braid
tugs turn to tickles to body melting pulses

Long evening walks before his shift at the mill
I hear the slow *kerplonk kerplonk* of the logs
I sleep on the verandah.
kerplonk kerplonk
I dream in his rhythm

The summer ends, he goes away
He cries, his head cradled in my arms
I am Cathy, he is Heathcliff
Wait for me, he says

Next summer, back at his summer job,
he has other girlfriends
but haunts every place I go
You're driving me crazy
he shouts
head tilted to the light
eyes welling
I only want to take you to a dance
Somewhere—amongst the kisses—I forget
I am teaching him a lesson

Saturday, a party
Another girl spread-eagled on top of him necking

Sunday, a phone call
I have to explain
Come over and I'll explain

It means nothing, he says.
She just jumped on me. You know her. She's crazy.
He cries
Don't do this to me,
Don't
He blocks my passage
grabs me by the throat
You can't walk out.
He grips tight and tighter.
I can't breathe
He shakes me
His hands so strong.
I know we're alone here.
I look at his frantic frightened eyes
painfully, slowly hiss the words past his strangling clamped fingers
Youu Geeeeet Youuuuuur Hannndss offff Meeee.
He releases his grip
I'm sorry, I'm sorry, I'm sorry
I move slowly, steadily, up the seven steps.
Outside, breathe again.

...

Mid-year exams
Saturday night home studying
Politics, Biology, History

Sunday noon I ring my girlfriend, best friend, confidante
Did you go?
Did you see him?
Yes. . . . He's here, she says, *with me.*
Somersault gut
(But he's mine, I thought he was mine)
Vision of him spread-eagled, half-wrapped, sun glowing on olive skin
(But you're my friend, I told you my secrets, you gave me advice...)

I speak to no-one, study
Six months later
I leave
...

He does not look at me
I'm sorry, he says
he rubs the back of his neck
Behind him a sign *Welcome home.*
I stand, white and motionless wordless

I do not say *But you said you loved me*
I do not say *But I've waited for you for a year*
I do not say *But our future stretches out in front of me in shining pictures of us together happy for ever and ever*

I say nothing, turn, walk to the headland.
The ocean inky dark below
Waves crashing somewhere in the blackness
No moon reflected on water,
just darkness and the waves on the rocks.

I take a deep breath and jump
free fall
crunch
land on one shoulder
bounce, somersault, bounce again
rolling through scrappy grass and stones
thump
a rocky ledge
slowly I move my arms and legs and sit up
hold shoulder and knee
rock with pain
slowly push myself up and start to climb.
scrambling
crying and clutching my wounds
to the top.
Torn jeans and shirt
blood seeping through

I sit looking out over the ocean
down into the darkness
nursing my leg and crying

After a while I don't cry anymore
I stand up
look up the hill,
turn
and start to walk again down the road

The composite collective girl is strongly embodied in the text—her skin bleeds, she bruises, her belly melts with desire. A collective story, particularly written in poetic form (Gannon, 2001), can have a greater sense of the "linkages" that Haug's group sought to recover, the "feelings, attitudes towards other people and towards the world, which have some connection to the body" (1987, p. 76). In the poem, this girl tells her own story in the first person, and it is both detailed and visceral. As this composite collective girl grows up, she experiences self-hate and violence, abandonment, lust/love, and betrayal but she also displays her power. She is vulnerable and the terrain is dangerous but she finds opportunities for resistance, makes conscious decisions about self-preservation, develops and maintains her integrity. She puts the knife down. She shouts over the strap and through the fingers around her throat. And she leaves, she leaves, she leaves. This was a constant in our stories and in our workshops which brought six women from Canada, the USA, the UK and different parts of Australia together in a place that we had come to from our other places, and as selves we had constructed through all our diverse lived experiences (Gannon, 2001). This girl is destined to leave and she is destined to live. She walks independently down the road to adulthood, towards her future selves, scarred but strong. Together in one text, ordered chronologically, the stories are a distillation of the struggle for agency in the lives of girls growing up into heterosexuality. Separately, surrounded by analysis and interrupted by theory, they might not have this impact. Written in narrative prose, they might not have these effects. The lines of the poem are breath length, the memories are immediate, details evoke the senses—sound, sight, and the sensitivities of skin. The space around the text, the slower reading that poetry requires, may give a little more space for readers to recognize their own younger selves alongside this girl. The dialogue of memories might continue beyond the text, as it did in "The Breast Project" play, and reach those others who were not at our workshop but who have themselves made mistakes, like our own, and survived them as well as we have.

Conclusion

Memory-work attends to the ways that discursive regimes are taken up and embodied in ways that become sedimented and naturalized. Within a poststructuralist paradigm that sees bodies as socially inscribed and performed, and a feminist paradigm that validates the personal and lived experience, memory-work provides opportunities for collective interruption of those regimes. In messing further with the memory texts that have been produced during some of the workshops I have convened, I aim to keep textual forms in play and to keep memories more open than more conventional scholarly forms allow. In messing with texts as I do, I am interested in the ethics and aesthetics of writing and of research. How might rigorous imagining assist us to enter into the space of the other (Gannon, 2007) in collective biography and in other research contexts? How might writing matter differently and take on different forms and contexts for different readers? How might my work provoke a dissolution of subjectivities, such that I see myself in you and you in me? And what effects might that have on our understanding of how we are and might be in the world?

Notes

1. Excerpt from Susanne Gannon, "(Gradual) Submersion" poem. In Bronwyn Davies, (2000), *(In)scribing body/landscape relations* (pp. 47-48). Walnut Creek, CA: AltaMira Press.

2. Condenada - daughter of the devil.

References

Barthes, Roland. (1977). *Roland Barthes* (R. Howard, Trans.). Berkeley, CA: University of California Press.

Barthes, Roland. (1989). *The rustle of language* (1st ed.). New York: Hill and Wang.

Britzman, Deborah P. (2000). "The question of belief:" Writing poststructural ethnography. In Elizabeth A. St. Pierre & Wanda S. Pillow (eds.), *Working the ruins: Feminist poststructural theory and methods in education* (pp. 27-40). New York: Routledge.

Butler, Judith P. (1990). *Gender trouble: Feminism and the subversion of identity*. New York: Routledge.

Cixous, Helene. (1998). *Stigmata: Escaping texts*. London: Routledge.

Davies, Bronwyn. (1994). *Poststructural theory and classroom research*. Geelong: Deakin University.

Davies, Bronwyn & Gannon, Susanne. (2004). Feminism/ Poststructuralism. In Cathy Lewin & Bridget Somekh (Eds.), *Research methods in the social sciences* (pp. 318-325). London: Sage.

Davies, Bronwyn & Gannon, Susanne (Eds.). (2006). *Doing collective biography: Investigating the production of subjectivity*. London: Open University Press/McGraw Hill.

Denzin, Norman K. (1997). *Interpretive ethnography: Ethnographic practices for the 21st century*. Thousand Oaks: Sage.

Denzin, Norman K. (2003). *Performance ethnography: Critical pedagogy and the politics of culture*. Thousand Oaks, CA: Sage.

Fine, Michelle. (1988). Sexuality, schooling and adolescent females: The missing discourse of desire. *Harvard Educational Review, 58*, 29-53.

Foucault, Michel. (1980). Two lectures. In Colin Gordon (Ed), *Power/ Knowledge: Selected interviews and other writings 1972—77 by Michel Foucault* (Colin Gordon, Leo Marshall, John Mepham & Kate Soper, trans.; pp. 78-108). Brighton, UK: Harvester Press.

Foucault, Michel. (1997). *Ethics: Subjectivity and truth. Essential works of Foucault 1954—1984. Volume 1*. London: Penguin.

Gannon, Susanne. (2001). (Re)presenting the collective girl: A poetic approach to a methodological dilemma. *Qualitative Inquiry, 7*(6), 787-800.

Gannon, Susanne. (2004a). Crossing "boundaries" with the collective girl: A poetic intervention into sex education. *Sex Education, 4*(1), 81-99.

Gannon, Susanne. (2004b). Out/Performing in the academy: Writing "The breast project." *Qualitative Studies in Education, 17*(1), 65-81.

Gannon, Susanne. (2004c). "Dream(e)scapes:" A poetic experiment in writing a self. *Auto/Biography, 12*(1), 107-125.

Gannon, Susanne. (2005). "The tumbler:" Writing an/other in fiction and performance ethnography. *Qualitative Inquiry, 11*(4), 622-627.

Gannon, Susanne. (2006a). *The breast project. Collection #6*. Hobart, AU: Australian Script Centre.

Gannon, Susanne. (2006b). The (im)possibilities of writing the self writing: French poststructural theory and autoethnography, *Cultural Studies <=> Critical Methodologies, 6*(3), 474-495.

Gannon, Susanne. (2007). Writing into the space of the "other." *Outskirts: Feminisms on the edge. 17* (Special issue on feminist engagements in other places) http:/www.chloe.uwa.edu.au/outskirts/

Gannon, Susanne & Davies, Bronwyn. (2006). Postmodern, poststructural and critical theories. In Sharlene Nagy Hesse-Biber (Ed.), *Handbook of feminist research: Theory and praxis* (pp. 71-106). Thousand Oaks, CA: Sage.

Gannon, Susanne & Müller-Rockstroh, Babette. (2004a). In memory: Women's experiences of (dangerous) breasts. *Philosophy in the Contemporary World (Special issue on feminist approaches to the body), 11*(1), 55-65.

Gannon, Susanne & Müller-Rockstroh, Babette. (2004b). In memory: Women's experiences of breasts. In Body Project (Eds.), *CorpoRealities: In(ter)ventions in an omnipresent subject* (pp. 195-214). Berlin: Ulrike Helmer.

Gannon, Susanne & Müller-Rockstroh, Babette. (2005). Nurturing breasts: Constructions of contemporary motherhood in women's breastfeeding stories. In Marie Porter, Patricia Short & Andrea O'Reilly (Eds.). *Motherhood: Power and oppression* (pp. 41-56). Toronto: The Women's Press.

Haug, Frigga (Ed.). (1987). *Female sexualization: A collective work of memory* (Erica Carter, trans.). London: Verso Press.

Lather, Patti. (1991). *Getting smart: Feminist research and pedagogy with/in the postmodern*. New York: Routledge.

Lather, Patti. (1994). Fertile obsession: Validity after poststructuralism. In A. Gitlin (Ed.), *Power and method: Political activism and educational research* (pp. 36-60). New York: Routledge.

Lather, Patti. (2007). *Getting lost: Feminist efforts toward a double(d) science*. New York: SUNY Press.

Linnell, Sheridan; Bansel, Peter; Ellwood, Constance & Gannon, Susanne. (forthcoming) Precarious listening. *Qualitative Inquiry*.

Probyn, Elspeth. (1993). *Sexing the self: Gendered positions in cultural studies*. London: Routledge.

Rabinow, Paul. (1997). Introduction. In Paul Rabinow (Ed.), *Michel Foucault: Essential works. Vol. 1. Ethics* (pp. xi-xlv). London: Penguin.

Richardson, Laurel. (1997). *Fields of play: Constructing an academic life*. New Brunswick: Rutgers University Press.

Rushdie, Salmon. (1991). *Haroun and the sea of stories*. New York: Penguin.

St Pierre, Elizabeth A. & Pillow, Wanda S. (2000). Introduction: Inquiry among the ruins. In E. St Pierre & W. Pillow (Eds.), *Working the ruins: Feminist poststructural theory and methods in education* (pp. 1-24). New York: Routledge.

Part Three

Dissecting the Mundane

Chapter 5

Actively Mathematical: Alienation and Delight

Betty Johnston

Gender can be understood by using a theory of practice (Connell, 1987) where it is assumed that people "invent" their lives, within certain constraints, and where both the inventions—actions—and constraints are of interest. I have been interested in exploring not only gender, but mathematics too, as a practice, focusing on how the two practices interact (Johnston, 1997) by using the particular methodology of memory-work.

In 1987 Connell pointed to a vast array of social analyses of gender in the literature of the previous two or three decades, and a number of ways of categorizing them. He argued that there were gaps in these theories that led to a need for a theory that gave importance both to the way that history shapes people, and to the way that individuals shape the history of gender—what he called a practice-based theory.

Using Connell's statements about gender theories as a base (1987, p. 55-61), I proposed to begin with parallel statements about mathematics and mathematics education:

- approaches that "focus on norms and give explanatory priority to will, choice and attitudes, avoiding questions of power and social interest, give no way of understanding the historicity" of mathematics—the structures in which mathematics has come to operate.

- approaches that have a view of mathematics as given, "leave out the element of practical politics; choice, doubt, strategy, planning, error and transformation"—the person as active participant.

The theory of practice thus suggests that we might usefully look at the intersection of personal experience and social structure, to examine what it might mean to say that mathematical practice is both constructed by active people, and at the same time structurally connected with other practices and involved in the constitution of social interests.

It would be neat to say that it was at this point that I encountered exactly the method I needed to address my concerns. But research is not neat, and in fact it was a prior encounter with the method—collective memory-work—that allowed me to refine my concern into a research question.

An encounter with memory-work

In the late 1980s, I became intrigued and excited by a series of seminars given at Macquarie University, Sydney, by the German scholar Frigga Haug, on research into women's experience. I was particularly excited by the method that she and her colleagues had developed to do this, memory-work. In the seminars, Haug spoke as a feminist and as a socialist; she drew on psychological as well as sociological theoretical frameworks. She talked about female sexualization, about technology and work, about daydreams, about memory-work, about women as victims or actors, about critical psychology, about gender and technology. One of the things that kept me going back to listen to more was her ability to make connections between—in fact, her refusal to treat separately—individual experience and wider social structures. In the structure and agency debate she and her colleagues refused to take sides; both structure and agency were important. The thread that bound all her interests was the question of how ideologies and social structures get into our heads: how we are constructed by them, and how in turn, we construct—or resist—them. "It is the fact of our active participation in social structures that gives them their solidity; they are more solid than prison walls" (Haug, 1987, p. 59).

Memory-work was the method that she and her colleagues evolved to illuminate that participation. Shortly after her visit, the book *Female sexualization* was published, giving a detailed account of the result of one such process of memory-work (Haug, 1987).

Two other refusals that are a feature of memory-work engaged my attention:

- the refusal to separate subject and object of research: our own experience—our subjectivity—she insisted, could be the object of our research;
- the refusal to separate knowledge and action: the point of the research was to increase our capacity for action, especially collective action.

The question of objectivity becomes not, "is this research objective?" but, "is any research objective?" Memory-work is not used to make statistically valid statements, but to explore possible relations and dynamics, and possible transformations.

Generated from feminist and socialist frameworks these challenges to the taken-for-granted separations of mainstream research were exciting in relation to mathematics. As humans we live quantified lives, where to be categorized, compared, ordered, measured is normal. Normality itself becomes measurable. The "normal" is seen as the true form from which we deviate in different, potentially measurable, ways. Memory-work can help us understand the limits of the quantifying methods so prevalent in maths and gender studies: their separation of the object and subject of research, their inability to theorize the processes of our daily lives, their pervasive individualistic approach, their customary distance from action and commitment to social justice. Using memory-work as a methodology might challenge the chasm between the separated, abstracted knowledge of mathematics and ourselves as knowers.

I had strongly resisted the idea that statistical methods could tell me anything I really wanted to know about how people construct and are constructed into the mathematical world. I did not want to measure. Memory-work was a relief and a challenge.

Coffee, croissants and mathematics: A memory-work group

In the 1990s I worked with two groups of women in Sydney to focus on the topic of women, rationality and mathematical practices. Through an examination of our own past experiences we tried to tease out the ways in which the discourse of mathematics—all the varied knowledge, practices and beliefs surrounding mathematics—worked to insert us into its world, whether as "successes" or not; and how we as individuals had woven ourselves into the mathematical world. One of the groups (Becky, Colleen, Julie, Kath, Louise, Marie and Sophie) met for two or three hours every fortnight, usually on a Sunday morning, over a late breakfast, for a period of four months. The women involved in the group were, as in Haug's original group, from a variety of educational and work backgrounds (high school science teacher, adult literacy teacher, librarian, engineer, design student, numeracy lecturer, research assistant). This variety brought a range of experience and theoretical frameworks to the discussions and analysis, but in no sense could we be seen as representative of our particular backgrounds. Like Haug and her colleagues we were not using memory work to make statistically valid statements, but to explore possible relations and dynamics, and possible transformations.

We wrote and analyzed memories using the cues *doing maths*, *cleverness* and *measuring time*. We examined and discussed relevant theories and opinions. We used many of the techniques that have become common in the method: writing and thinking about our own past as if it were the life of a third person, thus enabling ourselves to treat our memories with both distance and respect; scrutinizing and developing more precise ways of speaking/writing; recognizing that everything remembered constitutes a relevant trace, just because it is remembered, and can bring with it more details.

A challenging suggestion which we took up only towards the end of our research was that of re-vising the stories, literally seeing them again, where one or more members of the group rewrote one of the stories, their own or another's.

Many stories emerged, throwing light on the construction of our gendered mathematical identities. One account traced how the quantification of our society is woven into our lives, in particular how time and its measurement have a gendered element in relation to work, leisure, rationality and order (Johnston, 1998, 2002). A related theme was that of assessment, and how it defines and locates us—and how we sometimes resist it. A third theme was the journey that can be traveled from heteronomy to autonomy, from separation to ownership in relation to our mathematical knowledge (Johnston, 1995).

Here I will trace a theme of separation: aspects of the separation between maths and the everyday world, between symbol and sense, and between mind, body and feeling

Separations: Rules from outside

Mathematics, the school subject, was our starting place. From the beginning it was clear that alienation, separation, and lack of ownership of mathematical knowledge, were going to be recurring issues. I will present some of the issues that emerged, in particular in relation to pleasure, fear, emotion, and ambivalence.

Our first five stories were written and analyzed in response to the cue "doing maths." In exploring the separation between mind, body and feelings in relation to mathematics I would like to look at them initially for the contrast that they offer on the subject of mess:

Louise:
> *8.30 am. Convent school under a tree. The three girls are animatedly discussing their maths homework from the previous night. Not set homework. This was stuff they'd decided to do, they couldn't wait to do, a well-worn mathematics pathway that had been trodden by thousands before them, a journey of discovery.*
> *"Wasn't problem 23 terrific? I used the cosine rule, and tricky algebra"*
> *"Yeah, it was good, but what about 29?!"*
> *"Sure—how did you get it out??"*
> *"I used this lovely combination of. . . ."*
> *The usual hum of maths conversations for these three students. Louise could not get out problem 56, a tortuous piece of geometry which had left a smudgy trail of carbon pencil over the page. The same page was already indented by the pressure of earlier problems, so artfully deciphered that their presence could be felt as your hand progressed across the page. What a turn on! Sheila had fathomed 56, and proudly unveiled her solution with wide eyes*

and a smidgen of arrogance. All the better that Christine had not got up to it. Christine is quietly angry with herself, though apparently nonchalant. Boy, is she going to have a big maths night tonight. Louise can't believe she didn't think up the solution herself—shit! With a flurry of rubbers, Louise's page is erased. The now famous solution is recorded. The page is now even more smudged and creased—a beautiful record of human endurance and application. It looks fantastic! This is the best part—what visuals! Their own shared mathematical aestheticism.

Sheila is proud of her intellectual prowess and staying power. The other two are privately resolved that the tables will be turned tomorrow. All three girls cannot wait to get their books out tonight and work on something really taxing.

Marie:

She's about 11 years old, crouched over her work, arms around the outskirts of her books, hiding it. Palms sweating. The extent of her shame, not knowing, dirtiness, must somehow be contained and hidden. Then there is a figure behind her, towering, menacing: Sister Peter. Her voice is cold and low and in a few words the shame, not knowing, dirtiness of the young girl are exposed, public. "That's wrong. What do you think you're doing. Tear it out and start again." Repeat the shame, repeat the humiliation.

Becky:

She knew what he meant when he said, "It is worse, far worse, to get the right answer by a bad method, than to get the wrong answer using a good method." This maths teacher was different, he trod delicately, and surely, and he loved what he was doing. People said he was hopeless with the younger classes, he couldn't keep control. "The kids walk all over him," they said, rather scornfully. She thought that he shouldn't have had to teach those kids, it was a waste, and he must have hated it, when nobody wanted to do the maths. With the older class, however, he was quite at home. She found it very pleasing, the way you could do some things. Most of it seemed to be learning to fit the rules to the situation, and practicing recognition and that was quite satisfying, in its own way, tidy, organized. But there were glimpses of something far more delicate, more finely woven, the threads all coming together like the themes of a Bach concerto. There were times when the proof was so elegant—this was one of his words—you could hardly believe that such an apparently simple argument could have such power. Mathematical induction was like that: almost a cop out: let's pretend it's true in a general case; if it is, will it be true for the next biggest number? Right, if it is, then is it true for $n=1$? And if that's true, then it will be true for any number, any number at all. So many "ifs" that it should have been hard to find the substance, the actuality, but in fact it was very clear. She only wondered, with real pleasure, that the gossamer threads of its argument should have such strength, to prove true so many, often unwieldy, formulae. It was a sort of magic, not mystery, but tiny and powerful. A bit like proving that the square root of 2 was not a rational number, that you couldn't write it as a fraction: you said, OK, let's pretend we can write it as a fraction, and then proceeded to show that you got a contradiction. So the only possible *conclusion was that your original assumption wasn't possible, it wasn't a rational number.*

Nice, somehow. Too much maths had been trampling through the bogs in heavy boots—you knew you'd get there, but you had to put in the work. This was more like dancing.

Kath:

Her memories are more impressions: maths was part of the fluid world of being in a cocoon which was school—impressions of warmth, laughter, friends, the certainty of the sums and the rules. Chaos was not a part of this world. Order, cut grass, humming summer heat and security.

Colleen:

Another Saturday. C gathered her books and the work she'd completed and set off for another session of mathematics coaching. As she drew nearer her tutor's home her confidence waned. She wouldn't know the answers. He wouldn't be able to explain in such a way as to help her understand. She sighed. The exam wasn't far off. All she could hope for was that luck was with her on the day. After that she needn't deal with this sort of mathematics again.

Sewing on white linen: Two worlds

Both Louise and Marie describe themselves or their work as dirty, smudged, or creased, but the values that accompany those descriptions are polar opposites. For Marie, this mess is dirt, associated with sweaty palms, shame, humiliation and exposure. For Louise, mess is art: "a turn-on, . . . evidence of human creative endeavour, . . . a beautiful record of human endurance and application. . . . Their own shared mathematical aestheticism."

These opposite values afford glimpses into quite different worlds. One is a world where the writer is out of control, where the story happens to her, where in a sense maths happens to her. In the other world the writer is passionately active; she is doing the maths.

Marie talked about doing maths on the "pristine page:"

I had this problem a bit with sewing too, on white linen—it's something about being exposed . . . something I have about shame—and about being dirty—and I have a really big thing about being smelly as well which goes back a long way. But it's somehow like in a maths classroom, it's this thing about everything had to be laid out and ordered and mine just never was and everything was just sort of dirty and—quite out of control.

This fear of exposure and the feelings of shame, dirtiness, smelliness and lack of control were focused on maths, rather than other subjects. In maths, there could be no crossing out; work that might be wrong needed to be done on other little scraps of paper, if "pristineness and order" were to be preserved. Julie described an occasion like Marie's, when a friend's mother tore out her daughter's page "probably because it was so grotty." Even the technology of writing presented problems. Two of the women who had attended Catholic schools agreed

that "biros were looked on by the Catholic church as loose, and basically pro-
miscuous:"

Louise:
. . . and biros were just absolutely—they were like condoms—isn't
that right?

Marie:
Yes—we were not allowed to use biros—it was as though there had
been an encyclical on it.

Louise:
It was the new looseness.

Marie:
Right and wrong, good and bad—sin!
[There were] devastating experiences of ink everywhere, all that
stuff—but I think that with the maths is the added stuff, the thing of
the rightness and wrong . . . these memories are here around maths
but they're not around other things. There seems to be less of a mar-
gin for error with maths. . . . It had to be set out in a certain way and
you had to get the right answer. The right and wrong dichotomy is so
strong in maths, for me, and the thing about— the link with sin.

Not only, therefore, could the "pristine page" be physically messed up; the
content, the maths itself, could be a mess. In some subjects it was possible to
"find [your] own way there," to write an essay that made sense to you, but in
maths it was different. As Marie said: "I couldn't necessarily arrive at [it]
through my own process." The obsession with neatness and tidiness may be
partly illuminated by realizing that when we have no confidence in what we are
writing, then it is only over its physical presentation that we have any control at
all.

Mess for Marie is evidence of her failure. When the maths is meaningless,
then the sense of order is in its presentation. To fail there also is total failure. For
Louise, physical mess is treasured evidence of the creation of meaning, a different kind of control and order. It was not the page in itself that was valued, but its
use—not the white linen, but the old worn garment. As she said:

We used to love that—just say you'd written on this page—we used to rub the
back and say feel this, feel this! —because on the back side it was really
heavy—and this is what I can't believe about Marie's experience—you'd start
off with your exercise book, and the pristine pages, they weren't interesting, the
ones that you hadn't touched—it was the tortuous crunched stuff that you'd already done, that was.

From dirt to dancing

Mess is just one of the surprisingly physical, even sensuous, images that the writers use to talk about "doing maths." The images—actual or metaphorical—are associated with a range of occasions. Looking at all five stories we have:

> *fear*—a waning confidence, crouching, palms sweating, dirtiness, hidden, towering, low cold voice, shame, humiliation
> *hard work and following the rules*—trampling through the bogs in heavy boots
> *certainty and safety*—tidy, a fluid world, a cocoon, warmth, laughter, friends, order, cut grass, humming summer heat and security
> *appreciation*—a sure but delicate tread, glimpses of something far more delicate, more finely woven, the themes of a Bach concerto, elegant, gossamer threads, a sort of magic, not mystery, but tiny and powerful, dancing
> and finally *the excitement of creativity*—a well-worn mathematics pathway, a journey of discovery, a smudgy trail of carbon pencil, a smudged and creased page indented by the pressure, a turn on, visuals, mathematical aestheticism.

The literature on "maths anxiety" provides much evidence of the strong—negative—feelings and physical reactions associated with mathematics. Our stories echoed those experiences, and also provided evidence of strongly positive feelings and physical reactions and images. As Becky said: "amazing—this combination of the intellectual with the sensual."

As a teacher of adults who have returned to study after a time away, I am now accustomed to the ways in which "maths anxiety"[1] expresses itself, including its very physical manifestations: sweaty palms, headaches, physical tension, nausea. The literature on "maths anxiety" provides much evidence of the strong—negative—feelings and physical reactions associated with mathematics. What I was less prepared for in our research were the strongly physical, sensuous images and actions, associated with the positive experiences of Becky and Louise, and others, with "maths pleasure." But why not, after all? Why should we expect that the physical is related only to negative experiences? Perhaps part of the answer lies in the fact that "maths anxiety" does not allow its "victims" close to the maths involved. It is in its very nature to block understanding and appreciation. Mind (maths) and body are seen to be separated. "Maths pleasure" on the other hand emerges from a degree of engagement with the maths in question, where feeling is integrated with knowing and doing.

Connecting

There was for Becky and others a definite satisfaction to be gained from following the rules. "Most of [maths] seemed to be learning to fit the rules to the situation, and practicing recognition and that was quite satisfying, in its own way, tidy, organized," Becky wrote, but she likened it to "trampling through the bogs in heavy boots—you knew you'd get there, but you had to put in the work." What is it that happens to make some situations "more like dancing?"

Louise recognized her own aesthetic response in Becky's story:

> the thing about yours [Becky's] was that you had some sort of aesthetic appre-
> ciation for . . . [or] an intellectual appreciation of the simplicity of the solution
> and that it was beautiful, the simplicity was beautiful. . . . I really identify with
> that.

Another powerful factor in Louise's delight in maths, was that the work—the journey—was undertaken with friends. Together challenges were set, solutions were shared and worked on, and the written work appreciated, both for its content and its "mathematical aestheticism." It is clear too that one of the factors in her subsequent moving away from maths at university was the lack of an alternative group who could work together to construct a joint understanding.

Kath, highly qualified in a mathematically based profession, had been recently fired and delighted by coming to understand why $(x + a)(x + b)$ should be the same as $x^2 + ax + bx + ab$. She describes how a colleague had shown her how to think of the expression as the area of a paddock:

> You can actually draw it—yes, something physical—you can <u>see</u>—it absolutely
> stunned me, when she showed me that—and ever since then I've been thinking,
> oh wow, the rest of it must mean something. I finally got a meaning, but I was,
> what, 34. . . . I had [had] no problems with the mechanisms going through it, I
> could do that any time, but it didn't mean anything—why would anyone want to
> know how to expand. . .? I never even thought you could [ask why].

In this context, Marie makes a point about connections between maths and concrete situations:

> My first encounter with maths as a real thing was the maths anxiety workshop
> and the handshake problem . . . and this whole revelation, that it has a basis in a
> concrete experience, that is if I understand the reality of it then I don't need to
> know the rules because I can just get there again. . . . I could do that handshake
> problem and get back to that formula . . . because it made sense.

It was this very problem of maths not being her own process, of not being able to find her own way there, that so strongly alienated Marie from it at school.

Becky and Louise talked about inversive geometry:

Becky:
> So you could do things that would have taken an enormous long effort
> [otherwise]. . . . It was lovely, really nice stuff, but that's the only other bit of
> maths I remember that was like that—where I suppose I got an overview of
> what was happening. The rest I got in steps, and I followed the steps and I was
> inside it and I could keep on going—but the other one I could see.

Louise:
Yes, how it all works.

Instead of being on the ground—in the bog—following the separate steps, Becky had glimpses from above—an overview. As if flying, she could see the ground laid out below, the whole terrain.

Connections within the content giving an overview, connections between maths and real world objects, connections between people talking about maths—all these connections were working to contest separation and provide meaning, and in doing so, to make maths "more like dancing."

Dancing and delight: A forbidden pleasure

Colleen had no association of maths with pleasure. As Marie worked towards her School Certificate exams, she experienced a certain pleasure as she studied maths, but the pleasure was in the retreat it allowed her from her family rather than in the maths itself: "I just sat at a desk for hours and hours and hours and did endless examples, completely joyless."

Kath's images of "warmth, laughter, friends, order, cut grass, humming summer heat and security" evoke a strong pleasure, and one clearly associated with maths. It was not excitement, however, but the pleasure connected with what is known and secure: "they were no challenge. . . . There was no intellectual commitment at all." For Kath, that challenge was provided by subjects like English and history, which seemed freer, where she tried to extend boundaries in her writing and found her work rejected. There was after all a correct way to do it. In that sense, there were "formulae" in English too, but, as Kath said, "they were far more arbitrary to me than maths was." Kath's experience here has echoes of the "anxiety" usually associated with maths.

All these issues we discussed in some depth. However, as a group, we did not discuss in such detail the more unusual, extraordinary pleasure written about by both Becky and Louise. The stories were greeted with appreciative comments: "Wow! Wonderful, amazing. I like the notion of it being delicate and gossamer." But most of these comments were isolated, not part of the main discussion.

What is striking about the stories of Louise and Becky is their strong delight in maths, and the connections with music, art, dancing, and bodily pleasures discussed above. There is however for both women an element of "forbidden pleasure," of ambivalence, in their relation to maths. Becky realized that this was the first occasion for a long time in which she had allowed herself to talk publicly about how much she enjoyed maths. It also became clear that the different reality of university, which followed soon after this sixth form experience, served as a rude awakening for Louise. For both, the writing of the stories could be seen as a reclaiming of a lost delight.

A beginning of a deeper analysis is made when Sophie, who had been absent and had therefore only read the stories by herself, said: "I must admit I felt very guilty the way I reacted to Louise's, because I sort of groaned you know and it was like—oh God, somebody's into maths!" Others in the group identified with this reaction, and agreed that it was: "really sad that even while we're trying to find out why we're all so anxious about maths that somebody who wasn't and expresses enthusiasm is cut down by us . . . with a groan."

Ambivalence

Even those who enjoyed the greatest pleasure from mathematics, contributed to this devaluing. Becky, referring to not having previously allowed herself to say much about how much she liked maths, finished with the comment: "Because you're not supposed to . . . you shouldn't get such a kick out of it." Louise was particularly contradictory. Her story was extraordinarily expressive of her delight. Later, she described what she did in maths as merely "regurgitative . . . the reciting of catechisms," at another time it was simply "the result of hard work," and at yet another time she described herself like this:

> I was always the one who just did everything in my maths book, from go to whoa, I just loved it, I went home, every night I just couldn't wait to do it, it was fantastic, I loved it, it's really rather sick isn't it?

What happened to the pleasure? Why did we forbid it to ourselves?

We in the group, women ourselves, devalued Louise's excitement about maths. There was evidence in our experiences that this was a reflection of a much wider process where it is difficult for women to find support for non-traditional engagements, even from other women, even from other women who are aware of the problem.

Another arresting ambivalence in the stories emerged in the portraits of the three teachers. One is a male tutor who never makes it on stage. The other two, in the stories by Becky and Marie, provide a surprising contrast. Becky describes a male teacher who is associated, positively, with rather unmasculine images ("he trod delicately," "dancing," "gossamer threads"). Marie portrays a female teacher, Sister Peter, with a male's name and associated, negatively, with rather unfeminine images ("towering, menacing," a voice "cold and low"). Does this "cross-gendering" occur more generally in women's—or men's—experience of "doing maths?" Could it illuminate our understanding of the complex relationship between mathematics and gender?

Not only rules and abstractions

Emerging from these discussions are numerous strands of what it might mean to be mathematical, to do mathematics. Rules and abstractions, yes, the disciplined mind; but also creativity, frustration and delight, real world connections, political implications—a much more messy, less docile engagement. Marie is the one who makes explicit a range of these experiences, from her humiliating experience of drilled knowledge with Sister Peter to her experience of the hand-shake problem:

> this whole revelation, that [maths] has a basis in a concrete experience, that is
> if I understand the reality of it then I don't need to know the rules because I can
> just get there again. . . . It was absolutely my first experience of that really, it
> was actually of knowing in general and quite specifically in maths. . . . It is
> really exciting and sort of passionate and enjoyable, but we have people who
> are not socially controlled I think, in the end.

Not just frustration and fear, but also passion, delight and a kind of libera-tion. And a glimpse of what it might mean if we were to refuse the constructed separation between mind, body and feeling in mathematics.

Mathematics—produced and therefore transformable

What conclusions is it possible to draw from a series of memories related by a disparate group of women, a collection of particular stories told by separate individuals? Clearly it is not statistically valid statements that are either appro-priate or desired, but the exploration of possible relations and dynamics, and possible transformations. What decisions individuals will make, how they will deal with particular emotions, situations, conflicts are not predictable, but need empirical investigation. However:

> The notion of the uniqueness of experience . . . is a fiction. The number of pos-sibilities for action open to us is radically limited. We live according to a whole
> series of imperatives: social pressures, natural limitations, the imperative of
> economic survival, the given conditions of history and culture. Human beings
> produce their lives collectively. It is within the domain of collective production
> that individual experience becomes possible. If then a given experience is pos-sible, it is also subject to universalisation. . . . Our focus of interest was not
> unique personalities, but rather general modes of appropriation of the social.
> (Haug, 1987, pp. 44-45)

The evidence that is appropriate and powerful is not the evidence of num-bers and statistics. It is the evidence of Haraway's "positioned rationality:"

> Its images are not the products of escape and transcendence of limits (the view
> from above) but the joining of partial views and halting voices into a collective
> subject position that promises a vision of the means of ongoing finite embodi-ment, of living within limits and contradictions—of views from somewhere.
> (Seidler, 1994, p. 154)

The range of stories and analysis gathered from the two groups I worked with (Johnston, 1997) show that much of our experience of maths had been of a dominating practice that alienated us from our own knowledge and the everyday world, separating mind, body and emotion, and prioritizing abstraction and generalization over meaning. Examples of that practice have been illustrated in this paper. Understanding both maths and gender as practice, however, allows us to see them as produced by humans, in specific historical circumstances, and therefore as able to be different from the constellation of arrangements at any particular moment.

We came to see that the practice of maths can involve more than the single strand of knowing that is demonstrated and reproduced through incremental steps. It crucially involves knowing also through intuition and imaginative leaps, through experience, through playing with chaos: not either/or, but as Haraway (1991, p. 192) argues in relation to science, the necessary combination of the "imaginary and the rational, the visionary and objective vision." Its practice can involve not only deduction, order and reason but induction, mess and conceptual breaks. It is woven out of creativity and reproduction, it demands emotional engagement, it is transformed in use, for good or bad. This is not the "thin" maths practice of the maths/rationality/masculinity chain that was our dominant experience. The insights of our collective experiences worked to challenge that dominant vision and to refuse the necessity of either/or—either femininity or mathematics—in favor of the possibility of both/and.

Mathematics is not all-powerful, as it is sometimes portrayed. On the other hand, as some of us had experienced it, it does have power; it can be beautiful, and, in practice, it can increase our capacities for both democracy and delight. Through the use of memory-work we came to see that—like gender, class and race—mathematics is not given, not chosen, but produced, and therefore transformable.

Questions: Unfinished business

My use of memory-work grew out of a double fascination: the challenge posed by the question "What don't the statistics tell us about women and mathematics?" and the desire to explore how this method could help us both understand and transform our experience. The work with the two groups has only been a beginning and has left important questions open.

In particular I—like the majority of memory-work researchers—have not engaged explicitly with Marxist theory. That both feminism and Marxism were critical in the theoretical development of memory-work is clear, spelt out time and again by the original group (eg., Haug, 1987, p. 31). Anne Junor is one of very few who offers a discussion that elaborates on the method's Marxist context, when she contrasts:

> Derrida's model of women's free-floating resistance with the model of collective reconstruction developed by Frigga Haug and other women. . . . By contrast with the poststructuralist assumption that girl children are "inserted" into the social order, this alternative, Marxist, model is based on a view that women find ways of "constructing themselves into" the social order. Different views of resistance follow. (Junor, Hartwig & Sharp, 1990, p. 20)

She argues that memory-work challenges subjectivity by making individuality problematic, a challenge that is quite different from poststructuralism's "disappearance" of the subject. The kind of withdrawal envisaged by Derrida, is, says Junor et al., "the only possible response to one who sees social relationships as a ubiquitous deployment of pregiven male power" (p. 23). Memory-work on the other hand allows us to see such relationships as constantly being produced, and therefore able to be produced differently (p. 24), a position that accords well with Connell's theory of practice. A real engagement with the implications of the difference between "insertion" and "construction" could challenge and deepen our analysis, and its lack gives a less vigorous understanding.

Such a realization is not an argument for keeping strictly to the original theoretical frameworks or practical guidelines—certainly we do not wish to see the energy of the method, its concern with contradiction, silence and ambivalence, its richness and fluidity, in danger of being cemented into the safety of rules. However, it is a plea for revisiting those frameworks, for exploring the insights that may give. The field may be immeasurably enriched by being able to draw on a conversation about Marxist theory, as well as feminist theory, within memory-work research.

That a trend towards the safety of stages and rules might be detrimental (Johnston, 2001) can be seen by contrasting some of the more "rule"-oriented work in memory-work with that done by, for instance, the Scandinavian sports sociologists, in all its diversity and excitement. In an exploration of men's experiences in sport Laitinen and Tiihonen (1990) looked at how masculinity in boys is constructed through sport. Tiihonen, a student, used memory-work and other "techniques commonly used in the feminist movement" (life-experience, oral exchanges) to analyze "the latent social story beyond his personal sport history" (1990, p. 187). Sironen and his colleagues experienced memory-work as an "epoch-making event:"

> as if it were a natural extension of the age-old habit of women to conduct debates on everyday issues amid the tasks of cooking, looking after the children and doing the washing . . . its discursive technique of interpreting small narratives . . . was for us an extensively developed tool which we could use. (1994, p. 9)

The second, related, question that remains enticingly open for me is that of moving from "understanding" to "transforming," from analysis to the "greater capacity for action" that the original collective emphasized. The re-vising of some of the memories, something we did only a few times towards the end, several times generated a sense of exhilaration and a feeling that they worked as "practice runs" for potential future action. At the same time, we experienced a recurring concern that we were allowing ourselves to be diverted by Louise's school crises, and Marie's experiences in Technical and Further Education (TAFE)—by the real world. Gradually we realized that this "diversion" also needed be seen in relation to action. To have conducted "pure" discussion on the topic of "doing maths" or "measuring time," would have been to contribute to the same reductionist thinking that we were beginning to understand. We came to see that the analysis of the related issues was contributing to our ability to act, and our actions were deepening the analysis. Far from dismissing them as red herrings, we began to see the solving of these current and pressing issues as giving point to the whole process, as critically involving research in transforming lived experience. We were beginning, by the end of the research, to have greater insight into the aims of the original memory-work group:

> Since we are opposed to tolerating conditions that produce suffering—we argue instead for change, for active intervention– our attention will be focused here primarily on the process whereby individuals construct themselves into existing social relations. The question we want to raise is thus an empirical one: it is the "how" of lived feminine practice. . . . Our aim then was to counter heteronomy with autonomy, unhappiness with a struggle for the capacity to be happy. (Haug, 1987, p. 34)

Notes

[1] This is the common term in the literature. I prefer to use the term "maths abuse" that grew out of a conversation between colleague Jenny McGee and myself. We wanted a term that would take the blame from the "victim" and make the issue of power explicit. This term usefully carries connotations of maths as both abuser and abused.

References

Connell, R. W. (1987). *Gender and power: Society, the person and sexual politics.* Cambridge, UK: Polity Press.

Haraway, Donna. (1991). Situated knowledges: The science question in feminism and the privilege of partial perspective. In Donna Haraway (Ed.), *Simians, cyborgs and women* (pp.183-201). London: Free Association Press.

Haug, Frigga. (1987). *Female sexualization: A collective work of memory* (Erica Carter, Trans.). London: Verso.

Johnston, Betty. (1995). Mathematics: An abstracted discourse. In Pat Rogers & Gabrielle Kaiser (Eds.), *Equity in mathematics education: Influences of feminism and culture* (pp. 163-174). London: Falmer Press.

Johnston, Betty. (1997). *Maths and gender: Given or made? A study of women, rationality and mathematical practices.* Unpublished doctoral dissertation. Sydney: University of Sydney.

Johnston, Betty. (1998). Mess and order: Spotlight on time. In Christine Keitel (Ed.), *Social justice and mathematics education: Gender, class, ethnicity and the politics of schooling* (pp. 20-31). Berlin: Freie Universitat.

Johnston, Betty. (2001). Memories, normality & rules: The power of the mundane and the methodology of memory-work. In Jennic Small & Jenny Onyx (Eds.), *Memory-work: A critique* (pp. 31-41). Sydney: School of Management, University of Technology.

Johnston, Betty. (2002). Capturing numeracy practices: Memory-work and time. *Ways of Knowing Journal, 2,* 33-44.

Junor, Anne; Hartwig, Mervyn & Sharp R. (1990). *Marxism, science and poststructuralist fairytales*. Paper read at Socialist Scholars Conference, University of Technology, Sydney.

Laitinen, Arja & Tiihonen, Arto. (1990). Narratives of men's experiences in sport. *International Review for the Sociology of Sport*, *25*(3), 183-201.

Seidler, Victor J. (1994). *Unreasonable men*. London: Routledge.

Sironen, Esa. (1994). On memory-work in the theory of body culture. *International Review for the Sociology of Sport*, *29*(1), 5-14.

Chapter 6

Having a Go at
Memory-work as Sociological Method:
Experience of Menstruation

Glenda Koutroulis

In Australia (and possibly elsewhere, but I'm not really sure), the phrase "having a go at" can mean either to try at something or alternatively to criticize. When I undertook a PhD (sociology) in 1990, one of my supervisors suggested I "have a go at" memory-work, a relatively new methodology that had excited his interest. Six years later one of my examiners, also excited, "had a go at" memory-work. How precisely will become clear shortly. Some methods more than others seem inclined to provoke angst, shades of irritability, and various other responses not all negative. Especially likely methods are those that provide a space for creativity, introspection, self reflection, and encourage dialogue.

To recall, memory-work is largely a collaborative research strategy. During an initial task of memory-work, deciding on a theme about which to write, the discussion among collective members went as follows:

Menstruation, said Kate, "is not something I want to bring to the surface and wash the dirty linen in public." Jill asserted that the ordinariness of menstruation made it a not-worthwhile topic: "I don't want to come in here and have this heart wrenching thing because - oh, she got it on a Friday and there's some significance in that. To me, who the hell cares?" Rosa responded to Jill's

utterings with: "This is fascinating stuff," to which Jill interjected asking: "Is it
to you?" Rosa then continued: "We're talking about method and look what's
coming out." Jill replied with: "I think the methodology stinks." (Koutroulis,
1996, pp. 99-100)

Jill's statement, "I think the methodology stinks," might express a view shared
by one of my doctoral examiners who suggested that memory-work resembled a
lay form of psychoanalysis with nothing to distinguish it especially as sociological. Pungent words. The source of the stink is likely to emanate, at least in part,
from the heat generated by epistemological debates; as fuel for this malodorous
matter, however, memory-work is not alone. My approach to this chapter, then,
is straightforward: I want to explore the stink, discern, if I can, from where it
comes, and try to lessen its pungency.

   Thus the first section is devoted to elucidating how memory-work is sociological. I then explore the connection of memory-work to psychoanalysis, picking up on the reference to psychoanalysis made by Haug (1987) and other memory-workers. In the second section I move on to another "pollutant:"
menstruation, and air some (but not Kate's) dirty linen in public as I provide a
glimpse of us, the memory-work collective, doing memory-work—having a go at
it—as we grappled with understanding the embodied experience of menstruation.
I chose this topic because despite menstruation being a popular topic of anthro-
pological, psychological, sociological and medical investigation, particularly in
regard to more problematic areas such as premenstrual tension, there is little
understanding of the role this bodily experience has in shaping identity. The
memory I present and the subsequent theorizing traces the interplay between the
personal feelings and emotions inscribed in the memory, the body and social
factors. The third section emphasizes where problems were encountered, setting
the collective's experience against the complexities that existed for particular
individuals and how these problems were negotiated.

The place of memory-work in sociology

   From at least the beginning of the last century sociology has had an interest in
personal experience. The reflection on personal experience was characterized by
George Herbert Mead (1934) at the turn of last century in his classic text, *Mind, self
and society*. Mead analyzed how the self is constructed through social processes
emphasizing that the self could only be understood in relation to the social. However, neither sociology's interest in personal experience, nor what was considered
acceptable in the study of experience (Clandinin & Connelly, 1994), was absolute.
Memory has had a checkered history in relation to its sociological status and, according to Manning and Cullum-Swan (1994, p. 463), almost from the start of empirical work in sociology the use of personal documents such as diaries and letters
to study people's life experience, have been controversial.

A number of figures were influential in the development of the personal experience element of sociology, but one of the most important figures for more contemporary sociological thinkers is C. Wright Mills. Like those before him, Wright Mills (1967) in his classic work entitled *The sociological imagination* drew out the link between the personal and the public and the implications of this for a certain quality of social life. While a key feature of sociology is to analyze the relationship of the individual to society, the sociological task, according to Wright Mills, is to understand the interplay of personal troubles with problems of social structure. To have an "aware[ness] of the idea of social structure and to use it with sensibility," tracing the linkages among the various milieu, is to possess what Wright Mills calls "the sociological imagination" (1967, pp. 10-11). He proposes that "personal troubles [need to be translated] into public issues, and public issues into the terms of their human meaning for a variety of individuals" (1967, p. 187). Troubles refer to the self when cherished values are threatened. Issues concern wider social and historical life and the threat to values held by the public (Wright Mills, 1967). His notion of sociology, that personal experience is interconnected with social problems, corresponds with the feminist theme of the personal is political. These words embody the idea that there is no aspect of life, of the self, that is not worthy of public discussion.

Sociology, far from being a homogeneous discipline, is informed by a complex array of differing approaches that exhibit their own principles of investigation. Domain assumptions underlying these differences have seen the shifting of methods within the social sciences. These shifting frames of reference, Clandinin and Connelly (1994, p. 414) claim, "define acceptable knowledge and inquiry." One of the more enduring frames of reference is positivism. Clandinin and Connelly (1994) point out that proponents of positivistic models of inquiry sought to set the terms and limits of research, fueling debates over epistemological matters in the social sciences. A dogmatic commitment to "The Method," Wright Mills asserts, "has become the mere following of a ritual - which happens to have gained commercial and foundation value" (1967, p. 72). However, rituals can become convention and, as Richardson (1994, p. 520) points out, "conventions hold tremendous material and symbolic power over social scientists." The legacy, Manning and Cullum-Swan argue, is that sociology struggles to divorce from positivist "methods that take the external world as extant" (1994, p. 463), and deny personal or subjective experience as legitimate knowledge. Personal experience came to be suggestive of tainted knowledge and so experience as a focus of study risked criticism. Such criticisms, Clandinin and Connelly (1994, p. 414) argue, "constitute the politics of epistemology."

Epistemological debates informed by feminism challenged the theoretical and conceptual constraints that had taken a stranglehold on research (see Harding, 1987; Reinharz, 1992; Stanley & Wise, 1993; Weedon, 1987). Long before the emergence of memory-work, feminism had become an influential force behind a shifting of methods within social science. Some stalwart sociologists, for example Zola (1991), celebrated the effects of feminism on the way research is carried out and on how sociology is conceptualized. Zola wrote how he was compelled to re-think and examine his earlier writings in light of his own personal experience. The consideration of embodied experience in sociology sparked him to produce a con-fronting methodological critique, and call for personal experience to be placed at the centre of analysis.

Haug (1987) sought a means to impress the feminist principles of subjectivity and collectivity upon the dominant ways of researching. Thus, based on her own brand of feminist theory that grew out of her experience of oppression, Haug for-mulated a way of "doing" research that replaced the positivist locus of the object in research; and took researching women's experience one step further by employing women's own analysis and interpretation of their experience. The importation of poststructuralist categories and conceptualizations into memory-work facilitated the memory-worker's critical scepticism about the memory text, and deconstruction of the place of the self in reproducing what Haug (1987, p. 43) calls "the way indi-viduals live social relations." Memory-workers are directed not to seek explana-tions for their actions in their individual unique stories, rather, in the social produc-tion of their lives (see Crawford, Kippax, Onyx, Gault & Benton, 1992; Haug, 1987; Schratz, Walker & Schratz-Hadwich, 1995).

Memory-work is comparable to methods employed by other qualitative re-searchers and, like any classic social analysis, has a definable and usable set of tra-ditions. A memory is a written record of an experience much like that staple of so-ciology, the interview. Indeed, interviews could be considered a form of memory-work: experience is laundered through respondent's memories vis-a-vis the inter-view process. The specific research techniques used in memory-work are akin to standard sociological ones (e.g., thematic analysis, group interviewing). Memory-work shares similarities with literary criticism. In other ways it resembles ap-proaches to participative inquiry—cooperative inquiry, participatory action research, action science and action inquiry—that are premised, according to Reason (1994), on a commitment to cooperative inquiry, which emphasizes working with groups as co-researchers. These methods, Reason (1994, p. 333) argues, "unite to emphasize the fundamental importance of experiential knowing." Memory-work is at the same time a way of further developing these standard sociological techniques and yet an innovative, sociological way of proceeding to uncover the personal-social intercon-nection. The stages in memory-work represent logical steps in a systematic socio-logical analysis of the social construction of self, critically examining the social processes implicated in this commitment to understanding the self. The techniques are novel, but the process and aims are traditionally sociological.

Haug (1987) conceived memories to be the social text whereby an analysis by the selves, of the social production of the selves, was intrinsic. Memories, as social text, require reflection to make sense of experience by understanding the social context in which behavior occurs. This has been central to sociology since its earli-est days, exemplified for instance in Emile Durkheim's (1951) *Suicide*. Durkheim demonstrated, through much statistical data, that suicide was not a uniquely individual act but was shaped by collective social factors: the social environment had explanatory value in determining suicide and therefore suicide was fundamentally a social phenomenon. Thus, as Wright Mills (1967) recognized, personal troubles arise in the context of broader social problems.

Biographies of men and women are socially and historically located (Berger & Berger, 1976; Wright Mills, 1967), whereas what we know about the social is biographically acquired (Berger & Berger, 1976). Thus, a logical way of understanding the historical, social structures in which the milieu of people's everyday experiences are organized (Wright Mills, 1967) is to begin with the biographical (Berger & Berger, 1976). Although "memories appear to be at the extreme of what is personal and individual" (Schratz et al., 1995, p. 40) they are used as a basis of social knowledge. Despite how memories are used, the focus on biography or personal and individual experience draws attention to the arguments, of which Wright Mills says there is no end, about the relations between psychology and the social sciences. Negotiating these relations requires self-consciousness, or what Wright Mills calls "the sociological imagination." The sociological imagination, he claims

> is the capacity to shift from one perspective to another - from the political to the psychological;... It is the capacity to range from the most impersonal and remote transformations to the most intimate features of the human self - and to see the relations between the two. (1967, p. 7)

The memory-work and psychoanalysis connection

The psychology-sociology arguments, and the negative suggestion made by one of my thesis examiners of a similarity between psychoanalysis and memory-work makes it of interest to trace out any connection between them. Some energy has been expended by previous memory-workers (Crawford et al., 1992; Haug, 1987; Schratz et al., 1995) in detailing how memory-work is not psychoanalysis and any connection made is relatively indirect.

Here, it is useful to note that Freudian psychoanalytic theory has had an uneasy alliance with feminism and social theory. Some feminists have castigated Freud and psychoanalysis for being biologic, male centered, individualistic, and eclipsing economic and power structure. Others (for example, Juliet Mitchell, Gayle Rubin, Nancy Chodorow), however, have utilized aspects of psychoanalysis and Young (1990) herself considers aspects of psychoanalysis (desire and the unconscious) important tools for feminist social theory.

The practical task of psychoanalysis, in Freud's (1949) view, is focused on the study of disorders that derive from the early life and developmental history of an individual. Thus, psychoanalysis is a technique concerned with understanding individual disturbances and these are related back to early life. Within psychoanalysis, dreams are the most favored object of study (Freud, 1949). The process of understanding or interpreting a dream, Freud calls dream-work. Implicit in dream-work is the assumption that there is more to a dream than what is self-evident and the dream-work process described by Freud is to look beyond the obvious for what is concealed. Dream-working, Freud contends, requires collaboration between the analyst and the analyzed to fill in the gaps so that constructions about what happened can be made, even to say what might seem as unimportant or nonsensical or disagreeable. He points out that there may be resistance by the analyzed to unwanted interpretations. Overcoming such resistances, Freud argues, is that part of psychoanalysis requiring the most time and energy and he describes tactics for managing such resistance.

Substitute memories for dreams, memory-work for dream-work, researcher collaboration for analyst-analyzed collaboration and a very curious resemblance between Freud's conception of psychoanalysis and memory-work emerges. Add to this the analytical process that involves, among many other things, giving painstaking attention to the detail of a memory, seeing what is not said as important, and overcoming any individual's resistance to interpretations by adopting certain tactics to ward off individual or group destabilization (Haug, 1987). All of these techniques are within the province of dream-work or psychoanalysis. In addition, Haug (1987) refers to the conscious and unconscious, both of which are inbuilt constructs essential to Freud's conception of psychoanalysis. Despite these similarities, Schratz et al. (1995) begin to draw a distinction:

> Memory-workers claim that the work they do is research, not therapy; memories may play a role in memory-work that is comparable to the role that dreams play in psychoanalysis, but the allusion to psychoanalysis is misleading. Memory-work is not intended as therapy, nor is its primary concern with self-knowledge. It is concerned to close the gaps between theory and experience in ways that are intended to change the nature of experience, not simply to accept it. It is . . . focused on political and social action. . . . The key to the critical distinction between memory-work and psychoanalysis begins in the concept, derived from George Herbert Mead, of a duality within the self altogether different from Freudian conceptions of the individual psyche. (p. 41)

Thus, Haug's (1987) memory-work theory and practice, accounting for how individuals actively participate in their formation as social beings, the greater valuation of social processes in influencing who we become, and the political-social action dimension of memory-work is sufficient, in Schratz et al.'s (1995) view, to distinguish memory-work from psychoanalysis.

Nonetheless, while Haug warns memory-workers against "vulgar psychoanalytic models of interpretation" (1987, p. 56) those aspects of the process of psychoanalysis having some resemblance to the memory-work process might have been detailed. Haug asserts her strong dissent from psychoanalysis in part because she saw it as a self-centered perspective that impaired social analysis:

The aim of our collective research was to retrace in memory the patterns whereby individuals have worked their way into the social world, and since therefore our object was the process of women's socialization, . . . slipping into amateur psychotherapy clearly undermined our project. (1987, p. 57)

Amateur (or lay) psychoanalysis presents itself in everyday jargon in the form of questions such as: "How could you have done such a thing?" and glib reasoning, for example, "It's obvious you were forced to identify with your mother here" (Haug, 1987, p. 56).

Memory-work picks up where George Herbert Mead (1934) left off going beyond biography and interpersonal relations to tackle, in the spirit of Wright Mills, the broader context in which these relations and the individual are placed. Haug's (1987) theory traces women's oppression to their bodies, uncovering processes that contribute to construction of the self. On this base, "a method that required the critical reconstitution of individualism, . . . [that could] unravel, and then . . . challenge this (psychoanalytic) assumption of early experience as a prison of the self" (Schratz et al., 1995, p. 41) was built. Researching "at the interface between the individual and society" (Crawford et al., 1992, p. 4) in the way that memory-work does, necessitates not only a sociological imagination, but a sociological sensibility which may effect "a sort of therapy in the ancient sense of clarifying one's knowledge of self" (Wright Mills, 1967, p. 186). Researching via memory-work, I believe (unlike Schratz et al., 1995), is just such a therapy.

This "clarifying of knowledge of the self" or the complexities that exist for particular individuals, is set against the collective enquiry that forms the second part of the chapter as I shift from theoretical considerations to memory-work in process. In this focus on collectivity there is movement from the ideology of individualizing and atomizing life's experiences such as might be evident in psychoanalysis. Haug points out that the historical movement of individualizing is most apparent within State institutions that focus on individual responsibility for actions that differ according to gender. Noting that subordination to politically enshrined conventions works to a large extent through the body, Haug proposes that individualizing facilitates "normalizing" so that disparities can be measured. She provides the example of women's bodies and what she describes as the producing and the ordering of a certain "type" of woman. I begin exploring this idea by presenting Anastasia's memory of menstruation, which was written in response to the cue "significant moment," and the subsequent memory-work process of untangling its meaning.

First, however, I will provide some background to the collective and some ways in which we negotiated methodological requirements. This account of memory-work, begun in 1990 and completed in the mid 1990s, explored the menstrual experiences of eight Australian women with the pseudonyms of Jill, Kate, Rosa, Paula, Shane, Theresa, Rosemary and Anastasia, whose ages ranged from the thirties to the fifties. Five of the women were my long-time friends. Two were more recent friends. Several of my friends had met on previous occasions, whereas others did not know each other prior to the first meeting of the collective. At the time of the research six of the women lived with their partners and children; one woman was divorced and lived with her child; one woman was neither married nor had children and lived alone. We are from a variety of backgrounds, and although we could be described as middle-class, most of our parents were working-class or upper working-class. One woman is the daughter of Greek migrants, and two women (siblings) are the daughters of English migrants. Three of the women grew up in rural Australia: one woman in a Victorian country town, another in a New South Wales town and another on a South Australian farm. The remainder of the women spent most of their lives in a large Australian city. Some expressed strong religious affiliations (Greek Orthodox, Catholic and Protestant) and some no religious affiliation. All the women were in paid work (four nurses, one teacher, one violinist, and two social workers), and some were studying as well.

Prior to deciding on method and then establishing the collective, I had already settled on menstruation as my PhD research topic. Jill and Kate's comments (quoted earlier) about this topic took place at the first meeting where I discussed in detail the research process and requirements. After much debate within the collective about topic and method, the decision to take a broad reflective approach to the written memory through the sub-theme "significant moment" was reached. This theme, rather than one that was predefined as important to all women (e.g., menarche), we believed, would provide a degree of freedom for collective members to decide their own most memorable experience about which to write. We wrote only one memory and memory rewrite; my suggestion to write another memory was rejected by collective members because of the time involved in the analysis. We met 12 times: 11 meetings were in my home and one in Anastasia's home. These taped meetings took place over many months, each for several hours duration. All collective members were involved in the analysis, whereas I alone conducted the literature review, the meta-analysis, and wrote the study findings.

Memory-work: The process(ing of women)

Anastasia's memory:

It was one of those small lingerie boutiques, one that tried to stay tasteful but resulted in being bland. It was pretty much on the dead side of town, next to the old gun shop. It's a wonder people made a living out of it.

Her mother had insisted that Saturday morning that she needed a bra. They walked quietly, as if they were in separate thoughts.

The shop was pleasant as they entered. Counter to the left as they walked in, with various goods hanging along the right hand side. The changing rooms were nestled in the back of the store.

Both mother and daughter were ushered to the back of the store and waited patiently while the assistant went to collect a range of bras for the "young lady."

The "young lady" was feeling quite bored. She observed the jeans she wore in the mirror. . . . So did her mother!

"They need a wash; although I half expect they will dissolve in the wash—they're so bad!"

She just ignored these utterings and just continued to feel bored. She couldn't understand this need for a bra—there was nothing there.

The assistant returned with a tape measure and a number of samples.

"32a should fit," she said.

It didn't of course. The bra sagged in front making the whole exercise quite pathetic. She looked at her mum as the assistant raced off for some alternatives.

"Girls need support at an early age," returned her mother. "As a matter of fact lots of things will be changing soon, uh um . . . lots."

"Like what, mother?"

"Well, you will be changing soon, um . . . you will notice . . . um . . . changes."

"Mother! Are you trying to tell me about periods?"

The girl was definitely amused. "It's O.K. mum, don't worry yourself about it. I've known for some time now.

"But. . . ." Saved by the assistant. . . .

They eventually settled for a lovely pink one that sort of fitted.

The assistant promised faithfully that she would eventually grow into it.

Mother and daughter walked quietly back home in separate thoughts.

Even a cursory reading of Anastasia's memory suggests the range of possibilities and difficulties memory-workers might face with interpreting and theorizing Anastasia's "significant moment" of menstruation. In the discussion of the memory, Rosemary said, "I did feel like it was supposed to be some sort of initiation: your first bra, the discussion of your period. I think the way it was presented."

Rosemary's reference to initiation opens a space for reflecting on the linkages between growing breasts and growing up, and between breasts, a visible sexual sign, and menstruation, a hidden sexual sign. This space, however, is passed over as the group pick up on Anastasia's emotion. As the next excerpts of our theorizing show, Anastasia's reflection on her experience leads her to feel anger.

Anastasia: I was thinking that I was very aware of my anger, very aware that I was an angry person. . . . I think I learnt perhaps to suppress anger for fear that it would become rage and that it would become very destructive rage and that I would hurt somebody.

Rosemary: I think for women it's more than that, though. . . . Men can to a certain extent . . . channel it into a more open aggressive sort of stance with people, whereas women are more likely to adopt a less aggressive stance and become more passive. So for them it means greater repression of that rage. So I suppose you

could have been, if you hadn't been socialized to be a girl, more direct with your
mother than you were.

Anastasia: I was very direct with my mother . . . but not in this story. In this story I
am definitely suppressing anger and I'm not being direct. I'm just saying: "I know
about it, don't bother, can't be bothered even entering into a discussion with you . .
." and really feeling irritated. If I'm looking at it again, . . . I didn't really want to
do this. So why am I doing it? Why am I actually going? I'm walking down to the
shop, I'm looking at the shop, I'm observing, I'm almost irritated with the woman
who's serving me and yet I continue to do it.

Paula: Did your mother have power over you? Could you have refused to do it?

Anastasia: Why couldn't I have refused to do it?

Paula: Maybe you would have been punished. Maybe that was just a step which is
quite normal: that parents can tell their children what to do, and when, and how.

Rosemary: But is it saying that you would have been better off being overtly angry about what was happening?

Shane: You're not actually angry about the kind of things that are happening in the
story. It's an anger that pervades the relationship. So you're not likely to just target
it to what's happening in the story.

The focus of the discussion is relational as the group endeavours to uncover
the processes that contributed to Anastasia's anger. Paula's comment about
"normal" parenting is not queried and that Anastasia could have been defiant and
not worn the bra once it had been bought, remained unsaid. Shane makes an
interpretation that the relationship between Anastasia and her mother was an angry
relationship, but Anastasia does not hear this. The movement of the discussion
shows the flux and flow, the push and pull between the personal and the social.
Here it is useful to draw attention to how the group dynamic works to shape the
discussion and what role the facilitator might take in this.

Rosa continues the discussion and asks: "What made you angry? What do
mothers teach us?" These questions attempt to explore the issues around the
transmission of cultural mores from mother to daughter, which Rosemary follows
through:

> Well, I think in the story, it seems to me your mother was sort of introducing you
> to partly, being a good Greek girl. And that you've talked before about how your
> anger is partly fighting against it, sort of getting separate from her, and I don't
> know whether in this story you are consciously sort of fighting against that image
> of a good Greek girl or not. "Cause see, I would have given my eye teeth for a bra.
> I had to go to such lengths to get one."

Anastasia does not validate Rosemary's suggestion that buying a bra was an
introduction to being a "good Greek girl." However, Rosemary's spontaneous
analysis sits well with Haug's critique of female sexualization. Anastasia's body—
the breast—is one of the modes through which sexualization occurs:

The sexualization of "innocent" parts of the body takes place primarily through the generation of meanings around them, the building of signs into a referential system. Female breasts are never innocent, their socialization takes place at the very moment they appear—a moment that also signals the entry into adulthood.... These biological processes now enter into a social context, or rather it is within this context that they occur in the first place. They are tethered to the meanings through which gender is made. (Haug, 1987, p. 139)

The bra is the social practice through which gendered subjectivity is constituted. The acquiring of a bra in Anastasia's story is a referential sign in the way that Haug (1987) describes, assigning cultural meaning to her body changes: bra encased, uplifted breasts generate meaning. Breasts, as Young (1990, p. 190) asserts, are not only the most visible sign of femininity and symbol of female sexuality, they are the most fetishized aspect of her body "so the 'best' breasts are like the phallus: high, hard, and pointy." The unbound breast is fluid; thus, the bra helps to normalize the breast, producing the phallic look while at the same time, enclosing and containing that which must be controlled: female sexuality. Paradoxically, at the same time, the body becomes an object of male desire. Here we see the tension between the respectable and the sexual. The contradictions that shape female sexuality as an object of desire in our culture are clear: female sexuality is both hidden and displayed and both emphasized and controlled.

In her initiation into wearing a bra, Anastasia is reminded of the size of her breasts. Her comment on their size indicates recognition of a "proper size," a standard that Young (1990, p. 190) contends women have no part in establishing or controlling. The notion of having the "right sort of breasts" comes about through what Haug (1987) describes as a long process of habituation to "normality," or in Young's (1990, p. 191) view, "how they measure up before the normalizing gaze." Normality and deviations have an impact on experiences of bodily pleasure and wellbeing (Haug, 1992; Young, 1990).

In a discussion of moral socialization, Haug (1992) notes the tensions inherent in body functions and pleasure. On the one hand, integration into social groups depends on behavior centered on the body and its normality; on the other, there is the issue of body well-being and enjoyment. Whatever the intention of Anastasia's mother in consorting with fitting Anastasia's "inadequate breasts" into an "oversized bra," the process neither led Anastasia to pride or pleasure, nor a mother-daughter discussion of menstruation and sexuality. As Rosa noted, while Anastasia attempted to resist constructing herself in quite the way her mother had in mind, she was unable to for ultimately she wore, and still wears, a bra. The memory holds the initial moment of resistance only.

The above example of collective theorizing illustrates a certain sort of balancing between the personal and the social—the tug of the emotion and the question of an initiation. This balancing and the problems and dilemmas that transpire in the group dynamic share a quality similar to those that confront any group: there are some people who are loud, some who are quiet, some who are left out, and some who walk out. Anastasia's questions, "So why am I doing it? Why am I actually going?" were open to further exploration. At the time we struggled to unravel her questions and find how her personal troubles were linked to wider social life in the way Wright Mills (1967) and Haug (1987) ask. Haug's (1987) explication of female sexualization did this, though. And so did Young's (1990) analysis of "breasted experience." For me, the writer, as I drew on their analyses and placed this scholarly layer over our collective's layer of memory-work there was another "certain sort of balance" required.

Hovering at the boundaries, hovering at the hyphen

> When you write you are responsible. When you write you are sowing and you don't know where it's going to grow. Besides, writing has a special status: it's both repressed, rejected, despised, . . . but at the same time it has a huge hidden influence which we can never measure. There is something very tricky with writing. (Cixous 1990, p. 28)

In her essay "Difficult Joys," Cixous (1990) draws attention to the pitfalls, and oft forgotten ethics of being a writer. Her discussion incorporates words such as "intellectual violence" and "betrayal." These words express the intensity of feeling generated following my meta-analysis—constructing another layer of analysis that fits (well with) the data—of our stories and conversation produced in the creative yet seductive atmosphere of memory-work, where discussion and personal stories flourished as we compared, competed, enticed, and tried to make sense of experience. These were more relaxed times—jokes, laughter, a story, and another—a diversion from the more serious approach of "having a go at" the written memories, wondering if we were doing it right. Perhaps this is the time when we slipped into everyday jargon, glib reasoning and so forth—where Haug (1987) says amateur (or lay) psychoanalysis emerges. It was also the time when I slipped into another voice for unlike the written memories, the stories and conversation were not collectively analyzed. So, what began as an overlooked by-product of memory-work (Koutroulis, 2001) finished with a stink: treating the narratives and conversation differently to the written memories brought distinct voice-power ethical concerns.

Before I describe this voice-power "slippage" I will provide a context: I assumed responsibility for setting up the collective and the meetings, dispersing reading material to members, recording the meetings, transcribing the tapes, constructing the meta-analysis, and writing the research report. I did this because I was a doctoral candidate: I saw it as my responsibility and I did not want to "push the boundaries" of doctoral research too far and jeopardize being able to claim the thesis was my own and not the collective's work. I hovered at the boundary of memory-work and my own academic requirements so that for our collective it was never quite an equal enterprise.

I had put together a draft of some of the research, much of which contained stories and conversation (not written memories) about our experiences with men while we were menstruating, for the collective to review. The section on husbands drew an agitated response. Rosemary, after expressing vehement disagreement about the meta-analysis, covered a number of issues about group dynamics: "I think it's very difficult in a group to keep a logical flow going because everybody's got their own train of thought and everybody's jumping a bit from here, there and everywhere. So this is my beef, I disagree with this. I just think it's awful." The group joined with Rosemary to debate my interpretations and it is to this point that I turn, providing excerpts of the dialogue to demonstrate the range of opinion.

Anastasia points out that understandings of the self might not always be self-evident: "It may be somebody else interpreting my actions or my words in a way that I may never be aware. So, that meta-analysis, and maybe it isn't me saying it's right or it's wrong, it's just the way that people see that." Her last sentence, suggesting self-understandings and explanations need not necessarily be all there is to say about any given experience. Stivers (1993) acknowledges alternative interpretations, as Anastasia does, that may not fit with the subject's self-understanding. Whereas Ramos (1989) draws attention to the necessity of validating subjective interpretations so that information is not misrepresented, which is what Shane asks for: "One of the problems that I have with some feminist stuff is that you can always interpret it in an anti-male way . . . [and] it's not very satisfactory if the way Glenda is interpreting it is in fact nothing to do with the way it is."

While Shane, on the one hand, proposes that the individual whose experience is being examined remain the arbiter of whether meaning is adequately conveyed, Paula gives a more obscure response: "But I wonder if that matters. I've been trying to work that one out too. But in some ways it says more about Glenda than it says about the material." At first glance, her statement indicates a similar position to Anastasia. However, when she makes the comment "it says more about Glenda," another position manifests. It is possible that Paula's comment is expressing a change in the power dynamics of the group. What she thought would be an egalitarian textual process is turning out to be a voice-power issue that places me firmly in an advantaged seat. Paula's indirect message is that I controlled and recreated the stories within my own familiar feminist ideology, irrespective of what the rest of the group might have wanted.

Clandinin and Connelly (1994) capture the issues of voice that arise for both the researcher and the researched in personal experience methods. For the writer of the research they draw out

> a dilemma of voice in moving from field texts to research texts . . . as one struggles
> to express one's own voice in the midst of an inquiry designed to capture the
> participants' experience and represent their voices, all the while attempting to

create a research text that will speak to, and reflect upon, the audience's voices. (p. 423)

The author/researcher's voice, Clandinin and Connelly (1994, p. 416) suggest, is an issue of multiple I's: commentator, research participant, researcher, narrative critic, theory builder, man or woman. Successfully negotiating these I's requires a consciousness about voice—those that are heard and those that are not heard—essentially to be concerned with how we construct "others." This process Fine (1994, p. 72) calls "working the hyphen." It involves making a space for the researcher and participants to discuss whose story is being told, why, to whom, and with what interpretation. The hyphen at which we construct Self-Other, Fine (1994) argues, is the politics of everyday life.

While issues of voice and power are not peculiar to memory-work, I would argue that the voice-politics dynamic is subtle yet more complex than might be found in other methods. My experience with memory-work suggests that this, in part, is because of the meanings associated with being a co-researcher and how this is lived out in the collective (see Koutroulis, 1996). One way of negotiating this voice-politic dynamic is through collective as opposed to individual analyzing/theorizing. The advantage of collective theorizing is that it provides a critical balance of views, offers interpretations that might otherwise be overlooked, tests for plausibility and asks questions of the data (Crawford et al., 1992). Additionally, the collective acts as a corrective, challenging each other's day-to-day assumptions (Haug, 1987). Collective theorizing, though, might be an ideal that is difficult to realize, especially for a collective like that which I convened where there is not an equal interest in the product. This being so, there is an imperative not to hover, but to "work the hyphen."

Writing memories, rewriting the self

Rewriting memories is a formal part of the memory-work process but evidence to date tells that it has proved a stumbling block for some memory workers. Chapters such as this, I think, ought to be helpful to (prospective) practitioners of the method and so in this last section I will describe how one member of our collective interpreted and then put into practice rewriting. I shall begin with a reminder from Wright Mills who (1967, p. 72) argues that no method "should be used to delimit the problems we take up, if for no other reason than that the most interesting and difficult issues of *method* usually begin where established techniques do not apply."

The question: "Are the memories an artefact of memory-work?" suggests that the memories are not "true" memories. Memories, however, are part of the subjective, the self. Yet, in their production they are carefully crafted and in that sense, may be considered an artefact of memory-work. Haug's (1987, 1992) notion of mutuality in the construction of the social and the self is carried across into the research setting. Filling in gaps in the memories of the writer of the memory and the group members, invites the collective to participate by means of imagination in the construction of meaning.

Construction of meaning through imagination presented itself in Rosa's rewritten memory. Through fantasy she addressed *"the things that had come out for all of us . . . as if this is how I would like it to have been now, after going through the collective."* Fantasy as a strategy to escape or even destroy rather than reproduce a confining culture where women are subjugated is not a new narrative device. Walker (1990) details the attraction of fantasy by contemporary women novelists, whose playful depictions of differences among women mark a break with the unquestioning assumptions about women's identity and place, characteristic of many novels.

The incorporation of fantasy into memory-work can be seen as the deployment of an experimental literary device for sociological purposes. Haug (1992) proposes that daydreams or fantasies can be collectively worked on in the same way as memories. The fantasy, like a memory, is part of the self, a view consistent with a postmodern claim that the self is always present in what we write, even if only partially (Richardson, 1994). In other memory-work groups, participants have used collective discussion to inform the reworking of memories with "little reference to the memories themselves" (Schratz et al., 1995, p. 60). Creative acceptance of such texts shows that if the established techniques do not apply or do not work for any individual, the memory-writer is free to rework a memory through other means. Rosa's textual experiment with fantasy enabled her to experience the self-reflexive to develop a voice of resistance making possible a transformational process of self-construction.

This takes me to my final comments on "coming clean," to use Punch's (1994) term, where the problematic, the emotion and the angst, and how dilemmas were solved, a research concern encouraged by feminists including Reinharz (1992), Roberts (1981), and Stanley and Wise (1993) to name but a few, is exposed. Elsewhere (Koutroulis, 1996), I discussed at length the style of ethics that our collective engaged in and the ethical responsibility we believed we had to each other as we sorted out difficulties and negotiated agreements about group dynamics and facilitation, the layers of analysis and interpretation, and the meaning of co-researcher. In two important ways, my expectation of group research was not realized in the way that I anticipated it would be. This had disappointing consequences. First, through the meta-analysis, the ethos of collectivity central to memory-work, and the meanings that women give to their own experience, was diluted if not undermined. An ethical consequence of this practice brought to my attention by Paula was that the women moved from the expected position of co-researchers to objects with a specimen quality. Secondly, while I cherish the 12, intense and exciting meetings that took place over several months, in the overall scheme of the memory-work project, the time spent with the group was minimal in comparison to the time without them.

Ultimately, my experience over the last years without the group was probably as isolating and lonely as any postgraduate researcher might describe.

Finally, here in the pages of this chapter where I "came clean" I hoped to lessen the stink around memory-work. But as I write myself into this page with the focus on "I," me, me, me, I give form to another memory; it is of me, from me, plays through me, an individual. So, it is back to the analyst for a closer look. In the process of (be)coming clean a curious thing can happen—there is more to be aired. Remember the cleanly washed clothes left behind in the washing machine a little too long? What a stink!

References

Berger, Peter L. & Berger, Bridgitte. (1976). *Sociology: A biographical approach*. Harmondsworth, Middlesex: Penguin Books.

Cixous, Helene. (1990). Difficult joys. In Helen Wilcox, Keith McWatters, Ann Thompson & Linda R.Williams (Eds.), *The body and the text: Helene Cixous, Reading and Teaching* (pp. 5-30). New York: Harvester Wheatsheaf.

Clandinin, D. Jean & Connelly, F. Michael. (1994). Personal experience methods. In Norman K. Denzin & Yvonna S. Lincoln (Eds.), *Handbook of qualitative research* (pp. 413-427). Thousand Oaks, CA: Sage.

Crawford, June; Kippax, Susan; Onyx, Jenny; Gault, Una & Benton, Pam. (1992). *Emotion and gender: Constructing meaning from memory*. London: Sage.

Durkheim, Emile. (1951 [1897]). *Suicide: A study in sociology* (John A. Spaulding & George Simpson, Trans.). New York: Free Press.

Fine, Michelle. (1994). Working the hyphens: Reinventing self and other in qualitative research. In Norman K. Denzin & Yvonna S. Lincoln (Eds.), *Handbook of qualitative research* (pp. 70-82). Thousand Oaks, CA: Sage.

Freud, Sigmund. (1949). *An outline of psycho-analysis*. New York: W. W. Norton & Company.

Harding, Sandra (Ed.). (1987). *Feminism and methodology*. Bloomington & Indianapolis, IN: Indiana University Press.

Haug, Frigga. (Ed.). (1987). *Female sexualization: A collective work of memory*. London: Verso.

Haug, Frigga. (1992). *Beyond female masochism: Memory-work and politics*. London: Verso.

Koutroulis, Glenda. (1996). Memory-work: Process, practice and pitfalls. In Derek Colquhon & Allen Kellehear (Eds.), *Health research in practice: Political ethical and methodological issues* (pp. 95-113). London: Chapman and Hall.

Koutroulis, Glenda. (2001). Soiled identity: Memory-work narratives of menstruation. *Health, 5*(2), 187-205.

Manning, Peter K. & Cullum-Swan, Betsy. (1994). Narrative, content, and semiotic analysis. In Norman K. Denzin & Yvonna S. Lincoln (Eds.), *Handbook of qualitative research* (pp. 463-477). Thousand Oaks, CA: Sage.

Mead. George Herbert. (1934). *Mind, self and society*. Chicago: University of Chicago Press.

Punch, Maurice. (1994). Politics and ethics in qualitative research. In Norman K. Denzin & Yvonna S. Lincoln (Eds.), *Handbook of qualitative research* (pp. 83-97). Thousand Oaks, CA: Sage.

Ramos, Mary C. (1989). Some ethical implications of qualitative research. *Research in Nursing and Health, 12*, 57-63.

Reason, Peter. (1994). Three approaches to participative inquiry. In Norman K. Denzin & Yvonna S. Lincoln (Eds.), *Handbook of qualitative research* (pp. 324-339). Thousand Oaks, CA: Sage.

Reinharz, Shulamit. (1992). *Feminist methods in social research.* New York: Oxford University Press.

Richardson, Laurel. (1994). Writing: A method of inquiry. In Norman K. Denzin & Yvonna S. Lincoln (Eds.), *Handbook of qualitative research* (pp. 516-529). Thousand Oaks, CA: Sage.

Roberts, Helen. (Ed.). (1981). *Doing feminist research.* London: Routledge & Kegan Paul.

Schratz, Michael; Walker, Rob & Schratz-Hadwich, Barbara. (1995). Collective memory-work: The self as a re/source for re/search. In Michael Schratz & Rob Walker (Eds.), *Research as social change: New opportunities for qualitative research* (pp. 39-64). London: Routledge.

Stanley, Liz & Wise, Sue. (1993). *Breaking out again: Feminist ontology epistemology.* London: Routledge.

Stivers, Camilla. (1993). Reflections on the role of personal narrative in social science. *Signs: Journal of Women in Culture and Society, 18*(2), 408-425.

Walker, Nancy A. (1990). *Feminist alternatives: Irony and fantasy in the contemporary novel by women.* Jackson, MS: University Press of Mississippi.

Weedon, Chris. (1987). *Feminist practice and poststructuralist theory.* Oxford: Blackwell Publishers.

Wright Mills, C. (1967). *The sociological imagination.* New York: Oxford University Press.

Young, Iris Marion. (1990). *Throwing like a girl and other essays in feminist philosophy and social theory.* Bloomington & Indianapolis, IN: Indiana University Press.

Zola, Irving Kenneth. (1991). Bringing our bodies and ourselves back in: Reflections on a past, present, and future "medical sociology." *Journal of Health and Social Behaviour, 32*, 1-16.

Chapter 7

For the Sake of Knowledge: Exploring Memory-work in Research and Teaching

Karin Widerberg

To women of my generation entering the academic scene in the late sixties, feminism represented new openings. The male doxa gave us few and devalued roles, if any, in the makings of society. Social Science was all about men and their doings, expressed in abstract concepts where its gendered nature was concealed in the name of the Individual. Trying to read us as women into this picture was one of the first exercises feminism prescribed in the dismantling of our disciplines. Answering questions about how we were made invisible provoked questions on how to know and what to know from a woman's standpoint. Intertwining meta-theory, theory and method proved both necessary and fruitful to prove that there are other things to be known through other ways of knowing. To me as a feminist sociologist, two approaches have changed the sociological landscape fundamentally. One is the approach of Dorothy E. Smith and her critique of the sociological traditions for their way of "writing the social" (Smith, 1987; 1989; 1990a; 1990b; 1999; 2005) and the other is the method of memory-work developed by Frigga Haug (1987). Taken together, they are the dynamite that could set sociology on fire. But since they both present and propose "methods of inquiry" (Dorothy Smith's expression) rather than grand theory or doxic conceptual systems, their approaches are more demanding than other more traditional ways of writing the social. It is when put to use that its productive nature is illuminated or, in other words, it is the results that prove the value of the approach as such.

That is exactly the aim of this chapter. By here presenting my use of memory-work on different topics and in different settings, I hope to illustrate its productive nature, that it really is a method that makes a difference. But since my aim when using the method has been to explore all its possibilities in both research and teaching, I have allowed myself to develop it into a whole set of methods and techniques. This, I believe, is to be true to the very idea behind the method, if not strictly true to the model as it has been developed by Frigga Haug. Regarding the general issues raised in this book exploring memory-work, developing it and expanding its use the way I have done it, of course has both its merits and shortcomings. The pro's and con's of the various ways I have used the approach of memory-work are discussed here. Hopefully my liberties with the use of the method can inspire others to develop the approach to suit their own aims, for the sake of knowledge.

Memory-work as an individual enterprise: Two examples

As an individual enterprise—in writing and in analyzing the stories—the variations and complexities guaranteed by the gaze of the others in memory work as a collective enterprise is absent. And yet and to partly different purposes, which I will try to illustrate below, memory work as an individual enterprise can be quite fruitful.

Sexual harassment—a pilot study. Embarking on a research project on sexual harassment in 1987, I was determined to try out the method of memory-work, one way or another. I had just read Frigga Haug's book (1987) and was struck by the insights and knowledge produced by their use of the method. It was evident that the new knowledge they presented was a result of a new way of knowing. For me then the question was accordingly not whether to use the method, but how. With me on the project I had Harriet Holter—the grand old lady of Scandinavian women's research—and a group of enthusiastic female MA-students who were offered the opportunity to write their theses on the theme. None of the students knew each other or us beforehand and the issue of hierarchy had to be addressed. Harriet and I were not only much older but also belonged to another category—professors—while they were students. The idea of doing memory-work in this kind of group and on such a sensitive theme as sexual harassment encountered only embarrassment and silence when I raised the issue. Besides, the students said, they did not have the time it would take to do it "the Haug way" since they only had a year to work with the thesis. It was therefore decided that it was up to each participant to decide if she wanted to embark on an individual memory-work project but that the results—the insights won—should be shared within the group so as to benefit the project as a whole. In the end only two of us did a kind of memory-work, while all of us did bits and pieces of it. The purpose of using the method was simply for all of us to prepare ourselves for the interviews that were to be done later in the larger study.

None of us could have imagined how decisive this work would be, not only for the form and content of the subsequent interviews, but also for the entire design of the project and our understanding of the phenomenon of sexual harassment. How did we go about this individual memory-work, and what did we learn?

The theme for my own memory-work was sexual assaults, including sexual harassment. Over the course of half a year I wrote down all the different occasions I could remember—as stories, written one at a time. I tried to focus on what I could remember, how I remembered it and how I interpreted the situation—at the time and today. I found:

1. I remembered occasions I had forgotten. All the events were not remembered at once, but came to the surface over a longer timespan, triggered by the memory-process as such.

2. The number of such occasions and their variations surprised me. Is that so, I wondered, for other women as well?

3. I had problems defining some of the events as assault, even though they were clearly unwanted from my part. The problem was the language, the wording, and the connotations of assault.

4. I experienced some of the events as assaults even though "nothing" actually happened—for example, a situation of intense threat.

5. I felt shame in relation to several of the events. I would not wish to tell anybody about them, even though I knew I was not to blame. If I had been interviewed I probably would only talk about the situations in which I did the "right things," not the ones when I was "naïve" or "stupid," that is, situations in which I behaved as if there was no such thing as patriarchy.

6. The shame and contempt I felt towards myself as a victim. Didn't that indicate that I felt the same towards other women as victims? Feelings and thoughts I did not wish to have or to know began coming to the surface.

These insights brought about by the memory-work were discussed and confirmed in the research group. Although we did not read and analyze each other's stories, we did discuss our reflections and insights. And these collective discussions triggered new stories and further reflections and insights. These collective discussions accordingly had several consequences for the design of our research project on sexual harassment and for the interpretation process throughout the project (see our book Brantsæter & Widerberg, 1992). First of all, we made follow-up interviews with victims into a standard procedure. The memory and reflection process, triggered by the first interview, was included and documented. Any changes in the stories between the first and the second interview were registered and understood as being the way these things work, rather than as proof of deviations or untrustworthy statements/subjects. The result was an understanding of sexual harassment as experiences that are both interpreted and continuously reinterpreted in relation to other/new experiences, age, and varying gender-experiences and gender-relations, etc. Therefore, it is impossible to state or measure the consequences of assaults of harassment once and for all, even though this is what most research seems to imply. Experiences of sexual harassment are not a separate phenomenon in a woman's life; they are part of her self-image, her image of others and the relation between others and herself. This is something you have lived and are still living with.

This memory-work on sexual harassment had consequences not only for the research project, but also personally for us in the research group. The experiences that we remembered through the memory-work and the collective discussions changed our understanding of ourselves. We seemed to have lots of victim experiences, without having previously thought of ourselves as victims: we had no explicit victim identity. Maybe few of us actually have! Perhaps this identity is just as much a construction brought about by the traditional methods and approaches used within social sciences, where assaults are "phenomenized" instead of "relationized," personally and culturally. In any case, for us and up till then, our personal identity project and cultural identity contribution obviously had been to construct an identity that made invisible any personal or structural victimization; invisible to ourselves, and to others.

To study how this was done, in detail, the memory-stories would make an excellent starting point for further memories, reflections and discussion. In other words, the memory-stories can make us question our own identity-story, as well as showing exactly how the identity both shaped and was shaped by the experience in question.

Memory-work led me to question the earlier implicit version of my lifestory and identity. More specifically, it made me question my sexual history. Having written about my memories of assault, I became curious about my memories of sexual pleasure. How did they relate—in time and place—to the assault memories? So I started on another memory-work, this time on sexuality, and another one later followed that, this time on knowledge—a natural and urgent theme for me as a feminist researcher.

Sexuality and knowledge—a research project. For more than a year I wrote memory-stories on the two themes of sexuality and knowledge, in hopes of understanding myself and my social context, society, better. At first I had no intention of publishing anything; when there were no more stories that I felt urged to write, I simply put them away. It was not until a year later, when I was on sabbatical and had time to read them all through, that I saw them as material for a book.

Sexuality and knowledge are both about being in touch (Evelyn Fox Keller's expression, 1985): about pleasure, comfort, honesty, personal growth and fulfillment, and about being present. A wish and an effort that in reality often turns to the opposite: instead, we feel discomfort, distance, diminished personally, non-present, dishonest and oppressed. This happens both in the act of sexuality and in the act of knowledge. I saw all this when analyzing my own stories, but I also began to realize how gender links knowledge and sexuality together, connects them and sets them in motion. Knowledge, sexuality and gender are formed in the same process. In negotiations as to the kind of woman and man we want to position ourselves as, knowledge and sexuality appear as important pieces of the bargain.

Seeing these patterns in the memory-material made me wonder whether this could be used to explore and discuss issues of female subjectivity and objectivity. More specifically, I wanted to explore the kinds of experiences that might explain the contents as well as the forms of feminist knowledge of production, i.e., the feminist endeavor in academe.

With this as my purpose I wrote the book *The gender of knowledge* (in Swedish & Norwegian, Widerberg, 1995), where I present and make use of the material from the memory-work on sexuality and knowledge. Since the stories had been written one at a time with the purpose to explore and illustrate diversities rather than similarities and connections, the result is of course a picture of an "I" that is multiple. Thus this is a result of the method.

Summing up. I would accordingly like to stress that understandings of identity are formed not only by our theoretical approaches but also, although less acknowledged, by the very methods we use. Exploring methods accordingly implies exploring the social and the other way around. Different understandings of the I and the social will require different methods. Identity, theoretically understood as multiple I's, requires empirical methods that can contribute to the unfolding of the I into a variety, also in terms of voices. Here I have tried to argue that memory-work can be used as such a method. As such it can contribute to a fruitful challenge of the genre of auto/biography where a person tells or writes her story along implicit guidelines for a story of that kind (sequencing, coherence, a beginning and an end, the construction of an I, etc.) As an individual enterprise the researcher can let the stories and analysis expand in all the directions she herself finds most fruitful. But it is not until her work is read and commented upon by others that she will learn of other possible interpretations and experiences. As a collective enterprise this is guaranteed from the very start by the stories and gaze of ther others.

Doing body/texts: Memory-work as a collective enterprise

Early in the autumn of 1995, Drude von der Fehr (whose field is literature), Halldis Leira (psychology), Ulla-Britt Lilleaas (sociology) and I (sociology) met to discuss the possibility of working together on a new research project. We had all worked together previously in different constellations, and we knew of each other's research projects and approaches to knowledge. Just how well, though, varied, as did how well we knew each other personally. What we all shared, however, was a wish to work with the theme body/experience in a way and in a connection that could enable us to learn something new. The connection was clear from the start: we wanted to work together within an interdisciplinary dialogue where our disciplinary understandings could be challenged and expanded. The trigger in this process was to be the theme—the body/experience, a challenge to any disciplinary approach. In understanding body/experience, we aimed to use our academic disciplines as best as we could to see how far that would take us. Only then could the limits of our different disciplines become visible and we would find out what we each had to offer and what actually might fall in-between or even outside disciplines as ours. Disciplinary approaches were accordingly to be used when investigating the body/experience. On the other hand, we did not want these to restrict us in our search for new understandings. Of course, we also knew it would be unrealistic to try to turn off the disciplines in our way of working and thinking. They have by now become an integral part of us, whether we want it or not. But we wanted to widen our gaze, follow our curiosity and be open to the unexpected. To achieve this, we knew we would have to develop and make use of other ways of working than the ones we had grown accustomed to within our disciplines.

The wish to work in another way and using other kinds of methods and approaches was very much connected with the theme we had chosen for study. Although during the last decade the body had been the theme within the humanities and the social sciences, particularly its feminist branches, we still wanted texts that problematized and made the body visible as lived experience, and the other way around, that is, as embodied experience. There were of course one or two single and exceptional contributions, like the works of Frigga Haug, or in particular fields—like sexualized violence—but they had failed to leave any major traces in the dominant intellectual discussions "on" the body. We suspected that disciplinary thinking might be the culprit here; at any rate, it had not contributed the kind of knowledge we sought. Obviously we would have to proceed in another way.

Some of us had previously worked with alternative approaches to become aware of and to express, bodily or in writing, body/experience. We had tried them out and used them in exercises and workshops. As these had been very positive experiences, we now decided to make use of similar ways of working in our research group. At our very first meeting, we decided that we would do bodily exercises and then write them down as texts. It would be these texts and not the theoretical or meta-theoretical body-texts of our disciplines that would then form the material to be discussed in our interdisciplinary dialogue.

The approach. Over the course of two years, we did four different thematic exercises, some of which we did more than once or on similar themes, and wrote them all down as texts. The themes for these exercises were as follows: *having a good day, a day of turning, a day of low energy,* and *a day of "where am I in the body?"* in that order. Finally, we also wrote our "body biographies." The first exercises, *Having a good day* and *A day of turning,* involved trying to obtain pleasurable situations or turn non-pleasurable situations or work-tasks into pleasant ones for an entire day. Then we wrote a text where we related what we had done and experienced but also what it all, including its writing, made us reflect upon. *A day of low energy* involved trying to use less energy, that is to decrease our level of energy for a whole day. As in the previous exercise, this was to be an ordinary day; we were just to do the day differently. *A day of "where am I in the body?"* was an effort to try to feel and register which parts or areas of the body made themselves known to us throughout a whole day. "Body biography," finally, was an attempt to write an autobiography, taking the body as the starting point: what the body had been or meant to us and how we had lived, experienced and inhabited the body.

The themes for the exercises, the way we enacted them as well as the way we discussed and analyzed the texts evolved and varied throughout the process. We have searched for the most fruitful way of working and have taken the path that our desire for knowledge and its intoxication has led us. It has been work filled with pleasure and desire, not always easy and often both sensitive and conflict-generating. It was work we did in addition to our ordinary research and work tasks, in the evenings and at weekends. Our project—titled "The Body between Theory and Practice"—has been our "priceless pearl:" we have guarded it, tended it and enjoyed its radiance. From our meetings, to which we sometimes staggered, dead tired after a whole day at work, we have returned enlivened, energetic and excited. We believe that nursing the desire as we have done, in relation to themes as well as to our applications in exercises and texts, has been the precondition for the development of knowledge we have experienced throughout the project. For us, desire has not only been a driving force but also a tool to develop knowledge.

Here I will summarize our way of working in an idealized model, to inspire readers to try it out on other topics as well. Our way of working developed underway, so the description below cannot give a full or true picture of how we actually went about things. It should not be read and used as a set of rules, but rather as a set of guidelines to explore and develop the method further. In brief, then, our model can be summarized as follows:

1. The theme for the exercise was chosen collectively. We also decided on a particular day or time of day for the exercise. Knowing that all of us, separately in our different situations, would be doing the exercise we had decided upon was both comforting and stimulating. If, however, one of us forgot to do the exercise on the chosen day—this happened more than once—she picked out another day for herself.

2. The exercise was written down as text. Our only guideline here was that it shouldn't be too long. Each of us could write in the form and kind of language that seemed most fruitful. Inspired by memory-work, we all tried to be as descriptive as possible. An interesting question for us when analyzing the texts and for the reader of our texts and chapters in the report (Widerberg et al., 2001a) is whether the discipline makes itself known, and in that case, how this is done. To us, it was an attempt to de-emphasize our disciplines at this stage in the process. Later on, in analyzing our texts, however, we very consciously made use of our disciplines.

3. The texts were sent out to the others in the group and the group met to discuss them. We discussed the texts both separately and all taken together. These discussions were seen as preliminary. There was so much content in each text and so many angles and approaches to be taken when interpreting it that we could not hope to cover all in this first round. It became quite clear to us, early on, that each one of us would also have to work extensively with the analysis on our own. This was also the guarantee for a fruitful interdisciplinary dialogue.

In relation to traditional memory-work, memory-work á la Haug, there are some important differences affecting possibilities for analyses and arguments and knowledge being produced. First of all the stories were written about the immediate past—except for the body-biography—and not about what we usually conceive of as memories. Secondly, the story was sometimes of a situation but sometimes of the happenings of a whole day. This of course affects the descriptive character of the text. Besides, no instructions were given as to how to write the text, except a recommendation to be as descriptive as possible to obtain thick descriptions. In this aspect the stories greatly varied. Other variations occurred among us and in relation to the topic of the exercise. Thirdly, the stories were not written or analyzed anonymously, since the very aim was to investigate our disciplinary overdetermination in writing, reading and analyzing. Finally, based on our individual stories and collective discussions and analyses, we each wrote a kind of body-biography. Here we made use of the genre of biography but on a specific theme (the body). The insights won through the body project (exercises made and texts written and analyzed) played a decisive role in what was highlighted and how in the biographies. A hybrid method accordingly grew out of our explorations.

Since one of the aims of this project was to highlight disciplinary differences, let me just say a few words about it before closing this section.

Disciplinary differences becoming visible and fruitful. We had no intention of not making use of our disciplinary differences. Quite the opposite, we wanted to learn what other approaches had to offer, as well as becoming more aware through disciplinary comparisons, of the tools of our own chosen disciplines. We were of course not totally unfamiliar with each other's disciplines; we had read extensively within all of them. But knowing how sociology, psychology or literary study is done is quite another thing. As with most other disciplines, it is a question of a craft learnt through praxis, through making use of theories and methods when arguing, doing research and writing. It is a hidden agenda, not easily stated or pinned down. However, the results of this craft, the text, carry traces of the agenda, which are often quite easy to locate in disciplinary terms. This we knew and wanted to explore.

Even in the experiences of writing the texts, the disciplines made themselves known. Although all of us found it thrilling, joyful or painful, to write it all down (quite often the text was written all at one time), the finished product as a text to be read gave rise to reactions related to our disciplinary training. Roughly speaking, in literature a text is judged on its own terms (genre, structure, etc.); in sociology it is judged for what is said about reality (social structure and action); and in psychology, for what is hidden between the lines (about the person). And of course each one of us read our own texts as well as those of the others from our particular disciplinary perspectives. For a person from literature or psychology, presenting a text like this, that is, a text by and of oneself, is much scarier than for a sociologist. Judging a text from a text-perspective might make it seem naive, banal or pretentious, thereby embarrassing the literary scholar. The psychologist, on the other hand, might be afraid of what we others would find out about her, through reading between the lines, the way she herself always does. This we commented upon and discussed when we talked about the texts.

When we analyzed the texts, another aspect made disciplinary differences even more visible. In none of our disciplines is there a tradition for the researcher to use her own experiences as subject for investigation, at least not experiences written down as texts and treated as such, as material to be analyzed. In our disciplinary traditions, though, we tend to have very different readers in mind and therefore very different ways of relating to our audiences. In qualitative empirical sociology you often know—and indeed very often hope—that the subjects of your study will read what you have written about them. That means you take great care in how you present them. They can talk back and you must be able to relate to them face to face. You are accountable for the knowledge about them that you have produced. The topic is reality, that is, how things are, and it is your picture of their reality for which you are responsible. In literature, however, "the author is dead," often in more than one sense of the word. He/she can't talk back. Further, the topic or the aim of the text is not reality, so you aren't made accountable for giving a correct/true picture of it. You are free to love or hate the text, as long as your position makes sense within the various theoretical traditions. This freedom and lack of accountability, implicit in the traditions of literary study, came to the surface as a theme when we started analyzing our texts. We, the authors, were there and had to brace ourselves to handle the down-to-earth and direct treatment of our texts as delivered by Drude. Time and again she had to reassure us that it had nothing to do with us; it was just a text. Trying to see it as such was also in many ways liberating and enormously interesting. It helped us distance ourselves from our texts and see them from an outside perspective, that is, how you might perceive it if you are not "it." But still it was of course easy to take offence, having oneself analyzed, cut up, parcelled and labelled as if one weren't there at all. If we objected and tried to launch other interpretations, these were evaluated on the basis of whether or not they were fruitful, not whether they were "the truth."

The psychological approach proved far more restricted, perhaps more so than any other approach, since as a psychologist Halldis had been trained to evaluate clients' reactions and tread with caution. Halldis was careful to take up positive issues or themes and to try to get us to see things ourselves, rather than telling us about them herself. And what of the sociologists? Ulla-Britt and I were used to writing of and for our subjects and getting their reactions, making us accountable as the authors of texts for the interpretations we offered. Making the texts "social," that is looking for social patterns, gave us the chance to make them less touchy than a psychological and more personal approach would have been.

The merits and restrictions of these different disciplinary traditions were discussed and debated throughout our work. Using each other's analytical and

textual approaches would change the knowledge produced in our disciplines, but
that would also have been the result if we had taken our academic traditions to
greater extremes as well. If, for example, the subjects in sociological and psychological studies were to be invited to take a greater part in the analysis, also
reflecting on the researchers' analytical categories and concepts, our implicit
understandings would have been made more visible and questionable, probably
with new and other kinds of knowledge as a result.

Working in an interdisciplinary way thus meant trying to see what we could
learn from each other's way of proceeding, as well as trying to clarify, explore
and even strengthen our disciplinary traditions. The fact that we were using an
approach that none of us could claim to be experts in—it was in fact new to us
all—made this easier, not to mention the fact that we respected, trusted and liked
each other. We were the project, it was for us, and it was ours.

Learning by doing: Teaching memory-work in workshops

My own use of the method, as described above, had convinced me that this
was a method that could and should, for the sake of knowledge, be used and
explored on all themes and topics within sociology and probably within the rest
of the social sciences as well. But since the method so far has not been presented
in textbooks on qualitative methods, it is not well known or generally considered
as a "proper" method. To try to remedy this lack, at least in relation to my own
students, colleagues and research milieus, I started to give courses on/in the
method. Various techniques have then been developed to make the writing and
the interpretation as fruitful and rich as possible. Let me here briefly present
those that I have used, on different themes and in different settings.

I have given several three-day courses in the method for MA- and graduate
students. The groups have included 10—20 participants of both sexes, though the
majority tend to be women. After a short presentation of the method and how we
are to use it in the group, the theme for that particular memory-work is discussed
and decided. Since this is a temporary group and most of the participants do not
know each other, no sensitive topic should be chosen. Besides suggesting firmly
that the group should choose a "dull," everyday topic to test whether the method
can bring new knowledge to the things we take for granted, I do not interfere in
this process. What topics have the groups then chosen? They include topics such
as *anger, blushing/sweating, knowing/not knowing something, vacuum-cleaning,
dancing, getting dressed*, and, *travelling to work*.

Once the topic has been chosen, I ask the group to write what has really
happened, yesterday or long ago. They are told to try to be as concrete and descriptive as possible, by relating in detail everything about the situation. They
should also try to use the words they would have used at the time this situation
occurred. This might mean that the voice sounds stupid, mean or whatever, to
the ears of the writer of today. Of course writing a memory always means interpretation, I tell them, since interpretation is what drives the memory forward,
that is, how and what we remember. Every memory has layers of interpretation,

especially if the memory is of something that happened long ago. Even so, they should try not to analyze while writing, but give the story a chance to be told as straightforwardly as possible. Concepts, hasty analyses, immediately processing it academically—here these are more of a problem than a resource; they close more than they open for interpretation at this stage.

Participants are further instructed to write the story in three versions: in first person and in male and female third person. With today's computers, this is easily done. One simply writes one story and then orders the machine to replace, for example, the "I" with a "she" and then the "she" with a "he." Even though the language might become a bit odd, three versions of the story are thus easily made. One purpose is to see what happens when you objectify yourself (sometimes it is easier to write a story in the third person) or establish a distance to yourself. More importantly, by using the male and female forms, the gender of the text is made visible, often in ways not visible when the gender was "accurate."

The text is written then and there, usually within a time limit of one-half to one hour. De-dramatizing writing by doing it together, in a limited time and anonymously, makes it seem less pretentious and scary. Under such conditions, everybody can write something. The reason for writing the stories anonymously, however, is not only, or even primarily, to facilitate the writing process; it is meant to enrich the interpretation process. The stories are then interpreted collectively. No one can or is allowed to claim ownership of the story (or of the "correct" interpretation). The participants are further told that once the analyses have been completed, they can, if they so wish, tell each other which story was theirs. After the stories have been written and prepared in three versions for all participants, we read the stories together. We then discuss and analyze them as a whole. What kinds of situations and of what life-periods have we written about? And what have we not written about? Sometimes the silence in what we choose not to write about is just as interesting and thus worth analyzing, as what we did write about. For example, on the theme *to know/not to know something*, none of the 20 participants wrote about academic knowledge, although they were all students. Instead, knowing was here taken to mean being able to undertake and master, especially, bodily tasks in childhood or in youth. In the discussion, they all expressed insecurity in relation to knowing in academe as the probable cause.

In this first and more general discussion and analysis of all the texts, the gender aspect, made visible through the three versions she, he, and I, is also made a topic. What makes the gender appear correct or wrong? The acting or the wording? For example, on the theme *getting dressed*, which gender—when naked—starts by putting on the socks? And why do women always put on the underpants first, and not the bra? How we do gender all the time is here made quite clear. But it also illuminates how very gendered our way of wording and writing about something is.

To be able to make a more in-depth analysis of a situation and its language, one or two stories, usually rich ones, are chosen. Everything we see and learn

when analyzing the chosen story is written down on the blackboard, first uns-
ystematically and later organized into sub-themes, situations, relations, emotions
and so forth. Analysis goes on until nothing new comes up.

Besides in courses, I have used this method in other collective settings, in
the form of workshops, where the purpose was not to learn the method as such,
but where a particular theme was in focus. For example, in a half-day workshop
on fatherhood at a Nordic research conference, I asked the participants to write a
short memory story on *my friend's father*. Even though they were asked to write
in English—a foreign language for the vast majority of the participants—the stories were surprisingly rich in content, meanings and variations. Having no time
to copy all the stories for all of the participants, I read them aloud instead. Each
story was read twice and slowly, each after the other without any comments.
Participants were asked to write down their reflections when listening, and afterwards we had a general discussion about the patterns, relations, situations and
emotions that we found the stories revealed. The same pattern was used in another half-day workshop at a conference on drug treatment in a gender perspective. Here participants were asked to write a memory story about *a drunk person*. When reading these stories aloud, I also changed the gender in the story to
open up reflection on gender. In both workshops nobody complained about having to do writing. They could all write a story and they all had something to
write about. That the theme is concretely and not abstractly formulated is of
course of vital importance. Writing about fatherhood instead of *my friend's father*, is far more difficult; moreover, it would probably result in more abstract
and general stories.

Summing up my experiences of the use of the method in collective settings,
as in the courses and conferences described here, I find it extremely well suited
for grasping experiences. A major reason is that the topic for the writing is always a specific situation or an event on a theme. Writing about anger for example, means writing about a specific situation in which I was angry. When this is
used collectively, it is the situation rather than myself that is in focus. It is here a
method where the main thing is not the I, but rather the situation—the relations in
the situation—that make up the experience. This facilitates an interpretation of
social relations that form the experience, rather than looking for the causes in the
individual. Memories are written and interpreted to see the social relations, on
all levels, that shape the experience in question. It is precisely this aspect of
making the social aspect of the experience visible that makes the method particularly fruitful. It can indeed be used to unveil the things we take for granted in
everyday life—not least gender!

Memory-work as a methodological approach when teaching: From memory-work to experience stories

The enthusiasm I had encountered when teaching the method and the intellectual thrill of it all, learning so much about the social, inspired me to try to
develop it for use in regular teaching. I wanted to explore if and how I could use

it when teaching general sociology but of course also, and maybe especially, when teaching gender.

Well beyond the year 2000, the reasons why we feminists must still step in and give a couple of lectures on gender perspectives in our disciplines are always the same and I'm afraid quite familiar to most of us. In my own discipline, sociology, gender might be mentioned by the lecturers but is then treated as a variable or at most as a separate issue; something about women or women issues. Gender is definitely far from being understood and applied as a perspective when teaching the discipline, that is, as a fundamental social organizational principle, affecting all aspects of social life. Besides, the non-feminist male or female teachers succeed, by not being up-to-date, interested or involved in gender and feminist research, by turning it into a remnant from bygone days. They thus succeed in confirming the views of the younger generations in Scandinavia today; gender issues are traditional equality issues and as such are of no interest to a generation which "has all that" (that's what they think!), and which has moved beyond, to individual and subject positions and discourses. So, if we want to further gender perspectives in these generations, reaching them and engaging them in a reflexive dialogue about gender seems a highly urgent and political task.

But how can they be reached? Teaching sociology students at all levels over a number of years has taught me that if a theme is theoretically advanced and, if difficult, stated in sufficiently sophisticated terms—preferably handled meta-theoretically—the students will be thrilled. In this package even gender issues can be swallowed and the male students here are often those who show the most interest. They just love post-structuralist discourses! I do understand and can share their intellectual thrill for texts that open up totally new ways of understanding even though one might have to struggle with the texts to reach this understanding. The problem, as I see it, is just that these understandings are rarely related, implicitly or explicitly, to the lives and gender of the students themselves. As a result, gender is primarily considered an intellectual issue and not also a personal and political one. The fault is of course not theirs, but embedded in the discipline as such, something Dorothy E. Smith has highlighted in her work (Smith, 1987; 1989; 1990a; 1990b; 1999; 2005), and in the way it is researched and taught. The students learn about society from a ruler's perspective. Class and gender are accordingly something others "have." If asked about their own class and gender experiences, the first reaction is usually total blankness. Then they start searching for sociological concepts that fit and if none can be found, they condemn their own experiences as not Sociology. But if they can't read their own gender experiences into the concepts handed to them, these will of course not be the tools that they can use to understand their lives and their societies. And since Sociology's gender, which is formulated in abstract terms as the gender, is not their gender; their gender is made invisible and conceived of as "not gender," not only to them but also to us.

Knowing all this means that it is of little use to just step in and straighten things out, that is, telling them how wrong they are about gender and what gender is all about. Of course, they might learn about my understandings of gender, but they won't learn about their own understandings of gender and neither will I. To get them all to reflect and articulate understandings of gender, for us all to share, I have developed a technique which I've labelled "experience stories." It started out as a research method and technique, presented above, but as I here hope to show, it can also be used for teaching purposes of great interest to both teacher and students.

I want to illustrate the method through a description of its use in an undergraduate class in sociology on a particular occasion that I have documented in Widerberg (1998). I'm scheduled for two lectures on "Gender Perspectives in/on Sociology." I introduce myself and tell these about one hundred students that before I start my lecture, I would like them to take 10 minutes to write a couple of lines on the titled theme. "Describe (concretely!) a situation—today, yesterday or in the near past—when you felt/experienced/was made aware of being a woman/man."

I tell them to write no name on the paper, but just to indicate their sex. I also tell them that I will have read all the stories by the next lecture when I'll discuss with them my analyses of their material. After some initial restlessness, they all settle down to write. The way they hand in their texts shows that they have enjoyed the task and are looking forward to learning more about what this is all about. They'll have to wait until next time, I tell them.

Ninety-one (91) stories are handed in, 60 by women and 31 by men. The proportion of female and male texts corresponds to the actual gender ratio of students in the discipline. Among female texts are described more than 30 different situations, e.g.,

Wasn't heard/seen, dressing, in relation to a man, equality/gender talk, flirting, cleaning up, girls'talk, menstruation, chivalry, prejudice, doing gymnastics, in town at night (frightened), I'm cooking, he's cooking, having dishwasher installed, being talked to as good girl, being silenced in study-group, dancing, male computer-games, not coping with machines (computer), being more interested in sociology than men, feeling pregnant, showing emotions, men being unclean/ unhygienic, getting a women's job, weekend work division.

Only two texts expressed no reflections on gender. The men's texts were just as varied. The situations they wrote about included:

Opening doors/paying for her beer, shaving, washing up argument, reading about/discussing gender, complaints from girlfriend, taking a pee, when women expect one to know typical male things, e.g., fixing car, being object of woman's desire, men's talk/boys' talk, dirty talk, dildos, using the ladies room, heard women talking about menstruation and birth-control, flirting, watching male sex-offenders on film (embarrassing for the male gender), watching men's films, talking with the son about the tough sex, women dominating in the study-group.

Like the women's, only two texts reported no reflections on gender. The men's texts, however, were shorter and it was unclear in two whether they meant to be joking. Is taking a pee, for example, an effort to make fun of the task or is it a real answer? Some of the men's texts also expressed a sense of being provoked by women and equality themes. Similar expressions could not be found in the women's texts. Comparing the texts of the men and the women, however, the similarities are maybe most striking. They both reflect on gender when:

> Doing traditional gender tasks, "doing," that is, dealing with their bodies (as sex or gender), being together with their own sex, flirting, discussing gender or equality, perceiving the other gender as dominating.

Some men report reflecting on gender when listening to women talk about "women stuff," while we don't find corresponding stories by the women. The women on the other hand, write about being talked to or treated as an object by the men but also by each other. Such experiences are absent in the men's stories. Another interesting difference is that women reflect on gender when men do traditional female tasks, whereas men do not think about gender when women do traditional male tasks.

Focusing on type of relations more than tasks, both men and women express reflecting on gender in relation to/being with their own sex, in relation to/being with the other sex and being with the other sex when gender/equality is the theme.

The men report experiencing gender when acting. They don't report being treated as gender-objects in the same way as the women express in their stories. Both parties are embarrassed by their own gender and they both express a bad conscience regarding issues of equality. They don't do or feel what they "should" feel. They don't live up to the "equality standards" of either themselves or their sex. And they don't express any enjoyment or pride of their gender.

After presenting these results to the students, I asked questions. Is that what gender is all about to you? Is gender only about equality issues? Do you accept the official equality discourse and value your own behavior and feelings in its light, to the extent and in the way you express it in these stories? Aren't you ever happy or content that you are a man or a woman and hasn't that got anything to do with equality? Or are you just writing here what you think is expected of you as a student in sociology? That is, are you writing about gender in the way you've learned about gender through sociology? What else could gender be about?

The questions were consciously formulated in a provocative way. I had myself been provoked by the negative and self-critical tone in the stories. Gender conceived as equality was obviously no fun at all; it only made them feel bad or wrong. But was this really true? The students listened in dead silence.

Class was over, the students crowded in the corridors, engaged in lively debates. Gender—their gender—and Sociology—their sociology—was the theme. It would have been a great starting-point for further explorations of our, their, and my understandings of gender and sociology. With more and other stories on specific and selected themes, the students themselves, in groups, could have done the interpretation. But my time was up. I had given them some tools and they had given themselves and me materials and themes to reflect upon. Since then I have used this technique regularly and often on all kinds of themes such as class and emotions; documenting it all is a project on its own, unfortunately yet to be done.

Memory-work inspired methods investigating "The Sociality of Tiredness"

One thing leads to another, as illustrated above. The tiredness that surfaced as a topic in the Body/Texts project (presented above) caught my interest. Ulla-Britt Lilleaas and I embarked on a new research project to investigate it in depth, sociologically. In this project titled "The Sociality of Tiredness—on the Handling of Tiredness in a Class, Gender and Generation Perspective," we made use of a whole variety of memory-work inspired methods and techniques (Lilleaas & Widerberg, 2001).

To start with, different memory-work inspired pilot studies were undertaken to inform and enlighten the design and approaches of the empirical—quantitative as well as qualitative—research we had planned. These were writing pictures of tiredness from childhood, family and friends, family portraits of tiredness and a diary on tiredness.

Pictures of tiredness from childhood: family and friends. We wrote stories that aimed at giving a picture of how tiredness was expressed and handled in the families in which we grew up. What memories and pictures did we have of our parents and sisters and brothers in relation to tiredness? Our stories raised a variety of issues we then pursued in the subsequent empirical investigations: for example, the family history of tiredness, its inheritance and gender differences in how tiredness is expressed and handled; and the language, time and space for tiredness (what, where and when can different types of tiredness be expressed?).

Family portraits of tiredness: interviews. To find out how tiredness was perceived by the other members of the family, we interviewed them as well as our partners and children. With our parents we started with questions as to how they perceived themselves in relation to tiredness. Were they the tired type? How had they handled tiredness at different stages in life? And what about their own parents; how was tiredness expressed and handled by their parents when they grew up? With our siblings we added the focus of their work situations. With our children, we exchanged the focus on work situation for the school situation.

Besides confirming the relevance of the themes presented above and brought up by our earlier writings, the issue of tiredness at work rose as an iceberg in the dark. It seemed to be a most complex issue that needs to be pursued in detail so as to bring forth knowledge of how the causes, expressions and "mastering" of tiredness are determined structurally and culturally. Other issues also rose to the surface, such as:

- **Tiredness trauma.** Does it make sense to talk of such a thing? If one has lived through a period with little sleep and rest, can we talk about it lingering on as an embodied memory affecting future habits in relation to tiredness, sleep and rest?
- **Worry of tiredness.** Worrying of becoming tired seemed to be tiring in itself, sometimes even more so than the actual tiredness one felt when the worrying was finally over.
- **Tired persons.** Asking about tired persons among friends or in the family seemed a fruitful way to get information about how they perceived themselves as well as about value judgements relating to tiredness.
- **Diary on tiredness.** We then wrote a diary focusing on tiredness each day. What had made us feel tired, where was the tiredness bodily situated and how did we deal with it? For a month, we kept this diary, learning not just about ourselves but more importantly how we had to proceed in the later interviews. The diaries seemed to indicate that tiredness is about everything, one's whole life and way of relating. To make it into a phenomenon that can be studied isolated on its own, is therefore problematic and wrong in more than one sense. However, it is only by focusing on tiredness, trying to specify it, that taking it for granted is dismantled and problematized. Some things from my diary, which I intended to pursue as interview issues, were:
- **"Just finish-up type."** Working intensively to have time to relax when all is done. But when is work done? And for whom? Women's work is typically never ending, at both work and home. When can women rest if they are the "just finish-up type?"
- **Experiencing giving in to tiredness as something sinful.** Wasting time, making use of time and other such internalized cultural understandings might be hard to get rid of if they have been embodied as habits and parts of our identity. We are, in short, maybe not the kind of persons who "waste time."
- **Getting tired by, in and of social relations.** How do we handle it when our roles, professional and/or gender, are threatened? When we cannot be the kind of person we should or would like to be?

Summing up, the extensive pilot projects described above had a profound impact on the design of the subsequent empirical investigations[1]. Both the themes chosen and the very approach in the interviews were colored by what we learned through the pilot studies. To be thoroughly descriptive so as to avoid taken for granted statements and to pave the way to substantiated variation was a first step. The overriding question "how is tiredness done" was in the interview operationalized to questions about "what generates and what steals energy" during the day. We tried to trace our interview persons through their different work situations at home and work, during the weekday and weekend. We asked them to explain their different work-tasks in detail, from morning till night. We asked them to reflect upon the different types of tiredness, where these were bodily situated and how they were handled. Some of them even wrote optional tiredness diaries for a week, upon our suggestion, and had them sent in. Although tiredness is a favorite daily topic, especially among women and the younger generations, this was the first time, they said, that tiredness was the subject of serious reflection and investigation.

Making use of one's own memories, experiences and pictures when designing and doing research has more merits that are worth mentioning, e.g., becoming aware of one's own experiences on the theme makes it easier to be more genuinely interested in the research subjects as "others." There is less need to use them to find out about oneself. Equally important, one knows what it is like to be subject to investigation on the topic chosen. All this also informs both design and approach, which I have tried to illustrate above, perhaps most clearly when in the memory-work on sexual harassment.

Concluding remarks

For the sake of knowledge I have explored memory-work as a collective as well as an individual enterprise in different settings and on different topics, in both research and teaching. I have been interested to see how far I could take the method; where, when and how it could be used and still be productive. Besides ethical limits, other limits have triggered rather than hindered explorations of the method. Of course the kind of knowledge produced has varied with the forms and techniques being used. Using it as a collective enterprise favors knowledge of variations, especially if the group has been put together with that purpose, e.g., to illuminate class, gender, ethnicity, and generation. Naturally the longer the group can work together, the more in depth knowledge can be expected. Yet even when the group has limited time at its disposal, as was the case in my courses, substantial knowledge can be produced. Here specific techniques, such as changing the sex of the storyteller, can be most fruitful in making visible things we take for granted. While the collective form of the analysis unquestionably results in richer knowledge, I do not find collective decision-making on the theme to work with to be important. If time is short, it is much better to plan or try out the theme beforehand so that time is spent on the analysis instead. Formulating a theme that makes it possible for people to write easily and willingly takes experience from previously having used the method oneself. When using the method for a teaching purpose, the role of the student can be made more vital than in my illustration above. If the class is smaller and/or more time is available, one can invite students to participate in analysis. My example here shows that something can be done under the worst conceivable conditions for the method.

The method can be used as an individual enterprise with similar purposes as the collective enterprise, that is, making the social patterns—here of the individual and not the collective—visible in new ways. But as an individual enterprise it can also be used for other more biographical purposes, as I have argued. This might seem contradictory, since I and others repeatedly claim that the specific merit of the method is that it is not the I that here is focused but the social relations and patterns. And as such it is a method that can be widely used within the social sciences. However, the very focus on the theme in memory-work also has the advantage of making more visible the social and cultural aspects of the I, such as gender, class, ethnicity. Dealing with one memory at a time also helps make it visible in a more concrete and detailed way, which in itself furthers and stimulates the memory process, with the result that new insights can be gained. The focus on the theme also makes it easier for the I to unfold in all its varieties because the aim, the focus, is not to construct a coherent I throughout the stories. It is the history of the experiences on the theme chosen—not of the I—that is to be told. As such the method can be used to produce images of identity and the I as multiple and thoroughly social, different from what emerges from more traditional methods within the social sciences. On the other hand, the very focus on themes also makes other themes invisible, so the method can never give a full account of self-identity. But it can be used biographically, as I have tried to illustrate, as a kind of hybrid methodology (Widerberg, 1999).

For me memory-work is an invitation to methodological explorations that can further the development of qualitative research. It is an approach that can result in a whole variety of methods and techniques that can also be used as part and parcel of the more traditional methods and techniques, such as interviews and observations. It is a method that makes visible the social and the taken for granted. Thus it is one of the most fruitful methods available in making gender, class and ethnicity known to us in new ways, both in research and teaching. The lack within sociology is not theory but empirical knowledge of "how things are put together" (Dorothy E. Smith's expression). We need to know how the social comes about, how it is done, and here memory-work inspired methods can help us out.

Notes

1. The quantitative studies include questions in the national survey on living conditions (of a representative sample of the Norwegian population) conducted by the National Statistical Bureau in 1998 as well as questionnaires distributed to the work-places chosen also for qualitative studies. The qualitative studies include studies of different work-places—a firm, two schools, a restaurant and a bureau for community service—and different professions—engineers, teachers, waiters, domestic nursing personnel and leaders. A specific study of "changers," collective (workplaces) as well as individual ones (bosses) was also undertaken. About 100 qualitative interviews were conducted, including about 20 interviews with bosses and representatives of management on different levels. All the material is presented and discussed in our book *The times of tiredness* (in Norwegian), Oslo 2001, as well as in articles (for example Widerberg, 2006) and in several reports (in Norwegian) published at our department.

2. In this chapter I have made use of some extracts from some of my earlier writings where my various uses of the method have been presented. These are marked with an * in the Reference list below.

References

Brantsæter, Marianne & Widerberg, Karin (Eds.). (1992). *Sex i arbeid(-et)* (Sex at work). Oslo, NO: Tiden.

Haug, Frigga (Ed.). (1987). *Female sexualization: A collective work of memory*. London, UK: Verso.

Keller, Evelyn Fox. (1985). *Reflections on gender and science*. New Haven, CT: Yale University Press.

Lilleaas, Ulla-Britt & Widerberg, Karin. (2001).*Trøtthetens tid* (The times of tiredness). Oslo, NO: Pax.

Smith, Dorothy E. (1987). *The everyday world as problematic: A feminist sociology*. Boston, MA: Northeastern University Press.

Smith, Dorothy E. (1989). Sociological theory: Methods of writing patriarchy. In Ruth Wallace (Ed.), *Feminism and sociological theory* (pp. 34-64). Newbury Park, CA: Sage.

Smith, Dorothy E. (1990a). *Texts, facts and femininity: Exploring the relations of ruling*. London: Routledge.

Smith, Dorothy E. (1990b). *The conceptual practices of power: A feminist sociology of knowledge*. Toronto, CA: University of Toronto Press.

Smith, Dorothy E. (1999). *Writing the social: Critique, theory and investigations*. Toronto, CA: University of Toronto Press.

Smith, Dorothy E. (2005). *Institutional ethnography. A sociology for people*. Oxford: Alta Mira Press

Widerberg, Karin. (1995). *Kunskapens kön* (The gender of knowledge). Stockholm, SE: Norstedts; Oslo, NO: Pax.

*Widerberg, Karin. (1998). Teaching gender through writing "experience stories." *Women's International Forum, 21*(2), 193- 198.

*Widerberg, Karin. (1999). Alternative methods—Alternative understandings: Exploring the social and the multiple "I" through memory-work. *Sosiologisk Tidskrift, 2*, 147-159.

*Widerberg, Karin. (2001a). Introduction. From exercises to texts. In Karin Widerberg, D. von der Fehr, H. Leira & U. B. Lilleaas (Eds.), *Doing body/texts: An explorative approach* (pp. 1-9). Oslo, NO: Department of Sociology and Human Geography, University of Oslo.

*Widerberg, Karin. (2001b). Embodying intellectuality. In Karin Widerberg, D. von der Fehr, H. Leira & U. B. Lilleaas (Eds.), *Doing body/texts: An explorative approach* (pp. 10-34). Oslo, NO: Department of Sociology and Human Geography, University of Oslo.

Widerberg, Karin. (2006). Embodying modern times: Investigating tiredness. *Time & Society, 15*(1), 105-120.

Chapter 8

Mothers and Sons:
Using Memory-work to Explore the
Subjectivities and Practices of
Profeminist Men

Bob Pease

In this chapter I will outline the application of memory-work to understanding the subjectivities and practices of profeminist men. Profeminism for men involves a sense of responsibility to our own and other men's sexism, and a commitment to work with women to end men's violence (Douglas, 1993). It acknowledges that men benefit from the oppression of women, drawing men's attention to the privileges we receive as men and the harmful effects these privileges have on women (Thorne-Finch, 1992).

The research was undertaken as my PhD thesis and it began with questions that have been a personal challenge in my search to understand my place as a white, heterosexual man who is committed to a profeminist position[1]. What does it mean to be a profeminist man? What is the experience of endeavoring to live out a profeminist commitment? What do these experiences tell us about reforming men's subjectivities and practices towards gender equality?

I believe that men's subjectivity is crucial to the maintenance and reproduction of gender domination and hence to its change. The purpose of the research was thus to theorize men's subjectivities and practices to inform a profeminist men's practice and to enact strategies that will, in themselves, promote the process of change. So the research was driven by practical concerns as well as by the imperatives of intellectual inquiry.

Context of the study

The nature of my research interests and my commitment to praxis and change led me to develop a participatory approach to this exploration. This participatory approach was informed by feminist critiques of mainstream masculinist research. While it is generally accepted that men cannot do feminist research, they are encouraged to evolve approaches based on feminist standpoint epistemology to research men's lives and, in so doing, they must develop "their own standards, directions, meanings, space and name for what it is they are doing" (Kremer, 1990, p. 466). Wadsworth and Hargreaves suggest that "the methodological approaches of feminism will be relevant to men... seeking to transform subordinating practice" (1993, p. 5), whilst Maguire (1987) also encourages men to use participatory research to uncover their own modes of domination of women.

Inspired by these participatory approaches, to begin the research, I drew up a list of 20 men whom I knew personally from my involvement in profeminist politics and who I believed would identify with a profeminist stance. Ten of these men were, at the time of the research, active in Men Against Sexual Assault (MASA); the others were from a range of activist backgrounds including the non-violence movement, perpetrator counselling, and non-sexist educational programs of boys in schools. Because my focus was on both personal change and political strategy, I believed that it was important to choose men who were in some way taking a public stance with their profeminism.

I contacted each of the men, outlined the project to them and asked them whether they would like to receive a copy of a discussion paper outlining the project and come to a meeting to discuss it. All of the men I contacted expressed interest in the project and of the 20 men contacted, 15 men attended the initial meeting. Of those, 11 men committed themselves to the full project over a period of 15 months and 22 meetings.

Thus, I did not begin the study as a memory-work project. Rather, memory-work was one of three research methods that the group developed to carry out the intentions of the research. The other research methods were consciousness raising, and sociological intervention based on the social movement research by Alain Touraine (1977, 1988). All three methods involved group work, a precondition for participatory research and a preferred methodology for enacting the action component of the research process. Furthermore, the combination of the three methods provided a basis to bridge the gap between the individual and the social and between the subjective and the structural. Together, they avoided the danger of psychologizing masculine subjectivities at the expense of structural change, while at the same time grounding the discussion of political strategies in the subjective realities of men's lives.

Although memory work is a liberationist method (Onyx & Small, 2001), my concern was that the use of the method on its own would emphasize the individual biographies of the men at the expense of the collective social relations of patriarchy. By utilizing memory work alongside the social movement methodology of sociological intervention, which emphasized dialogues with interlocutors and collective strategizing about ways to challenge patriarchy, I was able to ensure that the links between the men's lives and their positioning with the hierarchies of gender were not lost.

The use of memory-work in the study

In many ways, memory-work was an obvious method to choose for the study. I had read Haug's (1987, 1992) work and the adaptations to the method developed by Crawford, Kippax, Onyx, Gault and Benton (1992). It seemed to complement the practice of consciousness raising, which I had originally formulated as the main research methodology. We used consciousness-raising as a method to deal collectively with what it means to identify oneself as a profeminist man. We started by generating a series of questions. What are the basic problems that profeminist men face? What are the dilemmas and issues we grapple with as profeminist men? What accounts for these problems and dilemmas, given the gendered structure of society? Why is it that some men take up a profeminist subject position? What kind of subjectivities will support profeminist men's politics?

For many men who support feminism, there is confusion about how they are supposed to act. So, we began the process of identifying dilemmas associated with attempts at living out a profeminist commitment and arising within our own psyches, in personal relationships, in workplaces or connected to our political activism. No attempt was made to resolve the dilemmas we identified; rather, this phase of the research sets the scene for the more in-depth exploration of the issues through memory-work and the further explication of them through dialogues with allies and opponents of profeminism.

The aim of this phase in the research process, following Vorlicky (1990), was to analyze our position and develop "a strategy for how [our] awareness of the difficult and contradictory position in relation to feminism can be made explicit in discourse and practice" (p. 277). This necessarily involved an interrogation of our masculinity and a questioning of the privileges that are afforded to us by our gender.

The men in this study were thus involved in a process of re-forming their subjectivities and their practices in the wake of feminist critique and challenge. Through the conversations recorded in my research, these men revealed what it means for them to be profeminist. They tell us something about the personal and political implications of being a profeminist man at this historical moment, thus demonstrating that non-patriarchal subjectivities are available to men. These subjectivities, however, involve dilemmas and contradictions, for they are formed out of conflicting discourses and practices.

Giddens (1992) has observed that men have been "unable to construct a narrative of self that allows them to come to terms with an increasingly democratised and reordered sphere of personal life" (p. 117). The stories that the men told to the group are stories in which they are attempting to do just this. As such, these stories also provide new narratives, which in turn have the potential to influence future stories and future lives. These men were self-consciously living the changes in gender relations.

It seemed to us that memory-work provided a vehicle to explore some of the unconscious elements of gender socialization. Haug (1987) had used memory-work to gain greater understanding of the resistance to the dominant ideology at the level of the individual, as well as how women internalize dominant values and how their reactions are colonized by dominant patterns of thought. Haug describes memory-work as "a method for the unravelling of gender socialization" (1987, p. 13). Her argument is that it is essential to examine subjective memories if we want to discover anything about how people appropriate objective structures (Haug, 1992).

By sharing and comparing memories from their own lives, Haug and her groups (1987, 1992) hope to uncover the workings of hegemonic ideology in their subjectivities. Her particular concern is with the ways in which people construct their identities through experiences that become subjectively significant to them. The premise is that everything we remember is a significant basis for the formation of identity.

By illustrating the ways in which people participate in their own socialization, their potential to intervene in and change the world is expanded. By making conscious the way in which we have previously unconsciously interpreted the world, we are more able to develop resistance against this "normality" (Haug, 1987) and thus develop ways of subverting our own socialization.

In my search of the literature on memory-work at that time, however, I was struck by the dearth of accounts by men using this method. Those accounts that were inspired by Haug's political project always focused on internalized gender identities of the oppressed and not on the dominant and privileged group. What would it mean to use memory-work to explore accommodations and resistances to privilege and social dominance? Onyx and Small (2001) raise the question of whether men can use the method as effectively as women and whether men's use of the method negates its designation as a feminist method. As I have indicated earlier, I think that men can use feminist methods to uncover men's modes of domination over women and to transform subordinating practices. Since publishing other accounts of this memory-work project (Pease, 2000a, 2000b, 2000c), Hearn (2005) has been inspired to use memory-work to interrogate and deconstruct his own experiences of nationalism and gender dominance in the context of colonialism and imperialism.

In the context of this research, we developed four memory-work projects to explore aspects of internalized domination. These projects focused on father-son and mother-son relationships and experiences of homophobia and sexual objectification. In this chapter I will illustrate the application of the method to mother-son relationships[2].

Mother-son relationships and the "mother wound"

There is a widespread view that mothers are a problem for men in Western societies. Men's distancing patterns are said to connect to unresolved issues involving mothers (Gurian, 1994). Similarly, Osherson (1992, p. 175) maintains that men's struggles with women in relationships are often based on "unfinished attachment struggles with mother—their simultaneous desire to be close and separate.

The tension between a desire for intimacy and connectedness with women and a desire to withdraw and shut them out was evident in a comment by Tony in the context of a discussion about our relationships with women. This comment was instrumental in our decision to explore the connection between our relationships with our mothers and our partners through memory work.

> I was thinking of how I relate to women and my sexuality . . . even how I define what being in a relationship is all about. One of the things I've been thinking lately is wanting to be intimate and relate to Pam and then wanting to withdraw from her, shut her out of my life. It seems like a real roller coaster. Sometimes I'm in it really deeply. Other times I start tuning out. I start removing myself. . . . Sometimes I want it all my own way. Sort of like wanting to feel safe and secure at the same time.

Tony's dilemma goes to the heart of many issues between men and women. A number of writers have commented on the tension men feel between their desire for intimacy with women and their fear of dependency, associated with their unresolved experiences with their mothers. Men fear dependency and commitment and are terrified of their own vulnerability (Jukes, 1993). They associate dependency with their mothers and the resultant feelings this generates hinder their ability to form intimate relationships with women.

The question is: What is the source of this problem? Is it too much of mother or not enough? A number of writers posit that separation from the mother is necessary and healthy for men (Keen, 1991; Farmer, 1991). Separating from mother is seen as the only way to manhood. Thus, mothers are seen by some writers as getting in the way of masculinity and are regarded as inevitably emasculating boys.

Whilst the men and masculinity literature admits that the boy's separation from the mother is a wounding experience, one has to ask whether boys *need* to separate from their mothers? Do boys need to repress closeness with their mothers to become masculine? Defining the issue in such terms portrays mothers as the problem.

One consequence of separation without attachment is that men are often unable to develop a sense of empathic identity with women. Furthermore, as some men distance themselves from their mothers and do not get enough nurturing, they later feel needy of women. On the other hand, while many men recognize their need for mother, they are often unable to openly express it (Osherson, 1992).

Men's unresolved feelings about their mothers have implications for men's capacity for loving and accepting women's love and consequently, men keep their emotional distance from women for fear of both entrapment and abandonment (O'Connor, 1993). Benjamin (1988, p. 52) even goes so far as to argue that domination "begins with the attempt to deny dependency."

In the context of the preceding, we were curious about the links between our relationship with our mothers and with women partners. I was mindful of Jardine's (1987, p. 61) comment, that "men have not even begun to think about their mothers." While men's relationships with their fathers have received considerable attention in writing about men and masculinity, there has been a resounding silence by men on their relationships with their mothers. It is certainly rare to see any examination of men's experience of the ambivalence and pain associated with distancing and separation.

Applying memory-work to mother-son relationships

At this particular session, five men (including myself), were present[3]. All of us identified as profeminist. We are all white, heterosexual and middle-class and at the time of the inquiry ranged in age from 30 to 56 years. All of the memories were written prior to the session. Each of them was read out loud to other participants. In this session, five memories were read and analyzed over a period of four hours.

The cue we used to evoke the memories was *to recall a situation with our mothers in which we felt a sense of discomfort*. The aim was to analyze memories in which there was a sense of distancing ourselves from our mothers, in order to explore the meanings we gave to those processes of distancing. What would memories of distancing from mothers tell us about our relationships with women?

Distancing mothers. The following memory from Tony demonstrates the theme of distancing:

> *Tony was about 13 and he was walking down the main street of Frankston (an outer-suburb of Melbourne in Victoria, Australia) with his mother. He didn't want to be there. He was annoyed with his mother that he was there. He was going shopping with her to buy clothes for him, which he didn't want to do. He didn't want to have new school clothes because he didn't like new clothes. He didn't want to be seen by his school mates. So he physically distanced himself from his mother. He was walking a few steps back in a similar way to which he*

had seen a school friend of his do the previous year but he could tell by the way
the boy was walking, that he was with his mother.

In discussing the memory later, Tony said that he lapped up his mother's
company when he was at home. He talked about how much he appreciated her
cooking and ironing and cleaning clothes but why did he have to go shopping
with her? Why couldn't she go out and buy the clothes without him? In an attempt to explain his experience he says: "I was meant to be a boy and I was
meant to have some sort of power. And my mother still seemed to have control
over me and I hated that."

It seemed to Tony at the time, that to accept his mother's authority was to
lose his self respect. He was asked whether there were any similarities in that
experience and his experience of shopping for clothing for himself with his partner:

just cringe like anything. It bugs me. I can really feel myself well up and think:
Oh hell. I suppose it is something about smothering or something. Wanting to
be grown up, feeling self-sufficient and feeling like I can look after myself.

The issue of women's perceived power in the domestic sphere brings up a
number of issues for men. Some of men's responses to doing their share of domestic work may be related to not accommodating to what they perceive as
women's control. As Tony pointed out, they are meant to be men and to have
some sort of power.

In the following memory, Michael recalls a similar experience:

Michael was about 13. He was living in a country town in New South Wales (in
Australia), going to a state secondary school. His parents lived on the fringe of
the town. It was too far to walk. Although there was an irregular bus service
that passed near the school, his mother insisted on driving him to and from the
school. It seemed as though he was the only boy in his grade who was driven to
and from school by his mother and his class mates commented negatively upon
this on various occasions. "Your mother drives you to school. Are you a
mummy' boy." After a while he went to his mother and said "Mum I would like
to take the bus to and from school." His mother said "Don't be silly Michael. I
don't mind driving you." Michael said "But mum I would prefer to go on the
bus." And his mother asked him why "Well I would just rather go on by bus
that's all," he said. And she said "No I'll drive you. It is quicker and safer."
His mother was adamant about it. There was nothing more to be said. The next
afternoon the school bell went and he walked out of the school building and
saw his mother's car parked near the school entrance. He ran more quickly
than usual, got in the front seat beside his mother and as he sat down, however,
he slid slightly forward so that he was not riding so high in the car. Over time,
he would gradually slide more and more forward. So that eventually his head
was about level with the dashboard. If he had to be driven by his mother, he
would decrease the likelihood of being seen.

Following Michael's memory, the group explored the significance of his being called a mummy's boy:

> **Tony**: So you didn't like being called a mummy's boy?
> **Michael**: No.
> **Harry**: Was it true?
> **Michael**: Well I guess it must have been true. If it was true, it wasn't some-
> thing that I was wanting to embrace.
> **Harry**: More importantly, what does it mean? Does it mean that mum loved
> you and cared for you and was close to you and wanted a close relationship,
> and that this was inconceivable given the peer pressure? Was there comfort in
> your relationship with her?
> **Michael**: Well, it is a bit similar to what Tony was saying. I saw all sorts of
> parallels between my story and yours.... Yes, there were comforts that were
> provided by my mother at home. And while those comforts were provided in
> the context of the home that was fine. But I didn't like those comforts to be
> seen more publicly outside the home.

Harry identified the issue clearly. Michael was torn between enjoyment of
his mother's nurturance and the stigma of being referred to as a "mummy's
boy." To be called a "mummy's boy" can be experienced by boys as being one
of "the worst things in the world" (Osherson, 1992, p. 175). "Mummy's boys"
are taunted by other boys and consequently, boys are forced to separate from
their mothers by the threat of humiliation, otherwise they would not choose to
make the separation (Kreiner, 1991, p. 6). There is thus a split between the private and the public manifested in the tension between the experience of the
mother and the experience of peer group culture.

As can be seen from this brief dialogue, the memories stimulated conversations between the men about the meaning of the memories. While on one level
the responsibility for interpretation rested with me as the narrator of our journey,
interpretation of the memories also took place within the group by the participants as they theorized the memories. This represents a form of what Kvale
(1995) call "communicative validity," where the validity of knowledge claims is
tested in dialogue through conversation and argument about the phenomena under investigation.

Devaluing mothers. As stated earlier, most boys observe their fathers' attitude of superiority towards their mothers. This is the context in which boys have
to decide whether to identify with their mother or with their father. A boy learns
that if he wants to be accepted into male society, he has to turn his back on his
mother. The following memory from Alan demonstrates this process:

> *Alan was about 12 or 13 years old. It was tea time and he was sitting around
> the kitchen table with some of his siblings and his father. His mother was cook-
> ing dinner. They were discussing an issue that was not of particular impor-
> tance. However, his mother said something that might have been construed as
> silly, that she didn't understand. So Alan and the others started hassling her,*

implying that she was stupid. Then to his surprise, his mother ran out of the room in tears.

I discussing the memory later, Alan described a strong sense of collusion in the incident, of men ganging up on the woman. He said:

> I recollect having a very close relationship and it really struck me as being so insensitive to her, being cruel. I feel like I was so cruel. I felt very ashamed, even now.

In Alan's memory, the mother was constructed as stupid based on an assumption about "male knowledge" being superior or "right." Michael related closely to this memory. His mother was a full-time housewife and while both his mother and father were poorly educated, his father read widely and was informed about the state of the world. His mother did not read as widely. She was only semi-literate and the story Alan told about his mother being seen as stupid occurred in his house as well; his father would be very condescending towards her. Before becoming critical of what was happening, he perceived his mother as being not very intelligent. There was pain in his voice as he recalled this experience and his inability then to feel proud of his mother, because of the way in which women were devalued.

Depending on mothers. How do sons address their dependency needs in relation to their mothers? We explored this question in discussing issues arising from other memories. Phillip's memory reveals his fear of having lost his mother's love:

> *Phillip was fighting with his brother, while the dining room at his house was being painted. He was 9 or 10. The crockery from the dining room was stored in his brother's bedroom. During the fight, Phillip threw a book at his brother. He remembers, in slow motion, the arch the book made as it slithered through a line of plates and cups. These plates and cups were special because his mum had saved up for them during the war, when her husband was away. So Phillip was a very sorry boy and was sent to bed that night without any tea.*
>
> *About 9:00 at night he came downstairs and saw his mum was sitting at the kitchen table crying. He hopped on her knee and they had a big cry together. Then he understood that it was alright. He was not going to be persecuted for this.*

In commenting on the memory afterwards, Phillip remembered crying in distress because he thought "I have really blown it this time." He has felt that feeling many times since then: "Feeling like a chastised little boy can be a big thing for me." When that happens, he feels defensive and wants to fight.

The reference to feeling like a little boy was a recurrent theme throughout the discussion about mothers. Phillip's memory elicited a recent experience from Michael; he had accidentally broken a special vase his partner had owned for several years. When he told her about the breakage, she was upset but he did not want to take responsibility for breaking it and emphasized that it was not his fault. In that situation, he described how he felt like a little boy who needed to be told that it was alright.

Phillip says that, in his view most men have not got over their reliance upon their mothers; they have shifted the focus to partners for emotional support and emotional security. When he has left or been left by a partner, feelings "of losing mum" come back to him. Michael reflected how some of the ways in which he cuddles with a woman were to do with his "unresolved dependency needs." Whilst many men are unable to accept their dependency needs, describing them as unresolved suggests a psychological weakness, whereas the notion of interdependence tends to affirm that in some situations we will be dependent and that is acceptable.

The following memory from Peter illustrates the tension between being depended upon and having one's own dependency needs:

> *Peter was about 20. He had a really good relationship with his mother. They had become quite close since his father died about 3 years earlier. He had been quite supportive providing some stability in an otherwise difficult few years for his mum. But she didn't have to worry about him. He was fine. Not so fine were a few of his siblings who for various reasons were having difficulties of one sort or another. His mother took an active interest in checking in with them, arranging dinners with them to offer an ear and to get to know how they were going. Peter had his own problems and it was at this time that he became aware that he needed support as well. He found it quite difficult to ask. This would go against the normal pattern of events, the normal way they related. He was too busy listening and supporting his mum. It was hard to change the dynamics of this relationship. She was a very busy and very giving woman and he knew that she needed to have this space. But he couldn't help feeling a bit resentful. He was supportive, stable, calm and had things under control.*

Interestingly, Peter's response to the cue of discomfort was more focused on a state of mind during a particular period in his life rather than a particular incident. In discussing the memory later, Peter connected this experience with his mother to his current relationship, where it is much easier for him to be supportive and to listen than to be supported. He says that the hardest thing for him is to acknowledge "that I am not in control, that I am in need and it is not all stable and calm."

The other group members could identify with this experience. Tony related his experience of working with partners of women who had been sexually abused as children. These men were able to be supportive with their partners, but at the expense of acknowledging their own needs and feelings and at times this became destructive in their relationships: "Of course I can't relate to that at all," he said sarcastically.

Michael recalled instances where in relationships with women he had put his own needs aside to be supportive to his partner's needs but his own neediness would "erupt" and he would then want her to put her needs aside. This would not always happen and he would experience himself saying "It is not fair. What about my needs?" This experience elicits an immediate response from Phillip:

> That is exactly what happens to me too. Unfortunately I am less conscious of it than I want to be, so it sort of comes up. I really enjoy that steadiness, you know. And then it comes up. It is totally demanding and the way I do it is very little boy demanding.

As men we are often unable to accept that at different times and in different contexts we need what women are able to offer us. To acknowledge our dependency at these times does not mean that we are weak men. However, because dependence on others, particularly women, is seen as a sign of weakness, men frequently are unable to develop genuinely interdependent relationships with women and often end up expressing their needs in a demanding rather than interactive way.

Blaming mothers. The memory work on one aspect of our relationship with our mothers enabled us to interrogate some aspects of men's tendency to blame mothers and the ways in which we had internalized dominant views about mother-son relationships. Mothers are often accused of dangerously enmeshing their own identities with those of their sons and of over-protecting them whereby they "indulge for their own gratification, in compensation for an unsatisfactory marriage" (Gomez, 1991, p. 49). Bly (1990, p. 18) posits that mothers typically exercise possessiveness over their sons.

A number of writers attribute the estrangement of sons from their fathers to the involvement of mothers. Biddulph (1994, p. 35) argues that a mother will often turn her son against his father and Bly (1990) blames mothers for getting in the way of boys' relationships with their fathers. In his view, this constitutes a conspiracy between mother and son. Tony responds to Bly's charge of conspiracy:

> To me it was about safety. It wasn't a conspiracy. It was more like a necessity, my relationship with my mother. I just saw my father for ten minutes a day and sometimes that ten minutes was something to dread. What's dad going to do when he gets home tonight? Is he going to be volatile? Is he going to be friendly? Sure I had a closer bond with my mother than my father, but I wouldn't call that a conspiracy.

As discussed previously, the major consequence of such over mothering is seen to be the creation of mothers' boys. Men who become "mummy's boys" are said to be "dominated by the desire to perform well to gain approval and to avoid female anger or rejection" (Keen, 1991, p. 21). Bly (1990, pp. 2-3) argues that "mummy's boys" were "too tied to women as children, and then as adults are too tender, too empathic, too interested in women's issues."

Profeminist men are often criticized by other men as mothers' boys. Corneau (1991) questions his profeminist client's reasons for embracing feminism. He argues that his client used feminism to ingratiate himself with women and the reason for this involvement with feminism was based on his desire to be rewarded with maternal affection.

Similarly, Forrester (1992, p. 106) suggests that the desire of one his clients to be a feminist man was "really a desire to be underneath, to be dominated sexually and politically by the feminist women he admires." His profeminism was regarded as "a kind of masochism, or a kind of fascination with the all-powerful woman figure."

It is important to challenge the framework within which these comments are made and to shift the terms of the debate about profeminism. It is likely that profeminist men will be closer to their mothers than their fathers and it is important for these men to acknowledge the strong influence of women, rather than to dis-identify with them. Such men can perhaps contribute the most to changing gender relations.

Reflections on the use of memory-work on mother-son relationships

In response to the cue of discomfort with mothers, the men produced memories of distancing, devaluing and dependence. In all of the memories there were connections between dependency issues with mothers and these men's relationships with women. The reference to feeling like a "little boy," at times, was a recurrent theme throughout the discussions. Through the memory-work, it was evident that there was a lot of ambivalence in these men's relationships with mothers. They, like most males, had received strong messages that they should distance themselves from their mothers or else risk ridicule as mothers' boys. Unlike most males though, who want to suppress the ways that they are like their mothers, these men had struggled to own the positive influences their mothers had upon their lives, although they were initially denied a framework within which they could easily do that. Profeminism would come to provide such a framework.

Given that the majority of men are pressured to distance themselves from their mothers, what can be done in working with men on these issues? Men can reflect on "how they would be different if they did not have to separate" (Carey, 1992, p. 68). Considering that, in losing touch with their mothers, men may have lost touch with parts of themselves could itself be a powerful force in provoking change.

It is also important that men endeavour to understand their mothers as women with their own life histories, expectations and needs. Such analysis can enrich their perception of women as a whole. Men can get to know their mothers better, to ask them about their experiences before they became mothers, especially in relation to experiences such as discrimination and harassment (Pasick, 1992). A lot of men have difficulty seeing their mothers as women with separate lives before and apart from motherhood. To acknowledge the truth of our mothers' lives requires us to recognize their oppression and our institutional power over women. To the extent to which we are able to do this, we will enhance the potential for partnership with women.

Reframing our childhood memories enables us to reconnect with our emotional histories and enables a critical stocktaking. Memory-work enabled us to examine the emotional and psychological basis of our relationships with women, including our unconscious feelings about them. Remembering is not only an attempt "to understand the past better but to understand it differently" and it enables us to challenge dominant social relations (McLaren & da Silva, 1993, pp. 75-76).

Memory-work enables men to reflect upon and shape their own experiences and, in so doing, it can contribute to the formation of non-patriarchal subjectivities and practices. The memory-work recorded here reflects sons' experiences of family life and, following Hearn (1987, p. 187), I believe that to reclaim our experience as sons, "through the self recognition of sonhood" is to challenge patriarchal constructions of fatherhood and manhood. Naming ourselves as sons, as threatening as it may be to some men, can provide the basis for the formation of alternative non-patriarchal subjectivities by allowing us to reposition ourselves against the dominant mode of identity reproduction.

Reflections on the method in the context of collaborative inquiry

Throughout the course of this inquiry, I occupied a number of conflicting roles at times: convenor, secretary, theorist, researcher and participant. Undertaking memory-work as part of a collaborative inquiry within the context of a doctoral thesis posed numerous problems. As a doctoral candidate, I was required to formulate a coherent research proposal that would then be translated into practice, interpret the results and draw original conclusions to sustain a thesis argument. As a facilitator of participatory research, however, I was required to be open to the interests and needs of the participants and to modify my research agenda, as appropriate, during the conduct of the study. While the participants and I shared a common interest in exploring personal and political issues facing profeminist men, the participants were not bound by my concerns about whether or not our inquiry would result in a successful thesis.

From the beginning, I was committed to share power with the participants, although this was always constrained by my greater investment in the outcomes of the group process. Towards this, I relinquished the role of facilitator after the first two sessions. Each subsequent session was facilitated by other participants on a rotating basis. While this was effective in sharing control of the research, it also meant that, at times, the sessions drifted into areas that were less relevant to

the major issues as I perceived them. Thus, the initial meetings of the group became open-ended exploratory discussions in which we canvassed issues and
dilemmas associated with living out our profeminist stance, as we experienced
them. During some group sessions, others identified particular issues and dilemmas that I would have liked to explore more fully but, as I was not facilitating, I was not always able to bring the group back to them, leaving many issues
insufficiently explored.

Furthermore, although I had the ability to raise issues for discussion along
with other participants, I was reluctant to actively influence the direction of the
group discussions. The questions that I did raise and the comments that I made
during the group discussions obviously reflected my evolving theoretical
framework. While it was recognized that I was spending more time between
group sessions reflecting on the discussions, I refrained from bringing what
might be regarded as abstract understandings to bear on our conversations. Nevertheless, as my theoretical understanding developed, I became a more powerful
influence in the group.

In the early stages of the inquiry, the collaborative group process and my intellectual immersion in the theoretical literature felt like two separate, parallel
journeys with little connection between them. As I had not initially set out to test
a particular theoretical framework, at times I seemed to be inhabiting two different worlds. This was not unusual, given the structural division of labor that usually separates theorists from practitioners. As the inquiry proceeded, however, I
found these two worlds coming together. My evolving theoretical framework
started to elucidate what was being said in the group and the issues arising out of
the group started to focus my theoretical work. Eventually, throughout the latter
stages of the process, the experiences in the group and the theoretical ideas were
constantly influencing each other in a dialogical relationship.

While there were limitations to the open-ended group discussion format, it
enabled issues to be articulated that would otherwise have remained submerged.
For those participants who took part in the memory-work, a high level of trust
developed within the group. This led to a great depth of self disclosure, as was
evidenced in the recorded memories and the subsequent stories that were elicited
from participants.

I also struggled with the issue of my own voice in the text. In the thesis, I
defended the view that the personal self has a place in scholarly writing and I
argued that it is important to write from inside the research situation rather than
from outside. Thus, I wrote the thesis in the form of a first person narrative. Furthermore, since this thesis was concerned with men's subjectivities, I considered
it essential that I identify how my own subjectivity influenced this research
process and has been influenced by it.

I had a dilemma, though, in using the first person plural "we" when discussing men and masculinities. Do I, as a male author, write about men in terms of
"we" or "they?" "We," in some contexts, may imply a false community between

men or suggest a connection with other men that I do not share. On the other hand, consistently referring to "they" implies a separation that denies my shared experience with other men and denies my own presence within the object of my analysis, whilst "we/they" is clumsy and does not address either of these issues. I chose, albeit with reservations, to write "we" when referring to both profeminist men and the men in the study and "they" when referring to men in general or men with whom I do not identify.

There was an additional dilemma related to my multiple voices in this research. As an active participant in the group and as a subject in my own research, my experiences, dilemmas and memories were data and my ideas as they were formulated during the group process were a part of the dialogues within the group and with the interlocutors. Notwithstanding my comments about writing personally, to describe my personal memories and stories disclosed in the group process I chose a pseudonym, giving myself, and my friends and family the same degree of anonymity as the other participants. There was no reason to separate myself out in that part of the research, as I allowed myself to be immersed within the group process. I retained my own identity, though, when I was talking in the group as a self-conscious actor in dialogue with other participants and interlocutors.

I was also in the group as a participant-observer, commenting on the process from my own subjective position. As I was engaged in a study of "my own people," my membership role in the group was what Adler and Adler (1987) call "complete membership," as distinct from peripheral and active forms of membership in field research.

Thus, there were multiple tenses and senses of self in this research: first, there were memories and biographical experiences told through my pseudonym; second, there were dialogues with participants told through an "I" in the past tense and third, there was the "I" as writer and interpreter of the research experience spoken through the present tense. Within each of these levels, there were further multiple "I"s, as I moved between total immersion as a participant and as a self-conscious researcher-participant in the group process and as I moved between disclosure of my personal self and scholarly narrator of the research experience. Undertaking research of the kind required a constant monitoring of subjectivities throughout all stages of the research process.

I was also aware that I had not followed the memory-work method strictly throughout the research because I was using it to complement other methods. Thus, my collaborative inquiry group was not strictly a memory-work group anymore than it was strictly a consciousness-raising group or a social movement intervention group. We did not always follow the rules that ideally pertain to any of these three approaches. Rather, we used each methodology as it became relevant to our collective project as we proceeded. Given the practical concerns of the research, noted earlier, I was interested in constructing research methodologies that would in themselves assist in the process of reconstituting men's subjectivities.

Memory-work provided an opportunity for the research participants to reframe some of the content of our memories. The process of recalling memories enabled us to elevate unconscious elements of our experiences to the conscious, as the immersion within a discourse "has implications for the unconscious as well as conscious remembered subjectivity" (Weedon, 1987, p. 112). Such remembering facilitates a process of challenging dominant social relations. By asking men to reflect on their understandings of the ways in which they accommodated to or resisted the dominant constructions of masculinity, through the process of memory-work we were able to understand the ways in which new subject positions could be created. The memory-work made more visible the discursive threads by which our masculinities were produced and it assisted us to identify forms of resistance to dominant masculinities.

One of the purposes of the research was to produce a praxis of how men can change and the methodological approaches employed became some of the very strategies being sought. That is, memory-work and the other methods used each represented pedagogical strategies for profeminist politics for men. Thus, in addition to contributing to theorizing men's subjectivities and to the insights about issues and dilemmas in profeminist men's lives, the research contributed to the development of these methodologies, both as research tools and as strategies for change in gender relations.

Postscript

When I finished this research project, I was very interested in using memory work again without the constraints imposed by the data analysis and writing up imperatives of a PhD thesis. Because I was so impressed with the impact that the memories had upon the participants (including myself) and the conversations that flowed from them, I was interested in setting up a memory work group with no specific research agenda in mind. Towards that end, since the completion of the research, I have used memory work to explore experiences of my body, reflections on the aging process and experiences of bereavement. No longer required to transform these memory group meetings into research papers, I have been free to experience the benefits without the tensions and pitfalls identified by Koutroulis (1993) and Onyx and Small (2001) as well as myself in this chapter. While the distinction is often made between memory-work and therapy, I have personally found memory-work as having the capacity to initiate a process of "unconsciousness raising," which brings the social dimensions of one's experience into the foreground. That being so, I think that memory-work warrants further investigation as a method of intervention in assisting people to link private troubles to public issues as C. Wright Mills (1959) encouraged us to do so many years ago.

Notes

1. The full research project is reported in Pease (2000a). An earlier version of some sections of this chapter appear in this book.

2. See Pease 2000b and 2000c for discussions of memory-work in relation to father-son relationships and men's experiences of objectification.

3. I used a pseudonym for myself in this study.

References

Adler, Peter & Adler, Patricia A. (1987). *Membership roles in field research.* Newbury Park: Sage.

Benjamin, Jessica. (1988). *The bonds of love: Psychoanalysis, feminism and the problem of domination.* New York: Pantheon.

Biddulph, Steve. (1994). *Manhood.* Sydney: Finch.

Bly, Robert. (1990). *Iron John: A book about men.* New York: Addison Wesley.

Carey, Maggie. (1992). Healing the mother wound. *Dulwich Centre Newsletter, 3 & 4,* 65-69.

Corneau, Guy. (1991). *Absent fathers, lost sons: The search for masculine identity.* Boston: Shambhala.

Crawford, June; Kippax, Susan; Onyx, Jenny; Gault, Una & Benton, Pam. (1992). *Emotion and gender: Constructing meaning from memory.* London: Sage.

Douglas, Peter. (1993, June). *Men = Violence: A profeminist perspective on dismantling the masculine equation.* Paper presented at the 2nd National Conference on Violence, presented by Australian Institute of Criminology, Canberra.

Farmer, Steven. (1991). *The wounded male.* New York: Ballantine.

Forrester, John. (1992). What do men really want? In David Porter (Ed.), *Between men and feminism* (pp. 105-117). London: Routledge.

Giddens, Anthony. (1992). *The transformation of intimacy.* Cambridge, UK: Polity Press.

Gomez, Joan. (1991). *Psychological and psychiatric problems in men.* London: Routledge.

Gurian, Michael. (1994). *Mothers, lovers and sons.* Boston: Shambhala.

Haug, Frigga (Ed.). (1987). *Female sexualisation: A collective work of memory* (Eerica Carter, Trans.). London: Verso.

Haug, Frigga. (1992). *Beyond female masochism: Memory-work and politics* (Rodney Livingstone, Trans.). London: Verso.

Hearn, Jeff. (1987). *The gender of oppression: Men masculinity and the critique of Marxism.* Sussex: Wheatsheath.

Hearn, Jeff, (2005) Autobiography, nation, postcolonialism and gender relations: Reflecting on men in England, Finland and Ireland, *Irish Journal of Sociology, 14*(2), pp. 66-93.

Jardine, Alice A. (1987). Men in feminism: Odor di vomo or compagnons de route?. In Alice Jardine & Paul Smith (Eds.), *Men in feminism.* New York: Methuen.

Jukes, Adam. (1993). *Why men hate women,* London: Free Association Books.

Keen, Sam. (1991). *Fire in the belly: On being a man.* New York: Bantam Books.

Koutroulis, Glenda. (1993). Memory-work: A critique. In Annual Review of Health Social Science: Methodological Issues in *Health Research.* Geelong, Australia: Centre for the Study of the Body and Society, Deakin University.

Kreiner, Charlie. (1991). Interview. *Achilles Heel, 12,* 6.

Kremer, Belinda. (1990). Learning to say no: Keeping feminist research for ourselves. *Women's Studies International Forum, 13*(5), 463-467.

Kvale, Steinar. (1995). The social construction of validity. *Qualitative Inquiry, 1*(1), 19-40.

Maguire, Patricia. (1987). *Doing participatory research.* Amherst: Center for International Education, University of Massachusetts.

McLaren, Peter & da Silva, Tomaz. (1993). Decentering pedagogy: Critical literacy, resistance and the politics of memory. In Peter McLaren & Peter Leonard (Eds.), *Paulo Freire: A critical encounter* (pp. 47-89). London: Routledge.

Mills, C. Wright. (1950). *The sociological imagination,* New York: Oxford University Press.

O'Connor, Peter A. (1993). *The inner man: Men, myths and dreams.* Sydney: Sun Books.

Onyx, Jenny & Small, Jenni. (2001). Memory-work: The method, *Qualitative Inquiry, 7*(6), pp. 773-786.

Osherson, Sam. (1992). *Wrestling with love.* New York: Fawcett Columbine.

Pasick, Robert S. (1992). *Awakening from the deep sleep.* San Francisco: Harper.

Pease, Bob. (2000a). *Recreating men: Postmodern masculinity politics.* London: Sage.

Pease, Bob. (2000b). Beyond the father wound: Memory-work and the deconstruction of the father-son relationship. *Australian and New Zealand Journal of Family Therapy, 21*(1), 9-15.

Pease, Bob. (2000c). Reconstructing heterosexual subjectivities and practices with white heterosexual men. *Race, Gender and Class, 7*(1), 133-145.

Thorne-Finch, Ron. (1992). *Ending the silence: The origins and treatment of male violence against women.* Toronto: University of Toronto Press.

Touraine, Alain. (1977). *The voice and the eye: An analysis of social movements.* Cambridge: Cambridge University Press.

Touraine, Alain. (1988). *Return of the actor.* Minneapolis: University of Minnesota Press.

Vorlicky, Robert. (1990). (In)Visible alliances: Conflicting "chronicles" of feminism. In Joseph A. Boone & Michael Cadden (Eds.), *Engendering men: The question of male feminist criticism.* New York: Routledge.

Wadsworth, Yolanda & Hargreaves, Kaye. (1993). *What is feminist research?* Melbourne: Action Research Issues Association.

Weedon, Chris. (1987). *Feminist practice and poststructuralist theory.* Oxford: Basil Blackwell.

Chapter 9

Pedagogical Uses of Memory-work through Family Immigration Stories

Naomi Norquay

This chapter describes an adaptation of memory-work, a study which explores 22 students' interrogations of their family immigration stories and their own social identities in relation to those stories. These stories were assigned as an in-class presentation with an accompanying culminating short paper. Here, I demonstrate how the assignment helped the students look at the world in new ways, seeing multiple meanings. In immigration stories the dominant theme of the rugged individual lends itself to an interrogation based on memory-work tenets: retelling and reproducing stories in a collective context, purposeful juxtaposition of stories to compare and contrast, interrogation of social identities in relation to the stories, and consideration of how new stories, new information and new interpretations shift our perspectives of self in relation to others. Family immigration stories have much in common with personal memories of past experience, the bedrock of memory-work methodology (Haug, 1987, 1992), in that, when interrogated, they can reveal the extent to which "individuals have worked their way into the social world" (Haug, 1987, p. 57).

Most students who graduate from York University's Faculty of Education obtain teaching jobs in the greater Toronto area in communities that are increasingly multi-racial and multi-ethnic and home to recent immigrants and refugees. This teaching context is overburdened with a general public discourse about immigration and immigrants that often demonstrates how racism is deeply connected to anti-immigration sentiment and to the largely unspoken belief that some Canadians are more Canadian than others. One of our mandates in the teacher education program at York University is to prepare our students to teach in these two contexts: in schools with immigrant and refugee populations and in the wider social environment that is often rife with racist understandings and approaches to those populations.

When I began teaching in York's teacher education program in the early 1990's, a colleague of mine, Marcela Duran, had developed a workshop on immigration conducted with our students at the beginning of their program. The workshop consisted of students sharing what they knew of their family immigration stories with a partner. Then the students were divided into groups, based on the era in which their families immigrated. Students shared their stories in these larger groups and then, in a whole-class plenary, each group retold some of their stories to the entire class. The students were required to consider: *Who came? When? From where? What were the reasons for immigration? What hardships did they face in settlement?* This workshop was intended to challenge students' misconceptions about when different groups came to Canada and the general assumption that immigration is an individual phenomenon that is not shaped by government policy. It was also intended to acquaint them with a range of immigration experience, past and present. The workshop also led to considerations of current-day immigrant and refugee issues, particularly in relation to schools and teaching and learning.

The workshop was a one-time-only event and the only place where students' family immigration stories were explored. Following a research study in which I interviewed 20 of those students about their family immigration experiences (Norquay, 1998, 2000), I determined that there was great potential to make further use of the stories. I expanded the initial workshop by adding a take-home assignment that required students to speak with a family member about the immigration story. In the expansion of the work I added a short culminating paper, in which students were required to interrogate the family immigration story and its impact on their own identities and their sense of entitlement within Canadian contexts, especially schooling. This expansion was enhanced by several more opportunities to further share stories in class and with a partner in on-line dialogue. The process was also influenced greatly by my adaptations of Frigga Haug's memory-work methodology (1987, 1992).

I had used a form of memory-work in the past to explore my own socialization as a white person (Norquay, 1993a) and women teachers' self-understandings of being progressive educators (Norquay, 1993b; 1999a; 1999b, 2000). Although neither research project had followed Haug's initial implementation of a memory-work collective, I had been drawn to Haug's premise that as individuals we work to insert ourselves into the social world (Haug, 1987) and that our stories contain the traces of that process and of our socialization, despite our belief that it is our individuality that shapes our engagements with the world. I was convinced that juxtaposing the stories of others was an excellent way to foster the interrogation of our own stories. I wanted to explore how such interrogation and collective sharing of stories might be a key foundation in bringing about social change. In my pre-service teacher education course, I wanted to harness students' family immigration stories to enable them to see themselves not only as individuals but as participants in social, political and historical contexts. I wanted them to begin to see themselves differently, particularly in relation to the immigrant and refugee students whom they would teach. It was my hope that, like Haug's assertion about childhood situations, students would discover that their family immigration stories "were not identical with the image [they had] hitherto formed of them" and that this "might allow them to be linked, not only with [their] as-yet-unremembered past, but also with a future [they] have not yet consciously thought through" (Haug, 1987, p. 51).

While juxtaposing and sharing stories is a common activity in the university classroom (at least in teacher education), what is not so common is the act of interrogation, nor the pedagogical intent to shift students' understandings of how their stories demonstrate their locations in the social world. These aspects of memory-work are highly compelling and easily transferable to the pre-service teacher education university classroom. Memory-work was employed for its pedagogical potential, rather than its efficacy as a research methodology. I believed it would be useful in supporting the aims of the immigration portion of the course. The aims were to correct inaccurate information and fill gaps in students' knowledge about Canadian immigration; signal that personal and familial stories are valid resources for teaching and learning; provide a supportive space for immigrants and children of immigrants to challenge the myths other Canadians have about immigration and immigrants; disrupt the largely unspoken assumption that not having an immigration story cements one's identity as always having been here. I should note here that the intent of the assignment was not to uncover the authentic ethnic or cultural identity of each student (which might be somehow revealed through access to an immigration story). Rather, we explored identity in relation to the myth of authenticity which operates as a device to deem some Canadians more Canadian than others, and to shackle the identities of immigrants to narrow stereotypes determined by the dominant groups.

Where my work differs from Haug's is in the focus on family stories, rather than on memories of personal experience. While there were always students in my classes who were themselves immigrants, and therefore the bearers of memories of personal immigrant experience, the majority of my students were not immigrants. What is interesting is that immigrant students also shaped their stories of their experiences in relation to the many myths of about immigration and immigrants. The assignment proved to be just as useful for them as it was for the 1st, 2nd and 3rd+ generation Canadians. Their lived experience was folded into the mix of stories that were juxtaposed. Collectively we worked "to prevent a simple duplication of the everyday, with all its prejudices and lack of theoretical insight" (Haug, 1992, p.17), wherein newcomers to Canada face a

range of prejudices and assumptions about who they are and who they can become within the Canadian landscape.

The data on which this chapter is based come from two written assignments
(an in-class assignment sheet and a small culminating paper), as well as class-
generated statistics on various aspects of immigration experience, from two co-
horts of students (1999–2000 and 2000–2001). (See Appendix A for details of
the assignments.) All student names and those of their family members have
been changed to pseudonyms.

In the sections that follow I take up the different stages of the overall assignment (the in-class activity, the take-home assignment, and the final paper)
and examine how students' initial responses and stories shift over the course of
the assignment. I end with a discussion about the possibilities and limitations of
memory-work within an educational context that calls stories of immigration
and identity into question.

"I don't have an immigration story:" Students' initial engagements with their stories

When students embarked on the in-class assignment, they did not yet
know each other and they did not know me. After going over the course syllabus
for the fall term, I handed out the in-class assignment sheet and instructed the
students to fill it in as best they could. "This is not a test." I joked. "You don't
need to answer every question to get an A." Anxiety levels were high at the beginning of the year and I knew that many students would have little or no information about their family's immigration history. My humor was intended to help
drop the anxiety level a notch or two.

I did not take lightly my request to students to divulge personal stories. I
was aware that students needed coaxing and encouragement to respond to this
request, as it was not an equitable one. Students' initial responses to it varied:
Some students who were themselves immigrants, or the children or grand-
children of immigrants, welcomed this assignment because they knew some
version of that immigration story. Others resented a request that they interpreted
as sedimenting (yet again!) the label immigrant, a label they felt they must wear
in Canadian contexts, especially in schooling contexts. Some students whose
families had been in Canada for generations, might have known their family
histories and were pleased to share them. But for others in this group the assignment often provoked puzzlement ("Immigration story? I don't have one!"),
frustration ("I don't know that history and no one in my family knows that history"), or anxiety ("How am I going to find this out? Can I do the assignment if I
can not?").

For this latter group of students the assignment summoned them to stories
they neither knew nor believed existed. Immigration did not factor in their identity construction. They were, for the most part, students whose families had been
in Canada for at least two generations, who were of Anglo or Anglicized origins,

and who were white. My experience has been that these students always found the story! They were always able to complete the assignment. Of interest to me here, is why at the outset they did not have a story and what sense they made of that over the course of the assignment. Their responses, such as enthusiasm, reluctance and anxiety, became important as we began to connect identity formation to the presence or absence of an immigration story.

In the week following the in-class assignment, the students read the first chapter of John Willinksy's (1998) book, *Learning to divide the world: Education at empire's end,* in which he explores why issues of ethnicity and nationality seem to matter to some students but not to others. In a study wherein he researched electronic communication in schooling, he collected the statements Vancouver (Canada) high school students had posted to their on-line pen pals in Australia. Sarah Huang wrote: "I have black eyes and hair. As you can tell from my last name you should know that I am Chinese" (p. 6). Another student wrote: "My name is Robert Campbell and I am a Libra" (p. 8). And another: "As to my appearance I'm chinese [sic] and very short. . . . Obviously I have long black hair parted down the middle and brown eyes." Finally: "I am 15 . . . with blonde hair and blue eyes. I'm pretty short. I was captain of the cheerleading squad. . . ." (p. 7). Willinsky notes that "the play of race and ethnicity in identity is not necessarily everyone's affair. . . ." (p. 8). For White-Anglo Canadians, identity is rarely troubled by the signification of here as opposed to there; their Canadian identity and sense of belonging are assumed. Summoning university students to recall and tell family immigration stories put here and there and the issues of ethnicity, nation and belonging on the identity map and challenged the unspoken assumption that some students had that identity just *is.*

By insisting that students share their stories, all students (even those who initially had no story) participated in the collective process of coming to a greater understanding of immigration and immigrant experience and how identity might be fashioned in the presence or the absence of a story. The students, as a class, became, as Haug suggests, "investigators with a common purpose, knowledgeable people who can supply fragments which [can be] used to create the social totality" (1992, p. 19).

Nothing taught this as well as the students meeting in "era of immigration" groups and sharing their stories. (See Appendix A, #2 for details of the immigration eras.) The first learning came when they looked around the classroom and saw how each group reflected Canada's immigration policies as they changed over time. For example, the sizable groups of white students in the immigration eras before 1952 reflected the preference Canada had in the 19th century and first half of the 20th century for charter group immigrants and immigrants from northern Europe. That there was rarely anyone in the group for 1929–1945 reflected Canada's decision to virtually shut down immigration at that time (Abella & Troper, 1982). The large number of students with Italian and Greek surnames in the group for 1952-1966 reflected the massive immigration from southern Europe that was encouraged at that time. Finally, there was a large heterogeneous group of students in the post-1976 group, when Canada established a refugee class and opened its doors to the world. This visual display of how individual immigration reflects immigration policy was very powerful and for many students the first realization that Canada's immigration policies have always shaped who have made their homes here.

While those without stories may have lacked knowledge of their own origins, the collective nature of this story-recall helped all students recognize that their individual stories were not their only source of information about immigrant experience and that other people's stories were rich resources for anyone who one day would be the teacher of immigrant and refugee children, and all those students who, like them, believe they do not have an immigration history. The assumption that our stories are the only source of our identity formation and that it is the uniqueness of the stories that makes them important to others was disrupted (Haug, 1992).

Through the sharing and juxtaposition of both similar and divergent stories, students learned that what they had assumed were individual hardships were actually experienced by many—across both time (immigration era) and space (regions of origin around the globe). For example, a student whose Mennonite ancestors fled religious persecution in Germany in the 1850's learned that a fellow student's Jewish grandparents also fled religious persecution in Russia in the 1920's. Both heard the story of an Ismaili classmate whose family fled Uganda in the 1970's. A student, whose name was changed by a well-meaning immigration officer when she emigrated from Hong Kong as a child, learned that a classmate of Italian descent has an Anglicized last name, courtesy of a late 19th century employer who refused to spell out the long family name of her great-grandfather. The daughter of a British "war bride" shared the story of her mother's hardships with a classmate whose wife was still waiting to emigrate from Pakistan.

In this initial public sharing, the students learned that their particular family stories were as much an effect of social and political forces, as they were the effect of personal choices, perseverance and rugged individualism. For those students who had no story, all this information gave them places to start looking and to start asking questions. For those who initially regarded as unfair my request that they engage stories they did not know, the in-class assignment provided a place where this state of initial disequilibrium actually could initiate critical questioning. One such student reflected on this in her final paper.

> I remember feeling so ordinary as I sat with my peers in class the day we broke into groups by immigration date. I was in the 1820—1860 group. Most of us had English/Irish/Scottish backgrounds—most of us knew little more. I wondered why it was our stories were not important to our families. Why were they not passed on?

What had begun as anxiety about not knowing an immigration story became a place to interrogate why that might be the case.

The sun never sets: The long arm of British imperial rule

Willinsky (1998) argues that although the British empire is a mere shadow of its former self, its legacies of language, education and traditions have made an indelible imprint on the parts of the world that it colonized. The empire created centers and margins through its shaping of various social identities, such as race, class, religion, and language, into haves and have nots. This became the process that destined certain subject positions to be "the other." It also made the pervasive power of the process seemingly invisible to those it claimed as it own. This has produced generations of anglophones who assume both the neutrality and centrality of their identities to what it might mean to be a Canadian. Just as Anglo students often believe that they do not have an immigration story, so is the Anglo aspect of their identity something they take for granted without being able to actually see it being reproduced in the immigration stories.

In the initial plenary discussion, students learned how Canada's relationship to Great Britain (first as a colony and then as a member of the Commonwealth) predisposed immigration to reflect that relationship throughout its immigration history. For students of Anglo origins, this connection was often invisible and taken for granted. Students who did not know their stories most often guessed that their families came from Great Britain. They stated this with an amazing certainty, convinced that the absence of stories of speaking another language and the presence of an Anglicized surname assured their origins as British. However, this assumption of origins did not translate into a hyphenated Canadian identity. Once stated, it disappeared into an identity of just Canadian.

In their final papers, many students commented on both the centrality and invisibility of this Anglo identity, suggesting that they had begun to question the assumptions about identity held in place by their stories. Morgan's paper demonstrates one of the effects of the assignment's requirements that the students engage course readings and discussions in their reflections on their family immigration stories and their own sense of identity and entitlement. She was hopeful that a relative's research into the family's past would help her better understand the extent to which privileged families like her own "became Canadians as an extension of their Imperialist heritage."

Although Camille's English mother "remained forever detached from England," Camille believed,

> England was my motherland and that England had saved the world from tyranny. . . . In my mind, the Queen was my personal queen to whom I sang every morning and whose picture hung in every classroom. I felt particularly special because I was the only one to have an English mother.

Even though her mother did not encourage the connection to England,
Camille knew that being English provided her with a particular cultural capital
when she was growing up, a cultural capital that made the English queen central
to Canadian identity, as head of state.

Rebecca's mother was the daughter of an English woman and her father
was the son of an Austrian-Italian woman "who immigrated to Canada with her
Irish husband." "I was raised with this story but was always aware that my
mother disparaged my father's family and thought hers was better." Joyce, a
fifth generation Canadian on her father's side, suggested that for her ancestors,
"arriving in Canada was almost like an extended trip to another part of England.
I feel we [didn't] deserve to call ourselves immigrants."

Non-white students, whose families had immigrated to Canada from other
parts of the British empire, also acknowledged the centrality of British imperialism to their families' experiences. Joanne's parents immigrated to Canada from
England hoping to escape the racism they had experienced growing up there, as
the children of Jamaican immigrants.

> My father said it was disheartening to transport yourself thousands of miles
> only to find the same people and attitudes you left behind. Canada was full of
> English, both United Empire Loyalists and recent immigrants, who did not con-
> sider themselves to be immigrants at all.

Monica's family had been a part of the elite in Pakistan. She wrote about
how her grandparents' families belonged to an elite class of educated and
wealthy people who were accepted by the closed English circle. They socialized
with influential people and their thinking was greatly influenced by their "Imperial rulers."

"Imperial rulers" as Willinsky points out, establish and maintain the
boundaries between the center and the margins by exoticizing the other. Sonya
observed how this practice helps maintain the boundaries between who belongs
and who does not.

> Even though my family has been here for nearly twenty-five years, and for the
> most part identify themselves as Canadians, we still keep much of our culture
> alive. . . . It is funny, because within the last year so many [white] celebrities
> have started to wear South Asian outfits, painting their hands and bodies with
> mendi, wearing toe rings, getting their noses pierced and wearing bindis on
> their foreheads (all forms of Indian culture) and it is considered cool and sexy,
> like a new fashion trend. But if an Indian woman were to walk around wearing
> stuff like that she would be treated or looked at like she did not belong. So on
> the one hand immigrants are expected to give up their culture to fit in, but on
> the other hand, light skinned people are looked at as trendy when they adopt the
> culture and styles of immigrants. This makes no sense to me.

These observations by the non-white students in the class did not go unnoticed by the white-Anglo students, many of whom used these critical lenses to reassess their own family stories. Pamela was one of two students in the study whose roots in Canada date back to the 1700's. Pamela's mother had told her that their ancestors were United Empire Loyalists. She did not know any more than that, but Pamela noted that her mother "has always only spoken of a British ancestry." Her family's long history in Canada produced a very particular kind of Canadian identity.

> Though I was taught from an early age that racism and discriminatory practices were wrong, there was still a discriminating line established simply by the fact that we did not consider ourselves immigrants.

What is key to all of these statements is the assumed centrality of an Anglo identity to a Canadian identity and more importantly, to a sense of entitlement to the center, not the margins of the Canadian social landscape (Bannerji, 1997; Roman & Stanley, 1997). Subsumed in this English identity is a racial one. Whiteness as a prerequisite for belonging surfaced in an interesting way in Tara's story. Her parents immigrated from Hungary in 1956 and Tara was born in Canada.

> I have never considered myself Hungarian. After one of our lecture discussions where we discussed visible versus invisible minorities, I thought about how when I look in the mirror, I see a Canadian face looking back. It surprised me and almost shocked me when I realized that if I was born in another country (Hungary), I would be looking at a Hungarian face.

Tara, I think, was pointing to context. But she was also signaling that a Canadian face is a European face—a white face.

"For a better life!" and other clichés

The in-class assignment required students to think about the reasons why their families came to Canada. Overwhelmingly, students listed "for a better life!" as the reason for immigration. The overuse of this term suggests that the students did not really know the reasons for immigration and "for a better life" seemed like a good bet. It is a cliché that supports one of the myths of Canadian immigration that Canada is always a better place than the immigrant's country of origin, and because it is better, immigrants should be grateful and should not complain. Other overused clichés included: "he thought the streets were paved with gold!" and "he thought he'd try his luck." These clichés might be seen to suggest that immigration is a choice, something someone chooses amongst other options, something that results from a desire for adventure, or something decided on a whim. The cliché, Haug suggests, "assumes consensus" (1987, p. 62) and "effectively puts a stop to thought and understanding" (1992,

p. 23), thereby working against further interrogation. The prevalence of these clichés could be readily illuminated for students with a simple show of hands. This process of situating individual stories within larger social contexts worked to enhance students' curiosity about the gaps in their stories, made invisible by the clichés "which ha[ve] lost any specific embodied reference" (Davies, 2000, p. 49). The collective work with the initial immigration stories encouraged them to probe beneath the often tidy versions of the story they remembered from earlier times.

In Irene's account of her conversation with her mother she noted,

> The first obvious question that I asked my mother is: Why did you and dad come to Canada? Without hesitation, she answered: For a better life. I immediately thought back to my first seminar with Naomi, where this reason, along with more opportunities, rated highest for immigration to Canada. I recalled Naomi saying how reasons for immigrating to Canada usually stemmed from something driving people out of their own country. This was when I learned that my father lost his job at the oil refinery in Greece.

Luisa, who had initially listed "for a better life" as the reason for immigration, learned, when asking her mother about the reasons for immigration, that her father's livelihood as an independent fisherman was ended when "he was threatened by men who wanted to control the fishing industry." In revisiting the well-known story of her family's 18th century immigration to Nova Scotia, Abigail was "surprised to realize that he left England in order to avoid debtor's prison." What is interesting about these three accounts is that they challenge the assumption that immigration is a choice among many choices and not a decision of last resort.

Also challenged was the version of events passed down from parent to child. It was only after Irene insisted, that her mother elaborated on her assertion that immigrating was "for a better life." She may have intended to shield her daughter from traumatic events that often accompany the immigrant's journey from homeland to Canada. That my students revisited their family immigration stories as adults increased the possibility that unsavory or painful details absent from earlier versions might be added to the stories, as their relatives weighed the benefits of such knowledge in the hands of future teachers. Simon, Rosenberg and Eppert (2000) suggest that such instances treat remembrance as a strategic and a hopeful return: if something bad is remembered, it is to help ensure that it does not happen again. As future teachers, my students might be able to play a role in ensuring a better future for immigrant and refugee children if they more fully understand the past.

Another prevalent detail hidden in these clichés is that they were most often about male relatives ("he thought the streets were paved with gold," "he thought he'd try his luck"). Female relatives (wives, mothers, daughters) were present mainly as followers and their stories were seldom told in the initial tellings.

They were usually seen as the passive bystanders of the decisions made by their male relatives (Haug, 1987, 1992; Chamberlain, 1997). Upon interrogation, Luisa learned that it was her mother and not her father who initiated their immigration to Canada. Contrary to her initial assumption that her father made the decision to emigrate, the family's immigration to Canada was initiated by her mother who was "worried about [her husband's] safety." Several students who had initially told the immigration story of a male relative decided to pursue the story of a female relative for their final paper. In every case, it was a story they had not previously known. Haug suggests that "[w]hen feelings, thoughts and experiences are ignored in their concrete reality, and are only spoken of, as it were, from a great height, it becomes difficult to speak of women's experiences in a narrative form without a special effort" (Haug, 1992, p. 24).

Another myth of Canadian immigration that is supported by clichés such as "for a better life" and "the streets were paved with gold," is that immigrants follow a "rags to riches" trajectory, starting from humble beginnings in Canada and, through hard work and determination, pulling themselves up by their own bootstraps. The immigrant is usually understood as someone in need, not someone of means. Rarely did students assume that their ancestors came to Canada from places of relative privilege. Bernice, for example, did not know that her grandmother, who had immigrated from the United States, married the son of her father's lawyer, or that her grandmother's "American relatives ensured that she maintained a comfortable life." Her assumption had been that because she had immigrated her grandmother would have faced some form of economic hardship. Upon investigation, Morgan learned that her great-grandfather had been a plantation owner and a member of the legislature, prior to his emigration from Jamaica in the early 1900's. Learning that her family came from this kind of privilege produced in Morgan the need to know more:

> [M]y history disturbed me because of the missing information. Did my family exploit black labour? Did they espouse slavery? A distant relative of mine is currently piecing together a history of this family and I hope to have these questions answered.

By taking a second look at their family immigration stories, the students learned that the clichés that populated their stories played an active role in holding in place "the well-trodden path of that which should be" (Haug, 1987, p. 63). By noting them, they were able to dig around them to uncover immigrant experience that challenged the pervasive myths of Canadian immigration.

Compare and contrast: The power of juxtaposition

The in-class and take-home assignments were purposefully supported by numerous opportunities to share and juxtapose immigrant stories, through sharing with a partner, meeting in immigrant era groups and reporting back what was learned in the take-home assignment. On-line discussion with a partner through close readings of weekly course material that included many first person accounts of immigration and the struggle for identity, class discussions, films, and lectures in which I shared my own stories of immigration and efforts to locate myself differently in relation to others provided additional opportunities. The final papers required students to engage at least two of these encounters; they had to consider other people's stories as well as their own. They were, in this way, forced to insert their individual stories into a larger collective context that ranged across time (immigration eras) and space (regions of origin). They were required to consider themselves in relation to others. The intent was to produce a complex reading of their stories that ruptured the assumption that experience is simply "telling" and that identity results from experience. Through this process some students experienced affirmation of their stories and their investments in them, while others experienced challenges, and some experienced both.

Affirmation was an important issue for Sharon.

Being Jewish, I never felt the need to question why my family came to Canada. I had never specifically asked anyone why our families immigrated until I received this assignment. Being a European Jew, it was simply assumed that my ancestors were persecuted in their place of origin. Of the classmates I spoke with, the only ones who could correctly and accurately assume the reason for immigrating were other Jews. In our case, the search for a "better life" meant searching for a place where life would not only be better, but also safer.

Sharon acknowledged the importance of having her family story affirmed by others, but in so doing, signalled the potential for others to learn from her story: her version of "a better life" included safety from persecution.

Colleen acknowledged how her mother's English as a second language (ESL) experiences were put into an important educational context by her on-line partner.

In her close reading of "Growing up Ukrainian in Toronto" (Diakiw, 1994), [my on-line partner] states that she is amazed by people who are intolerant of "new Canadians" who do not speak English very well. It is interesting that we are amazed by people's intolerance when we experience it everyday in some form or another. [My on-line partner] also discusses how this intolerance impacts the ESL student and how many of us do not realize the challenges an ESL student must face. My mother was treated poorly and often experienced prejudice because of her inability to speak English.

Often, students did not recognize their immigrant relatives as ESL learners; they usually saw them as lacking, rather than as individuals who had a substantial skill set in their first language. Colleen's on-line partner's comment enabled Colleen to make a connection between her mother's experience and those of the ESL children in her host classroom. In comparison, the focus on those immigrants who struggled to learn English, highlighted in Fiona's case, her father's advantage. By comparing his experience to that of other immigrants, Fiona reflected on her father's "lovely Irish accent" and how his experience of having an accent differed from that of some of her classmates.

> My father's accent was considered charming, instead of mitigating against him, it was an advantage. Some of my classmates reported that their family members experienced discrimination based on their "non-Canadian" accents. My father's experience illustrates that accents and ethnicities are valued differently. . . . I conclude from the seminar discussion that my father indeed experienced privilege, having a "lovely accent" and [an] appealing ethnicity.

Rebecca gained an interesting insight into her family's immigration when she contrasted the story with those of others in the class.

> I was struck with the fact that people whose forebears immigrated at roughly the same time as my grandmother had much humbler socio-economic status than later immigrants. Perhaps this is due to the state of the world then, but I think not. I'm aware that Canada's immigration policy with its point system now favours the skilled, educated and even prosperous emigré. I feel humbled to think that, if judged by today's criteria, my relatives wouldn't have made the cut.

Similarly, Monica reassessed her family's good fortunes.

> When I view my family history from the perspective of discussion in class about meritocracy and "bootstrapism" I begin to wonder whether my parents really did pull themselves up by their own bootstraps. It seems to me they had always been above everyone else to begin with. Yes, my father worked hard in his job in Saudi [Arabia], but so did the Pakistani street cleaners who were treated like dirt. My family was "extended the gift of civilization" and they were privileged enough to have an "educated view of the world" allowing them to belong to the "civilized" elite and not the disadvantaged "primitive" (Willinsky, 1998).

Students, across immigration eras and regions of origin, utilized other people's stories to interrogate their own. Pamela reflected this way.

> For me, the culmination of our course readings and discussions has made me critically examine "who is a Canadian," "how can one Canadian's experiences in the educational system be vastly different than another's," and most importantly, "why?" Over the past month I have covered a lot of ground in my personal pondering of these questions. For every time I have asked myself these questions, I have formulated a new and different answer. Admittedly, I feel less and less comfortable with my previous assumptions about who I was in relation

to who everybody else was, here in Canada. A close inspection of my immigration story reveals an obvious lack of information. My upbringing was based on
a blatant understanding that I was "from here".... I thought I had egalitarian
views, I thought I embraced multiculturalism in this country. What I see now
was me, behaving as if I was a hostess, welcoming everyone to my country.

Joyce's reassessment of who she was in relation to others also suggests that
the assignment challenged her identity and her assumptions about others in important ways.

Interrogating my family story in relation to our course has caused me some discomfort. I realize that my family had it relatively easy when I read and hear
some of the stories of other immigrants who arrived in Canada. . . . As Diakiw
said in his article, "It's always a WASP who understands what a Canadian is.
They want us to be like them" (Diakiw, 1994, p. 55). I grew up with this view-
point. I can remember saying exactly the same thing about more recent immigrants to Canada. I couldn't understand why they couldn't just be like us. . . . If
they wanted to keep their language and their culture, I couldn't understand why
they couldn't go back to where they came from and leave us with our nice
WASP country! What universe was I living in? . . . I have carried throughout
my life my perceptions through Anglo eyes. . . . Now I have faced these perceptions I have changed my views so I will look at myself and others from a
Canadian outlook instead of an Anglo one.

I suggest that Joyce has repositioned a "Canadian outlook" to be a multicultural one.

Final discussion

Here, I discuss three issues that I believe are important to the pedagogical
uses of memory-work methodologies: student resistance, uncovering past
trauma, and using research methodologies pedagogically.

Although I found that most students learned in transformative ways from
the assignment, some students resisted the assignment and, instead, sedimented
their subject positions and their views of the world. (These instances are hard to
study because resistant students rarely take up my invitation to give me a copy
of their final papers for research purposes.) Generally speaking, resistant students refused engagement with their family's stories, providing only summary
comments instead. Many of these comments were akin to the clichés of "a better
life" that populate the initial in-class assignment. Injustice, intolerance, inequities of any kind were not revealed, assumed, or imagined. These students usually
viewed their own identities and circumstances as solely the result of individual
hard work or personal luck. Their analyses of their family stories often mirrored
those found by Sleeter in her study of white American teachers.

Sleeter (1993, p. 165) observes that "the symbolic meaning Euroamericans
attach to ethnicity today upholds the ideology of individuality and mobility with

an open system and the myth that everyone came to the U.S. in search of a better life and had to work equally hard to better themselves." One of her research participants, a daughter of Italian immigrants, expressed this view.

> One of my pet peeves, that I know if you want to work, you can work. . . . I know what my father did when he was in need, . . . and we didn't have the free lunches and we didn't have the clothes that other kids wore (Sleeter, 1993, p. 161).

One student who did give me a copy of her paper echoed Sleeter's student.

> [My great-grandfather] immigrated to Canada in 1906. He came by himself, at the age of 14 years, hopefully to find a job. He found work in farming and must have felt good enough about Canada because 6 years later he went back to England to get his mother and father. . . . He worked hard and always had a job. . . . He saw, in Canada, a country that had opportunity and he was willing to do his part to make it great. . . . I came to realize, long ago, that many people don't start out life with advantages that many people take for granted. Not everything, however, can be put down to class or cultural identity. I believe strongly that attitude and self-confidence contribute greatly to the process.

I have often read this kind of response as resistance, stemming from narrow-mindedness or mainstream defensiveness, which is readily supported by the widely held belief that the successful integration of the immigrant into mainstream society depends solely on that individual's willingness, gumption and hard work (Harney & Troper, 1975). Schick (2000) suggests that this kind of student resistance is both predictable and pervasive. Schick found that amongst her white middle class students, the desire not to know and the need to maintain a kind of liberal do-good innocence drives student resistance to course materials that engage evidence of inequity and injustice (Schick, 2000, pp. 84-85). Despite my attempts to challenge this belief through readings, class discussions and opportunities for students to share their families' stories with each other, some students resisted entertaining the possibility that their ancestors' "hard work" for a "better life" might have contained any injustice, violence or loss, or that they had had opportunities denied to others. Perhaps student resistance is a good indicator of Haug's insistence that we often iron out the contradictions in our lives so that they become "forgotten and omitted; left unperceived" (1987, p. 40). While this resistance did sometimes wear down as the year progressed and subsequent seminars and assignments engaged other aspects of identity and issues of equity and social justice, it seems to me that the old adage "you can lead a horse to water but you can't make him drink" rings true here. When presented as a pedagogy, rather than a research methodology which people may choose or not choose to partake in, memory-work is not immune to resistance. An irony here is that resistance is one the best justifications for employing memory-work as a pedagogy! Whether manifested in the form of clichéd responses or in the form of uninterrogated gaps and silences within the stories themselves (Haug, 1992), student resistance reminds me that my power as the teacher in the classroom is always up for challenge.

It is that power that summons students to find out about their family's pasts. This is never a neutral or innocent request and it is one that always runs the risk of having students come face to face with past trauma. Reasons for immigration often contain some kind of violence: political, economic, familial, etc. Settlement in Canada almost invariably includes experiences that are traumatic for the immigrant. Consider Luisa's revelation that what she thought was simply a choice "for a better life" actually had been a flight from violence. Morgan learned that her ancestors had been plantation owners and worried about their connection to work place violence: "Did they exploit black labour? Did they espouse slavery?"

When Irene spoke with her mother about her immigration experience she learned for the first time that her mother had had an abortion.

> My first attempt at filling out the sheet on my family history produced a skeletal outline with many gaps. It was not until I sat down with my mother that I really learned of some of the hardships that my parents experienced. . . . During my family's initial few months in Canada, my mother became pregnant. Women she hardly knew, told her that landlords in Toronto would never rent a place to a family with three children. As a result, she had an illegal abortion, which almost killed her.

It is stories such as these that give me pause and have me wondering whether the benefits of the immigration assignment outweigh the risks. While such risks are present in any memory-work endeavor, I wonder what my responsibilities are when I unleash the summons to tell family stories and to interrogate them. To ponder this question I turn to Roger Simon et al. (2000) who explore pedagogical uses of traumatic remembrance, particularly of the Holocaust. While they are concerned with the purposeful summoning of traumatic events, not the accidental, they make the point that "remembrance is aligned with the anticipation of a reconciled future in which one hopes that justice and harmonious social relations might be secured" (p. 4). I would argue that Irene's mother judged that her daughter was old enough to know about the abortion, and that in telling her about it she possibly signalled a desire for a better future for other immigrant women. That her daughter, Irene, was a teacher candidate perhaps made it even more urgent to tell this story.

I will close with an anecdote about a former student, who participated in a research project about beginning teachers[1]. When a student in my class, she had been one of those with an unknown immigration story, one who had initially questioned the use the family immigration assignment would have for teachers. On a field visit to her grade five classroom, I witnessed the students participating in a sharing time in which they took voluntary turns reading pieces they had written for a unit of study called "We Welcome All Nations." The unit was part of the Family Studies program for grade five students, in a Catholic elementary school. The students had had a choice of either interviewing a senior family member about their family's immigration history, or, writing a reflection on a poem about acceptance and tolerance they had read in class. Several students shared their writing.

The pieces on family immigration histories were very interesting. One student had a Jewish grandmother who had survived the Holocaust; another's grandparents had spent time in a DP camp after the Second World War; another told a story about her parents' first encounter with Canadian winters; and another talked about his older brother's struggles to make friends after his family immigrated to Canada from Bosnia. The reflections on the poem were very sincere, and the students reflected on the poem's message in hopeful ways. It was, however, the family stories that sparked a very interesting class discussion about social difference, equity and justice. I noted that the students wanted to know so much more than the written stories had told. For example, they wanted to know what a DP was and how the grandmother had managed to survive the Holocaust. One child compared the devastation of WWII to his knowledge of a tornado that had struck a camping ground. Unfortunately, other time demands of the day brought this lively discussion to an unfinished end.

In a later interview with the teacher, I asked her about her decision to give students a choice. She explained that she had given the students the choice because she knew some children would not have access to family stories, either because the people who could tell them were not around or because families might not even know the stories. By giving her students a choice, she concluded, no child would be put in the situation of having to seek out stories that his or her family might not wish to tell.

Besides learning much about Canadian immigration and her own identity as an Anglo-Canadian in my class, she had also come to appreciate that asking children to tell the story of their families' immigration is not an innocent request. Her strategy was to make that request one of choice for her young students. While I believe no educator summoning students to memory-work should ignore the risks involved in such a summons, I do believe that there is more risk when children are involved. While I do not advocate that my students replicate the family immigration assignment in their own classrooms, many, such as the teacher in my anecdote, find themselves compelled by the province of Ontario's standard curriculum to elicit such stories from their students. By the end of Grade Two, for example, students must "trace a family tree, conducting interviews with family members to learn a lesson about their place in history" (McCann, 1999, p. C5). Critics of this particular requirement question its age appropriateness and its ethical dimensions.

While I made it quite explicit that my family immigration assignment was not to be repeated in my students' practicum placement classrooms, I am heartened that the complexity of the lessons learned through the assignment produced thoughtful and careful pedagogical decisions such as the one described above in the work of this beginning teacher.

Memory-work comes with complex requests and elicits unexpected results. I foresee replicating the immigration assignment within the context of a graduate course wherein memory-work is taken up as a research methodology, with the immigration assignment as the vehicle for exploring that methodology. Such a project would enable further probing of not only the family immigration stories, but also participants' iterations of those stories. No doubt, even deeper insights into immigration and immigrant experience would be gained.

Notes

1. The research project, *Beginning teachers constructions of social equity and social difference*, received funding from the Social Sciences and Humanities Research Council of Canada, 2000 - 2004.

2. Items marked with an asterisk (*) in the References are required material for the family immigration assignment.

References

Abella, Irving M. & Troper, Harold M. (1982). *None is too many:Canada and the Jews of Europe, 1933–1948*, Toronto: Orpen & Dennys.

*Atwood, Margaret. (1993). First Neighbours [from The Journals of Susanna Moodie]. In Peter Fanning & Maggie Goh, (Eds.), *Home and homeland: The Canadian immigrant experience* (pp. 34-35). Toronto: Addison-Wesley Publishers Limited.

Bannerji, Himani. (1997). Geography lessons: On being an insider / outsider to the Canadian Nation. In Leslie G. Roman & Linda Eyre (Eds.) *Dangerous territories: Struggles for difference and equality in Education* (pp. 23-41). New York: Routledge.

Chamberlain, Mary. (1997). Gender and the narratives of migration, *History Workshop Journal, 43*, 87-108.

Davies, Bronwyn. (2000). *(In)scribing body / landscape relations*, Walnut Creek, CA: Altamira Press.

*Diakiw, Jerry. (1994). Growing up Ukrainian in Toronto. In C.E. James & A. Shadd (Eds.), *Talking about difference: Encounters in culture, language and identity* (pp. 49-55). Toronto: Between the Lines Press.

*Fukushima, Michael. (1992). *Minoru: Memory in exile*, National Film Board of Canada (video).

Harney, Robert & Troper, Harold. (1975). *Immigrants: A portrait of the urban experience*. Toronto: Van Nostrand Reinhold.

Haug, Frigga (Ed.). (1987). *Female Sexualization: A collective work of memory* (Erica Carter, trans.). London: Verso Press.

Haug, Frigga. (1992). *Beyond female masochism: Memory-work and politics*, (Rodney Livingstone, trans.). London: Verso Press.

McCann, Wendy. (1999, March 4). Tracing family roots can hurt kids, advocates say, *The Toronto Star*, p. C5.

*Meyers, Mary. (1994). *Teaching to diversity: Teaching and learning in the multi-ethnic classroom*. Reading, MA: Addison-Wesley Publishers.

*Norquay, Naomi. (1993a). The other side of difference: Memory-work in the mainstream. *International Journal of Qualitative Studies in Education, 6*(3), 241-251.

Norquay, Naomi. (1993b). *Uses of memory: Women, schooling and social difference.* Unpublished doctoral dissertation, University of Toronto, Toronto, Ontario, Canada.

*Norquay, Naomi. (1998). Family Immigration (hi)stories and the construction of identity. *Curriculum Studies, 6*(2), 177-190.

Norquay, Naomi. (1999a). Identity and forgetting. *Oral History Review, 26*(1), 1-21.Norquay, Naomi. (1999b). Who rebels? Gender and class in stories of irreverence and resistance. *International Journal of Qualitative Studies in Education, 12*(4), 417-431.

Norquay, Naomi. (2000). Where is here? *Pedagogy, culture and society, 8(1)*, 7-21.

*Norquay, Naomi; Tran, Thang; & Tachuk, Laudie. (1994). *Van can use chopsticks!* Unpublished manuscript, York University, Faculty of Education.

Roman, Leslie G. & Stanley, Timothy J. (1997). Empires, emigres and aliens: Young people's negotiations of official and popular racism in Canada. In Leslie.G. Roman & Linda Eyre (Eds.), *Dangerous territories: Struggles for difference and equality in education* (pp. 205-231). New York: Routledge.

Schick, Carol. (2000). "By virtue of being White: Resistance to anti-racist pedagogy". *Race, Ethnicity and Education, 3*(1), 79-94.

Simon, Roger I.; Rosenberg, Sharon; & Eppert, Claudia. (2000). Introduction: The Pedagogical encounter of historical remembrance. In Roger Simon, Sharon Rosenberg & Claudia Eppert (Eds.), *Between hope and despair: Pedagogy and remembrance of historical trauma* (pp.1-8). Lanham, MD: Rowman and Littlefield Publishers Inc.

Sleeter, Christine. (1993). White teachers construct race. In Cameron McCarthy & Warren Crichlow (Eds.), *Race, identity and representation in education* (pp. 157-171). New York: Routledge.

*Szepesi, Katalin. (1994). I want to call myself Canadian. In Carl E. James & Adrienne L. Shadd (Eds.), *Talking about difference: Encounters in culture, language and identity* (pp. 29-30). Toronto: Between the Lines Press.

*Szepesi, Katalin. (1994). "Hello. . . . My name is. . . ." In Carl E. James & Adrienne L. Shadd (Eds.), *Talking about difference: Encounters in culture, language and identity* (p. 31). Toronto: Between the Lines Press.

*Willinsky, John. (1998). *Learning to divide the world: Education at empire's end.* Minneapolis: University of Minnesota Press.

Appendix A

In-class Assignment / Activity

1. Students fill out a sheet on their family immigration history. They must choose one side of their family's story to tell. The sheet asks them to provide information about the following:

> When did your family come to Canada? Country/region of origin.
> Who came?
> Age at time of immigration.
> Languages spoken.
> Education/Occupation (in country of origin).
> Reasons for emigrating.
> Who was left behind?
> Contacts upon arrival. Initial settlement in Canada.
> Employment.
> Schooling opportunities.
> Difficulties encountered.
> Experiences of "becoming a Canadian."
> How do you know this information?
> Look at the similarities and differences between you and your
> partner's experiences and consider the reasons for these. In the
> space below record your thoughts on this discussion and what
> you have learned about yourself and your partner.

2. The students then meet in "immigration era groups" that correspond to migration and immigration practices and policies in New France, British North America and Canada: pre-1600; 1600-1820; 1821-1860; 1861-1890; 1890-1913; 1914-1929; 1930-1945; 1946-1951; 1952-1966; 1967-1976; 1976 to the present.

In these groups they share their stories and fill out a group chart that asks for information regarding country/region of origin and reasons for immigration.

I do a statistical analysis of these charts and use this analysis for further exploration and class discussion.

3. The students interview a family member about their family immigration story and fill out a sheet. The sheet is the same as the in-class assignment with the added question: What information recorded above is "new" to you? Once completed, the students return to class and compare it with the sheet they filled out in class and they discuss their findings with their initial partner.

4. Students interrogate their own stories and others' stories, supported by class discussions, lectures about immigration policies and practices, a film about the internment and subsequent deportation of Japanese-Canadians during and after World War Two, several first person accounts of immigration and immi-

grant identity, scholarly articles about immigrants and schooling. (See bibliography for a complete list of readings, which are marked with an asterisk*.)

5. The students write a culminating paper (5-7 pages in length) in which they must: seek out information regarding their families' immigration (hi)stories and reflect on their own identity in relation to those (hi)stories. Using the "family immigration history" forms, provided in class, students investigate and then interrogate their family immigration history, in relation to weekly readings, lectures and seminar discussions; and reflect on how that history has shaped their identity and their experiences within schooling, particularly in relation to their sense of authenticity (being a Canadian), entitlement (having a sense of belonging and cultural agency), and identity (national, cultural, ethnic, etc.).

Chapter 10

Schooling and Socialization: Memory-work with Preservice Teachers

Judith S. Kaufman

In 1998, I began using memory-work with preservice teachers in an undergraduate course that emphasizes child development, culture, schools, and community. This is the first course that students take once they are admitted into the teacher education program, usually in their third year of college. One of the components of the course is to engage students in critically examining the reasons they have chosen to teach and their assumptions about learning and teaching. Students come into teacher preparation programs having been immersed in their profession of choice for at least 12 years. This apprenticeship of observation (Lortie, 1975) leads to a host of assumptions about teaching and learning that, when left unexamined, influence and necessarily limit preservice teachers' understanding of the scholarship on learning and teaching.

The lesson that Freud draws from Oedipus is that when we are ignorant of our past, we are determined by it. According to the myth, Oedipus ignored the inscription, "know thyself" on the Temple of Apollo at Delphi. To "know thyself" is to uncover the past so that we are freed from it. In teacher education, personal histories traditionally have been employed to help students examine and challenge their experiences in school. Personal histories reveal tacit beliefs about teaching and learning. As Knowles and Holt-Reynolds (1994) write, teachers can make real decisions about who they want to become as teachers, "only when they have an opportunity to look at the differences between what they have always believed teachers should do and what they can now envision that teachers could do" (p. 5). In this way teachers can become "crafters of their pedagogies and the conscious authors of their lives in classrooms" (p. 5).

The choice to engage students in memory-work as opposed to having them write narratives of their school experiences pivots on the distinction between memory-work and narrative. As noted in Chapter 1, narratives are often carefully crafted stories that are full of omissions and evasions. They are edited summaries of lives with causal and logical sequences of events that resonate with our present views of events and ourselves (Evans, 1999). In contrast, the discrete memories generated through memory-work are intended to illuminate moments as opposed to causal strings. These memories can interrupt the tight connection between experience and the self. In this interruption lies the possibility of new connections or reinterpretations. Discrete memories prompted by a one-word cue are no more true than autobiographical narratives, but they can point to experiences that are less shaped by familiar discourse. They can reveal an alternative discourse that rests on the forgotten or the not valued and thus, is not a part of the discursive practices of our communities. Discrete memories can present a contrast to the usual, to what we expect to remember. It is in the contrast that we see the ways in which we have constructed ourselves.

In the context of the undergraduate course, the process of how we have been socialized to think about schooling may be studied because the complexities of our early experiences in school survive in these discrete memories. The effects of economic class, ethnicity, gender, sexual identity, physical limitations, experiences of inclusion and marginality, values and ideology may be unpacked in these early memories of schooling.

An additional advantage to memory-work over personal history is that the narratives produced through memory-work are much more manageable. Because students work with a very detailed structure in producing memories, those memories are more amenable to analysis. The memories are precisely focused in the sense that all students begin with a cue such as *lunch* to narrate a discrete school memory. Knowles and Holt-Reynolds (1991), in their seminal piece on personal histories and teacher education, note that for preservice teachers, "putting their experiences in perspective helps recall, more specifically, the origins of some of their contemporary thinking about becoming teachers, an activity that helps clarify some of their newfound insights" (p. 106). Surely, this is an activity with many potential benefits; however, with memory-work, we can engage students in probing their histories in very particular ways in order to answer specific questions having to do with how we are socialized to think about schooling.

Personal histories are by definition very personal. A colleague, who has used both personal histories and memory-work, observes that with memory-work, it is much easier to move from the personal to the social when the intent is to ask questions about how we are socialized to think about some aspect of schooling. Using personal histories, students are hard-pressed to move away from the personal to consider how their experiences relate to the larger social context of schooling (Rosebud Elijah, personal communication, June 19, 2007). To be sure, the university professor has different purposes in mind when engaging students in writing personal histories as opposed to engaging them in memory-work. As Knowles and Holt-Reynolds (1991) describe, they derive numerous insights when they carefully listen to students' personal histories and this increases their effectiveness as teachers of preservice teachers. With memory-work, the goal is to engage students in collectively theorizing about a particular set of their own personal experiences and then considering how that theory can inform their thinking about appropriate classroom practices. The intent is that students move from the personal to the social to application.

Power relations and memory-work

Multiple questions regarding power are raised when requiring students to engage in memory-work. Several of the authors in this volume speak to the issue of power as they undertake memory-work with colleagues (Gannon), friends (Johnston) or research subjects (Koutroulis) and the imbalance that results when one member of a memory-work group appropriates the work of the group and writes it up for publication or as a dissertation. All members of the group may be amenable to appropriation, but if they ultimately are not a part of the writing process, the memory-work at this point is no longer collective and cannot be said to represent all the voices that were a part of the original collective.

Using memory-work in a pedagogical context presents a somewhat different set of issues related to power. My students are not freely choosing to come together to explore their experiences as a way of rethinking their participation in the social structure of schooling. In fact, many of my students come to this first course in their preparation as teachers without a significant critique of schooling. They tell stories about bad teachers and their desire to be different from those teachers. In the current climate, they are becoming aware of the onslaught and negative impact of standardized testing; however, for the most part, they have not considered the reproductive nature of schooling in relation to gender, class, ethnicity, sexuality, and ability. Nor have they considered their own participation in and appropriation of the structure of schooling. Cultivating this awareness is, certainly, one of the purposes of this course and the point of education. The question for me, particularly when I first began to use memory-work in this context, was whether it could be an effective experience for students in helping them rethink their beliefs about teaching. In the almost ten years that I have been using memory-work with my students, I believe it has been an effective and an empowering experience for many.

The course

This course meets for three hours a week, over a 15-week semester. I generally spend a total of 10-15 hours on memory-work across the term. The students spend the first few weeks generating memories and doing some preliminary analysis. I gather them into small groups of four to five that they maintain until the end of the semester. In the fifth week of class, we leave memory-work aside and begin working with the assigned readings. In the class, they read texts on learning (Bransford, Brown & Cocking, 1999), critical theory applied to the classroom (Hinchey, 1998), and inclusion and Down Syndrome (Kliewer, 1998). They also read chapters, articles and watch films on queer issues in the elementary classroom (Chasnoff, 1996; Letts & Sears, 1999), diversity and curriculum (McIntyre, Rosebery & Gonzalez, 2001), and English language learners (Tse, 2001). With about four weeks of class left, we return to the memories and engage in a more formal analysis. The students now are more prepared to theorize about their memories and connect their theories with existing ideas. Relying on their memory-work, they begin to reflect on their participation and socialization within the institution of schooling. They consider how they have been taught to think about learning, teaching and classrooms. They consider how all of this relates to existing theory and popular culture notions of schooling. The memory-work culminates in a group presentation and formal group paper that details their findings and analysis.

I introduce the methodology in the first meeting and discuss the idea that memory-work will help us examine not only how we all have been socialized to think about school, but how they, as students in school, make sense of and participate in the institution. I emphasize that students are not passively shaped by schools; but rather their beliefs and identities emerge through active involvement and appropriation. In this way, we cannot think of school as independent of our own involvement in it. I explain that their experience ultimately will form the basis for theorizing about schools and socialization. They may then scrutinize their beliefs about schooling and make conscious and informed decisions about the kinds of classroom practices they consider appropriate.

For the second class meeting, students read the introduction, methodology chapter, and a findings chapter in Kaufman, Ewing, Montgomery, Hyle and Self (2003). They write a first memory using the cue *gym*. I select the initial cues based upon their lack of context for memory-work at this point. Most recently, I asked the students to write memories cued by *gym*, *recess*, *tests*, and *lunch*. The students suggested *science project* and *times tables*. The structure for writing the memories is adapted from Haug (1987) and Crawford, Kippax, Onyx, Gault and Benton (1992). I direct students to write one of their "earliest memories; of a particular episode, action or event; related to the identified cue; in the third person; in as much detail as is possible; but without interpretation, explanation, or biography" (Kaufman et al., 2003, p. 31).

In what might be an indicator of Freud's waning influence at the beginning of the 21st century, students in the 2005[1] class responded to the chapters in Kaufman et al. (2003) reporting that they hardly thought about their memories and were surprised that their memories could be meaningful. One student wrote, "not often that I sit and think about how my past memories reflect the person that I am today." Another student observed, "I always thought that memories were simply recitations of things that happened in the past." Other comments included the following: "I have never thought about my memories in such a way. It's surprising to me that when I looked back on my memories, I actually remembered them;" "thinking about my memories and the connections to the person that I am today is something that I never really thought about before;" and "I never thought of memories having a deeper meaning." One student in the class connected with the text and wrote, "the way we can scrutinize our values and see how patriarchal values have restricted our ways of thinking and our ways of knowing the world. . . . I can see how memory-work can help get rid of the traditional patriarchal values we have imprinted [on] our socialization."

I organize the students into their memory-work groups and give them a simplified set of steps to analyze their memories. The process is based on Crawford et al. (1992). The students begin by expressing their opinions and ideas about the memories. They look for similarities and differences, and then look for clichés and generalizations. Here we spend a bit of time defining clichés and looking for examples in their memories. Finally, they think about what is missing from the memories and/or the questions that remain about the memories. They have about a half hour to work on this and then I model some whole class analysis. I invite four or five students to volunteer to read their memories. As they read, I take notes on the board and then I walk the class through a possible analysis using the procedure. Two of the gym memories appear here.

She thought gym was a little boring, but nothing was worse than sitting in class. She stands up when she's told and does the warm-up exercises with the rest of their class. She laughs to herself and her friends, as they are all making fun of the gym teacher because he was so out of shape. When it came time to play the game we all listened to the rules, but we never seemed to follow them. The gym teacher would set us up with something to do and then walk away somewhere. Once the game started, she was a little timid because she wanted to get in on the game and be an active part of what was going on, but on the other hand she would rather just watch because the boys never pass the ball anyway. They played rough and she really did not want to be a part of that. She liked gym because her and her friends could sit and talk.

She was there in the gym with her fellow classmates waiting for the teacher to come in. She was wondering what will he say when he found her not completely prepared. She remembered that all the students were supposed to have on either sweat pants or shorts and she had neither one. Just what she thought, he embarrassed her because she did not have on her sweat pants or shorts, but she has her sneakers on. He scolded her as she began to tell him the reason that she did not have on the clothing that he requested. She exclaimed she could not wear pants or shorts because of her religion. He still did not listen and sent her off crying. She had to return with her parents to straighten out this matter. She remembered because of her differences she was made a laughing stock of the gym class.

Issues related to diversity and gender were raised with these two memories. The diversity issue is apparent in the second memory, but gender comes up in two different ways in the first memory. The boys who were competitive and played rough reinforce these popular conceptions of gender. The girls who liked gym because they "could sit and talk" reinforce a popular but declining image of girls as uninterested in physical activity.

I want to raise again the issue of power in this particular context and the balance between memory-work with a collective and memory-work in a classroom. When I modeled analyzing these memories with the class, the aspects of the memories that I focused on and the questions I asked, particularly in the first memory, were about gender. I noticed the gender issue as soon as I heard the memory. In this instance, I assumed power through authority and through subtle questioning, led students to consider gender in this memory and the other gym memories. Gender is an important consideration in the course and something I want students to think about in their preparation as teachers. Ultimately, students began to see how gender played out in their experience and how that linked to theories about gender and schooling, but they did not arrive at their insights through collective probing. This is not to say that I intervened in all of their small group discussions of the memories, but I circulated among the groups as they worked and thus engaged in some amount of regulation. As a teacher, I can call this facilitation, but anytime I draw their attention to something they otherwise would not notice, I am in a sense, regulating their gaze and thus exerting power. I raise this, not to discourage memory-work with students, but to point out that when used in this way, the distinction between memory-work as a pedagogical tool and memory-work as a research methodology, is very clearly highlighted.

Prior to the next class meeting, I asked students to watch television, scan magazines, the newspaper, novels, or other media and begin to collect artifacts and ideas that indicate how "school" is represented in the popular culture. They brought images of the following: bullies, teasing, competition, pressure, standardized testing, homework, fear of math and science, the popular crowd, friends and clothing. They found from their artifacts, "only students who do well, enjoy school and students who don't do well aren't cool and experience fear and lack of self-esteem." Additional ideas included, "schools are not the way they used to be." "Teachers are to blame." "Learning is not fun and schools are not places that children want to come to." Toward the end of the semester, the students scrutinized these ideas, along with their memories and established theory as they developed their analysis of their participation and socialization in schools.

The students' analysis

With about four weeks left in the semester, students had about an hour in each class period to work in their small groups. They went back through their memories and considered their initial findings in light of the course readings and popular culture. In the remainder of this chapter, I provide a sample of the students' work with the memories.

Science project. One group's analysis of their memories cued by *science project* led to some interesting insights.

> *Mrs. Green handed out blue construction paper to each student. They were told to take out their cotton balls. They were going to make clouds! The blue paper was the sky and the cotton balls were obviously going to be the clouds. They made big puffy clouds and clumped a bunch of cotton balls together, and they made thin clouds by stretching out small cotton balls. They even colored some cotton balls and made dark rain clouds. She and the rest of her table had so much fun doing this project. She did so well on it, that she got a "Great job!" and four gold star stickers.*

The group concluded from some of their memories that they learned very little about science in elementary school and when they engaged in projects such as the one described here, they were really doing crafts, not science. From some of the literature on science teaching (Bransford et al., 2000) and positivism (Hinchey, 1998), they concluded that many teachers did not want to teach science. "This might be because they did not like science due to the way they were taught science and therefore relayed this dislike to their students. These teachers were probably taught in a positivist way which is extremely boring."

When the group probed the memories of two of its members who recalled what they had learned from their science projects, a link was drawn between the memories and research on learning. They concluded that the projects were taught in classrooms that were knowledge-centered and thus rich in diverse resources that support learning in content areas. The teachers were constructivists and taught scientific ideas that were relevant to the students' everyday lives.

Tests. The students in another group concluded about their memories cued by *tests* that they were "socialized to believe that school is about doing well and not about learning."

> *She was in second grade now. . . . She impatiently waited for the test to begin. On her desk, she had two number two pencils ready to go. . . . She thought what will happen if I do bad on this test. Will people know my score? . . . She listened for the teacher to say they can open their packets. . . . The teacher wrote the time on the board and said, "Begin." With her little heart racing, she began to fill in the bubbles. . . . She wondered what everyone else thought of the test. She looked at all of her friends to see if they were flying past the questions or if she was at the same speed as them. She was more concerned with whether or not she was behind her other friends than she was giving her full attention to the test. The teacher said time was up. She stared at her page, blank circles. She quickly filled in the remaining empty circles and handed in the test.*

The group linked their experiences of tests to Hinchey's (1998) discussion of positivist classrooms, where they learned that memorizing facts is what counts as knowledge. They observed that tests determine identity, i.e., whether you are a good student or a bad student, and thus provoke anxiety and some-times cheating. They drew connections to a film that depicted students stealing the SAT. "They do not care if they learn something from the test. . . . All they care about is doing well and getting into the school they desire."

The students in this group considered their own participation in their analy-sis of their test memories. They wrote, "Teachers fail to recognize that tests are unnecessary and do not benefit students; however they still insist on giving them and conform to the orders of their superiors." They go on to explain that teach-ers are modeling conformity for students when they administer classroom tests. "Students conform to the system and do not question their teachers as to why they give tests." Students in another group discussed the idea of "constructed consciousness" (Hinchey, 1998, p. 21) and observed that they accepted "a value system based on ranking and memorization" that placed them at a disadvantage in relation to the dominant group. Both of these ideas represent a shift in their thinking because as Haug (1987) notes, in this recognition of participation there is still "an element of resistance, a germ of oppositional cultural activity" (p. 42).

With this critique of their own experience, the students begin to apply the theory we have been discussing and can envision their own classrooms. One group discussed using portfolios and how this form of evaluation not only dem-onstrates to a "teacher and school administration what the student is learning," it allows students to self-monitor and self-assess, "which allows them to take re-sponsibility for their own work." Another group focused on how little is learned when required to memorize information for a test. The group members argued that memorization prevents many students from "transferring their knowledge." Relying on Branford et al. (2000), they concluded that teachers need to approach a topic with breadth and depth, thus allowing for mastery and a high probability of transfer.

Lunch and recess. Bullying, fitting-in, gender stereotypes, and release from the classroom were among the themes that students found in their lunch and recess memories.

> *She sits alone while she waits for her friends to return with her lunch. She was afraid to go on the lunch line to get her lunch because the boys will make fun of her. She was known to be the fat girl in the class. They made remarks so cruel that she does not want them to see her eat. . . . The lunch teachers tried to help, but they just did not understand that when you tell the teacher it just makes matters worse. . . .*

With regard to bullying, the students critiqued their own belief that bullying is natural to school. They cited research by Khosropour and Walsh (2001), which showed bullying was accepted by teachers, students and school staff. One group tied together bullying and fitting-in and pointed out that both of these stem from the way difference is devalued in classrooms and schools. Linking the discussion to our readings on disability and queer issues the students wrote, "Society wants everyone to fit into a certain mold, and when you do not fit that mold you are looked down upon, and feel like an outcast." For this group, constructivist classrooms where students are actively engaged in learning and socializing throughout the school day would accustom students to working with each other in productive ways. In the classrooms these students envisioned, difference is embraced as a value in the curriculum, literature, and discourse.

Freedom or release from the classroom was something I raised in relation to recess and the students pursued this in their analysis. One group cited a comment from one of the students who said, "Recess is the only part of the day where kids get to express themselves." Another group asked, "Why has society and the school shaped students' minds to feel one way about recess and the total opposite for subjects such as math and English?" This group referenced the movie *School of Rock* (Aversano, 2003), in which a substitute teacher transformed a boring classroom with robot-like students into a fun, interesting and exciting place because he used his knowledge and passion for rock and roll as a teaching tool. The group explained that if classrooms were centered on students, learning and community, the contrast between the classroom and recess might not be as great.

Conclusion

My use of memory-work as a pedagogical tool has evolved over almost ten years. The challenges involve helping students develop a broad enough understanding of the method so that they come away with a substantive and ultimately useful critique of their early experiences in school. I define usefulness here in the sense that they can conceptualize and implement teaching practices that reflect their critiques. Tied to this is the challenge of demonstrating to students that the method has meaning and relevance to their practice as teachers. Towards the end of the semester as they are pulling together their final analyses, many begin to see the relevance. They are able to use and connect established theory with the theory they are developing, and they can forge connections to what they are currently seeing in elementary school classrooms. I continue to be impressed by the work that my students accomplish using memory-work. In the spirit of collectives using the method, they come to regard their personal experience as a valid source of knowledge in coming to theorize about socialization and schooling, and they develop fairly sophisticated analyses based on experience, theory and popular culture.

The issue of power will always arise as a challenge when using this method. For students who are naïve to issues of power in their own lives, it is difficult to walk the fine line between facilitating the emergence of voice and shaping voice. The lesson may be trite, but it is important to stay conscious of how I might shape the discourse before the students have even had a chance to hear the sound of their own voices.

A final thought concerns impact. Using memory-work, my students have interrupted their traditional notions of schooling. In the course of a semester, they have investigated the ways in which they were socialized to think about school and as a result, many have developed new and critical ways of seeing classrooms. My hope is that what they have learned will emerge in their practice as they become teachers. However, the classrooms and schools they will enter as preservice teachers are specialized sites for socialization. Unless students have opportunities to practice and implement what they have learned, much of it will fall by the wayside. When the collective that I worked with wrote about our own memory-work, we closed with ideas that are applicable to these preservice teachers.

It is easy to fall into the old ways of seeing because we continue to live in a social world that constantly reinforces old boundaries and meanings. Nevertheless, the interruptions occasioned by this work have changed our narratives. We will continue to tell very different stories. (Kaufman et al., 2003, p. 140)

Notes
1. All of the student quotations, memories and text references are taken from the fall 2005 class.

References

Aversano, Scott (Producer), & Linkater, Richard (Director). (2003). *School of rock* [Film]. Los Angeles: Paramount Studios.

Bransford, John D.; Brown, Ann L. & Cocking, Rodney L. (Eds). (1999). *How people learn: Brain, mind, experience, and school.* Washington, DC: National Academy Press.

Chasnoff, Debra & Cohen, Helen. (1996). *It's elementary: Talking about gay issues in school* [Film]. (Available from Women's Educational Media, 2180 Bryant Street, Suite 203, San Francisco, CA 94110). San Francisco: Women's Educational Media.

Crawford, June; Kippax, Susan; Onyx, Jenny; Gault, Una & Benton, Pam. (1992). Emotion and gender: Constructing meaning from memory. London: Sage.

Evans, Mary. (1999). *Missing persons: The impossibility of autobiography.* London: Routledge.

Haug, Frigga (Ed.). (1987). *Female sexualization: A collective work of memory* (trans. Erica Carter). London: Verso.

Hinchey, Patricia H. (1998). *Finding freedom in the classroom: A practical introduction to critical theory.* New York: Peter Lang.

Kaufman, Judith S.; Ewing, Margaret S.; Montgomery, Diane M.; Hyle, Adrienne E. & Self, Patricia A. (2003). *From girls in their elements to women in science: Rethinking socialization through memory-work.* New York: Peter Lang.

Khosropour, Shirin C. & Walsh, James. (2001, April). *That's not teasing-tha's bullying: A study of fifth grader' conceptualization of bullying and teasing.* Paper presented at the annual meeting of the American Educational Research Association, Seattle, Washington.

Kliewer, Christopher. (1998). *Schooling children with down wyndrome: Toward an understanding of possibility.* New York: Teachers College Press.

Knowles, J. G., & Holt-Reynolds, D. (1994). Personal histories as medium, method, and milieu for gaining insights into teacher development: An introduction. *Teacher Education Quarterly, 21*(1), 5-12.

Knowles, J. G., & Holt-Reynolds, D. (1991). Shaping pedagogies against personal histories in preservice teacher education. *Teachers College Record, 93*(1), 87-113.

Letts, William J. & Sears, J.T., Eds. (1999). *Queering elementary education: Advancing the dialogue about sexualities and schooling.* Lanham, MD: Rowman & Littlefield Publishers, Inc.

Lortie, Dan C. (1975). *School teacher: A sociological study.* Chicago: University of Chicago Press.

McIntyre, Ellen; Rosebery, Ann & Gonzalez, Norma (Eds). (2001). *Connecting curriculum to students' lives.* Portsmouth, NH: Heinemann.

Tse, Lucy. (2001). Why don't they learn English? *Separating fact from fallacy in the U.S. language debate.* New York: Teachers College Press.

Chapter 11

From Being Excluded to Giving Voice: Memory-work, Gender and Marketing

**Mary FitzPatrick, Lorraine A. Friend
and Carolyn L. Costley**

In our academic discipline of marketing, scholars conduct research from three main perspectives. One is strategic. Traditionally, we have studied the effects of marketing variables and how to market effectively. This research typically has practical applications for businesses, non-profit organizations, or policy makers. More and more, it is applied to social marketing issues aimed to make society better off.

Consumer researchers (often housed in academic marketing departments) represent the second dominant perspective of research in marketing. More often than not, consumer researchers focus on theory building; they study all aspects of consumers and consumption for the sake of understanding consumers. Some of this research leads to practical implications for business, but these tend to be de-emphasized. These two perspectives, the strategic and the consumer perspectives, represent the practice-theory dichotomy, which has characterized marketing scholarship for much of the last century (Rust, 2006).

The third perspective has recently been christened "transformative consumer research" (TCR; Mick, 2006, p. 2). Like the strategic perspective, TCR is application-oriented. However, it differs from the strategy perspective in that TCR specifically seeks applications to benefit consumers. Recommended topics include vulnerable consumer groups (e.g., poor, illiterate), harmful lifestyles (e.g., excessive alcohol consumption, overeating, compulsive buying, materialism), consumer activism (e.g., pro-environment behavior, consumer resistance), and marketing system issues (e.g., financial planning, media consumption, privacy, product safety, product and package labeling) (Mick, 2005). This perspective has even produced journals that cater to this orientation, such as the *Journal of Research for Consumers* (www.jrconsumers.com).

We approach our research from the second and third perspectives, with hopes that it can eventually apply to marketing practices. We have used memory-work to study topics that we believe can enhance consumers' well-being: satisfaction (FitzPatrick, Friend & Costley, 2004; Friend, 1997; Friend & Rummel, 1995; Friend & Thompson, 2000, 2003), trust (FitzPatrick, 2004; Fitz-Patrick, Costley & Friend, 2005), materialism (Roper, 2000), and respect (Costley, Friend & Babis, 2005).

Our research has evolved as we experienced using memory-work. Initially, Friend (1997) focused on adding women's voices to her holistic examination of the everyday complexities of consumers' experiences with marketing. Collective and interactive aspects of the memory-work method fit the goals of her work at the time interpreting the relational meanings of service encounters. Feminist aspects of her work surfaced in 2000 (Friend, 2000; Friend & Thompson, 2000). We began focusing on relational dynamics related to gender (FitzPatrick, 2004; FitzPatrick, Friend & Costley, 2004; FitzPatrick, Costley & Friend, 2005) just as the relational marketing paradigm (Vargo & Lusch, 2004) was becoming a discussion topic. As we experienced memory-work on these topics, our commitment grew to advocate for responsible consumer-marketer relationships. For instance, we chose to study respect (FitzPatrick, Costley & Friend 2005; Costley, Friend & Babis, 2005; Costley, Friend & Tsarong, 2006) and happiness (Costley, Friend, Meese, Ebbers & Wang, 2007) so we can help consumers and service providers understand and transform their own behavior in ways that enhance both individual and societal well-being.

In this chapter, we do three things. First, we argue for the relevance of memory-work to strategic marketing research, theoretical consumer research and transformative consumer research. We briefly describe topics we are pursuing using memory-work. Finally, we illustrate in detail how we used memory-work to give voice to men, extending the application of memory-work while retaining its core philosophy. Our contribution to memory-work is this extension of its application. In particular, we advocate that memory-work can give voice to groups marginalized by the marketplace, including the academic marketplace. Memory-work can benefit marginalized groups, and we are actively at the forefront of this movement.

Memory-work as a methodology to broaden the scope of marketing research

Memory-work philosophy parallels certain ideas in the recent relational view of marketing. Much contemporary marketing thought is moving to this paradigm, which elevates consumers from objects on which to enact strategies to co-creators of value. Marketing's focus is shifting from the production and delivery of goods to relational dynamics in the process of creating value for mutual benefit. "Customers are active participants in relational exchanges and co-production" (Vargo & Lusch, 2004, p. 7). This perspective is decidedly relational and challenges marketing scholars to adopt different research methods. Memory-work is an ideal method for understanding intricate relational phenomena in a complex social system. Vargo and Lusch (2004) envision that iterative learning by both the enterprise and the consumer enhances the value derived by both parties. Hence, marketers and consumers socially construct (co-create) value. Haug et al. (1987) designed memory-work to learn about socially constructed meaning, making it an appropriate method for the maturing marketing discipline. The co-researcher approach of memory-work parallels the co-creation of value in the relational marketing paradigm. However, while the method is useful, the relational marketing paradigm does not necessarily have a critical feminist perspective. In this aspect, memory-work and marketing's consumer and transformative research perspectives are better matched.

Consumer research has been calling for broader methodological approaches, particularly feminist approaches, for decades. Memory-work appears to be a relevant answer. It incorporates a feminist ideology that counterbalances the traditional masculine capitalist approaches that the academic marketplace has favored (Hirschman, 1993). It answers the call for participatory and dialogic methods (Penaloza, 1994). It facilitates examination of the presence and nature of biological, social, and cultural categories (Bristor & Fischer, 1993). Memory-work is useful for understanding consumers, building theory grounded in narratives of consumers' lived experiences. Consumption can only be fully represented if researchers recognize "the panoply of otherness" (Stern, 1996, p. 144), and memory-work can help us do this. For a discipline internally struggling to find ways to hear consumers' voices over the voices of retailers, marketers, and academics voices, memory-work gives feminist scholars a process for giving voice to marginalized groups (Catterall, Maclaran & Stevens, 2005). We think the method can amplify not only the voices of women, but also those of other muted groups such as social classes, ethnic minorities, economically, physically or mentally challenged, and men.

Memory-work facilitates transformation and thus is ideal for transformative consumer research. It was purposely designed to emancipate by giving voice to women, challenging and reforming traditional research practice, generating new knowledge, and helping change inequitable social relations (Haug et al., 1987 Haug, 1992). The memory-work method can help consumers to understand social relations, such as those of the marketplace, which are characterized by power hierarchies, and to transform their understanding of themselves (Friend & Thompson, 2000; Willig, 2001). The memory-work process helps researchers see how power and social relations work within the research process and helps transform us as researchers.

Specifically, memory-work can broaden the marketing discipline by expanding the domains of what and who learns from the research process. Consumer researchers possess and use methodologies that help them understand phenomena such as consumers' everyday lived experiences and symbolic consumption. But, memory-work adds a way to understand the relational, social, and cultural processes that contribute to experiences and their meanings.

Treating research participants as co-researchers enables participants to see the social and cultural constraints within which they live and construct their identities. They can critique their own stories and transform their personal stories as well as advocate social changes and social policies. Hence, participants learn more about themselves than they do by participating in more traditional research projects. Both researchers and research participants learn about structures and processes underlying their identities and come to envision ways to enhance people's well-being. In addition, the philosophy on which memory-work is based advocates the use of the researcher's own voice, as a participant as well as a researcher. Incorporating researchers' voices into data collection, analysis, theorizing, and writing processes, memory-work frees researchers to draw on their own knowledge and experiences at the same time as it challenges researchers to take responsibility for their roles in the production of knowledge (Markula & Friend, 2005). In sum, the memory-work process treats participants and investigators as equals in power, responsibility, respect, and reward, which can enhance the ethics of the research.

Memory-work offers an equitable way of understanding who consumers are, how people create who they are, and in particular, how people use consumption to create identities. But it is not just stories of how people create identities that is relevant. Also important are the social and cultural structures that contribute to the process; we can learn how gender is socially constructed in the marketplace context. Furthermore, memory-work is a useful process for learning how individuals construct identities regardless of gender. This can help marketing research expand beyond superficial treatment of gender. Understanding people's experiences in the context of marketplace hierarchies has potential to broaden marketing research and transform consumers. Attending to issues of market-initiated power inequities can help citizens and policy makers transform social and cultural structures and change lives. For instance, ethnic stereotyping (a socio-cultural phenomenon) constrains the range of consuming experiences for those stereotyped and limits how one creates identity. In our research, although Sweetie, a Pacific Island participant, tried to create identity by consuming, she was fully aware of how ethnic stereotypes overrode her efforts (Friend & Thompson, 2003). Through the memory-work process, Sweetie learned how she helped facilitate and reproduce the system by not speaking out. Others in the group came to understand how the system confined Sweetie every day of her life. Learning this prompted them to social activism and they came to treat people they encounter with equal respect. Specifically, Sweetie prompted us to pursue the topic of respect in marketplace relationships (see Costley, Friend & Babis, 2005; FitzPatrick, Friend & Costley, 2004).

Examples of memory-work in consumer research

Since the mid-nineties, we have used memory-work in four consumer studies. Two were PhD research projects: one that studied women's satisfaction in clothing shopping (Friend, 1997) and one that studied trust in relationships between patients and health care providers (FitzPatrick, 2004). A master's thesis focused on materialism (Roper, 2000). Currently, an academic collaborative project is studying respect and disrespect in marketplace relationships. In this section, we provide brief descriptions of these projects and explain how each contributed to the consumer research discipline.

Satisfaction is an important consumer topic, historically examined from objective marketer-oriented perspectives. Most research on satisfaction and dissatisfaction had overlooked the subjective nature of people's lived experiences. Friend's research was designed to give voice to women in this context. This is the first known application of memory-work in consumer and marketing research. Women's shopping experiences have been trivial to marketers, but not to women. Friend's work showed how consumers' experiences, individual identities, and socio-cultural contexts contribute to satisfaction and dissatisfaction. The participants chose trigger topics of *a quick exit, exhilaration, an impulse buy, a pressure experience, an unusual experience,* and *a nasty shopping experience.* Through their work, the women learned how they supported the system, giving away their power. For example, they learned that the system teaches that beauty is power and they decided that they should not judge themselves by the standards set by others. Over the course of the memory-work, they began to tell stories of standing up for themselves and regaining their power in the marketplace. This research began a re-examination of satisfaction from diverse perspectives, particularly socio-cultural perspectives, which has introduced women's voices to the marketing literature. It offered the marketing discipline an alternative methodology for understanding concepts from consumers' points of view and illustrated a transformative agenda in action. Others have cited this research for its contributions to "an area of vital importance to marketing and consumer research—the role that marketing, consumption and gender play in the formation of identity, and the impact of identity upon consumer behavior" (Schroeder, 2003, p. 3).

Because we rarely hear individuals' perspectives on how materialism affects them and society, one of our master's degree students used memory-work to learn how individuals express, experience and view materialism and how gender colors those experiences. Groups of women and groups of men wrote about *purchasing or using a good or service that was of high materialistic value*

to you or *a time when you felt displeasure/ill-will about another person's materialistic values or attitudes*. Unlike results from other methods, the individuals
did not feel that their materialism reduced their well-being. Instead, it helped
them belong and made them happy. At the same time, they also began to wonder
about how to get out of the materialism trap. In another paradox, they were out-
raged by others' displays of materialism, but jealous. While they understood
themselves to be judged in positive ways by what they possessed, they judged
others negatively by displays of materialism. They saw injustices, greed, and
exploitation in others' materialistic displays. While it provoked thought and
stimulated ideas, this was a small project with limited analysis and theorizing
possible by the participants.

Currently, a research collaborative made up of academic researchers, similar to Haug et al. (1987), is studying respect and disrespect in the marketplace.
Friend's (1997) and FitzPatrick's (2004) memory-work narratives raised the
notion of respect as an important aspect of marketplace relationships. We set out
to learn what respect means and how it works in the marketplace context. Using
memory-work, we are seeing how respect is socially constructed and how we
create and fit into the structure depending on our different social positions (men,
women, physically disadvantaged, students, consumers, service providers).
Showing how respect works in the marketplace to enhance or diminish consumers' well-being is an important contribution.

Finally, FitzPatrick's doctoral research revealed complex interactions between gender and trust in patient-practitioner relationships (FitzPatrick, 2004).
These patterns were framed by a range of social forces, such as individualism,
consumerism, and patriarchy, at work in individuals' life worlds outside the
consulting room. She worked solely from patients' perspectives because, like
satisfaction research, health care research has traditionally excluded patients.
Memory-work gave the participants a chance to have their say. Their stories
were rich in detail and many were of profound personal significance. Some of
these stories had not been told before. Gender appeared as a social process
within individuals' construction of trust. Gender shaped the way men and
women lived and attached meaning to their interactions with their health care
providers.

Gender is not only a phenomenon worthy of research attention; Fitz-
Patrick's research found that gender also is a powerful force at work within the
research process itself. Gender shaped research processes and experiences in the
research design, recruiting, and data collection stages including effects on the
researcher's behavior. These observations raise issues that researchers should
consider. How might methods favor one gender? How does a sample's gender
composition affect the data? How does gender influence the researcher?

Memory-work with men

As marketing has moved beyond a hard capitalist orientation, memory-work has moved beyond women. Originally used with middle-class white women, scholars are now using memory-work to include a wider range of excluded voices. We learned a lot from using it with men.

From FitzPatrick's research with both women and men, we learned that research itself is a gendered process. When we treat research as a coordinated activity of interpersonal interactions and recognize that social conventions shape those exchanges, we see that participants enact gender throughout the process. Scholars from all disciplines need to be aware and sensitively respond to gender dynamics in the entire research process. This is a chance to enhance the research experience for both participants and researchers and improve the quality of our research. Furthermore, this is a chance to develop the flexibility of the memory-work method and allow memory-work to be a gendered process.

This section describes our insights into the gender dynamics in FitzPatrick's study. The views expressed here come from Mary FitzPatrick's experiences as a white middle-aged, middle-class female qualitative researcher. We present them in an intimate style because the memory-work process and the health care topic were intimate and personal for her and the men and women who participated. We present them as a reference for personal reflection and methodological dialogue.

Setting the research topic

Mary planned for two groups, one male and the other female, to be involved in a study of patients' trust in their general practitioners (GPs). Mary chose this topic because she was intrigued by the apparent reluctance of New Zealand males to visit their GPs—a reluctance reflected in our country's growing rates of cancer and cardiovascular disease for men. Furthermore, health research has tended to ignore men's everyday experiences, excluding their voices from knowledge about men's health (Watson, 2000).

Mary began the research assuming that New Zealand men would be happy to tell her about their personal experiences of health care. In the face of her bewilderment at a zero response from males, one astute colleague asked gently if she had thought about why no one had previously conducted research in this area. Realizing that she might be struggling to find male respondents who were firstly, experienced and secondly, willing to talk about a trusting relationship with their GPs, she revised the research topic, broadening it to any primary health care practitioner instead of only GPs.

As researchers, we need to ensure we design our research to be gender-friendly. Mary realized that certain dimensions of gender might mean that it is difficult for men or women to respond. To what extent can women and men understand the topic? What are the experiences in the topic? To what extent will they be at ease responding to the research questions?

Choosing the method

In determining to use memory-work for her research, Mary reflected that her initial decision had incorporated no thought about how comfortable respondents would be using the method. After several men had declined the opportunity to be involved, she began to consider that memory-work, with its emphasis on personal stories, full details of the emotions experienced, and intense group work, might be a method that New Zealand men would find difficult. Haug et al. (1987) indicated that the method should change according to the situation; there is not a hard and fast right way to use it. Noting this, Mary decided to relax the rules (see Crawford, Kippax, Onyx, Gault & Benton, 1992). She decided to say less to prospective participants about preordained processes and allow them to develop the process in ways that were comfortable for them.

Recruiting participants

Mary believed that gender had the biggest impact on the research process in this stage, where no one anticipated a gender effect. Initially, she printed 80 posters calling for research volunteers, and put them up around campus. She personally gave them to department secretaries and asked that they be posted in high-traffic staff areas such as tea-rooms, mail-rooms, photocopying rooms. Eight women contacted her in response to the poster, two of whom went on to become participants. No men responded to the posters. So she waited for a month. She talked to her supervisors about it, to friends and colleagues, to a sociology professor, a psychology professor, her dad.

> Notes from Mary's personal diary. Talk to Dad about accessing volunteers. Trying to get a sense of how to engage the interest of males in the research ads, and subsequently in the Memory Work. Dad explained that for men (particularly of his generation) breakdown in health was perceived as weakness. Having to go to the doctor was even worse! Have had a sense of this for a long time but previously had never really taken it on board. Had almost dismissed it as an over-reaction, a sympathy call, an excuse—how could it possibly be true? Men these days are educated, aware, in control of their own lives!
>
> This time I got it. Me and Dad. I had asked him specifically to tell me the truth, not what he thought I wanted to hear. My Mum and my children were away. A window in time. And in getting it, I learned I had to step out of my shoes, and into his. Properly. No token gestures. No lip-service. Started to understand the power of socialization. For how long are the "sins of the fathers" visited on the sons?? How strong is this macho attitude to illness/GPs for subsequent generations??
>
> After: I have learned about honouring the confidences invested in me by others. And learned empathy. Gentleness. And humility too.

Another recruitment plan began to take shape. Mary decided to stay out of the public places—the tea-rooms, the photocopying rooms—and go small, discreet, and private with an ad in our university's electronic events newsletter.

Because she already had enough female participants, she was able to target males specifically. Her strategy advisors at this stage were her supervisors, both specialists in consumer research; an expert in gender studies; a marketing strategist; and one of the university's authorities on teaching and learning. She was consulting with assorted sympathetic males. She designed the ad very carefully. She got rid of the fuzzy words like story, trust, and relationship. She stated one of the goals of the research was to improve health care delivery to New Zealand men. On the advice of the marketing strategist, she left out of this ad any specific details of the method. For instance, she omitted that it involved writing stories and participating in group work, that each group session would last for three hours, and that there would be five group sessions. This plan aimed to engage the men's interest enough to have them phone her, at which point she made a time for a face-to-face meeting when she proceeded to market the chance to be a part of this research.

The ad went in. Three men responded to it. A fortnight later, the ad went in again. Two men responded to it. No men signed up. She was left with two choices: Give up on men entirely or come up with another plan.

Applying both marketing and gender concepts to the experience so far, she came to realize that her product was in fact being regarded by the men as very high-risk (perceived personal risk, ego risk, social risk, time risk), and involved a considerable gender-stretch. Marketing understands that the most effective promotion for such an offering is word of mouth. So she abandoned the ad approach and concentrated solely on strategic snowballing, identifying likely participants, talking through the research project with them, and asking them to recommend any males they thought might be interested. It was hard work, but three months after the poster ads went up she had a group of four men sitting around her dining room table ready to do memory-work.

Although advice cautions researchers to ensure data quality by building trust with their participants once they have gathered, it is not the norm to think about building trust, especially doing it differently with different genders, in the recruiting process. From Mary's experience, we learned that it should be.

Implementing memory-work

Mary took the role of facilitator with the group of four males, and worked as a participant in the group of five females. Differences emerged in how the men and women used the method as they worked through the memory-work process. We believe these differences illustrate gender at work in the research process. These differences were most apparent in the groups' choices of trigger topics, the content of their narratives, and in their analysis and discussion styles.

Trigger topics. In choosing trigger topics, the men's decision-making processes seemed to be more focused and faster than the women were. The men produced very specific topics, such as *The first visit to a new practitioner*. The

women's choices of trigger topics involved more discussion and resulted in topics that were quite broad, such as *Being vulnerable*.

Narratives. The most noticeable difference between the men's and
women's narratives was in the number of characters. The women's narratives
were heavily populated, peopled with significant others, partners, spouses, children, friends; as well as the other people present at various stages in the service
encounter. In one particular narrative written by a woman about a visit to a den-
tist, there were 11 children and three adults present. The narratives of the men's
group tended to focus on the individual male, in the role of patient, and the particular healthcare practitioner involved in the encounter.

Sessions. These women and men worked the method differently. The men
decided as a group to experiment with the structure of the method. One session
they chose to begin by reading all the narratives first, then went back and analyzed them separately to see if this gave them a clearer overview of the points of
similarity and difference between their narratives. They expressed concern that
during the group work they were losing points or not developing ideas to their
full potential. They decided to use a whiteboard during the next session to record
main points. During one session, these men discussed modeling their findings so
they could clarify connections between the points they were making. Midway
through the project, the men incorporated a collective narrative, composed towards the end of the session. This helped them theorize how men (not themselves specifically) live relationships with health care providers. Such adaptations of the method by these men to make it better for them to use, are not
surprising when we consider that memory-work was designed originally by
feminist researchers as a method specifically for women.

The groups differed in the focus of their work. The men seemed to enjoy
working with their stories as a group of narratives, and collectively theorizing
how the individual stories taken together displayed male experiences of trust.
The men used a car metaphor to talk about and make sense of their health care
experiences. The women appeared to enjoy working to uncover the intimate
details of the network of relationships underlying each individual narrative. In
their discussions, the women often juxtaposed positive and negative experiences
of trust. Comparison seemed to help them express the subtle nuances.

Several times during the course of data collection, one or another of the
men would check with Mary that she was "getting what she needed," or that
they were "doing the job right." These regular checks suggested that the men
had a task-orientation toward the research. The women relished the social aspects of their sessions and it was not unusual for the session proper to start 30
minutes after everyone had arrived.

Closure. Finally, each group accomplished closure quite differently. Mary
was aware that because of the intimacies shared and the bonds established, it
was important for her to take a proactive role in managing the groups' closing
ceremonies. She very carefully scripted the words beforehand, put much thought

into choosing personal thank-you gifts, then structured the closure so that it flowed naturally and had the participants leaving with an appreciation of individual accomplishment, and pride in the value of the work they had done together. But, this was not enough for the women. "This feels really strange—I don't want to go," wailed one participant. They did not leave the room until they had made arrangements to meet for lunch six months on, an arrangement that effectively continues their relationships with each other. The men, on the other hand, seemed quite comfortable saying their final goodbyes to each other on the day.

Gender of the researcher

The researcher does gender too. While theorists acknowledge that the gender of the researcher influences participants (Denzin, 1989; Fontana & Frey, 2000; Oakley, 1981), Mary observed the inverse as well; participants' genders influence the researcher.

Because each memory-work session was three hours long, she provided food and drinks for the participants: sushi for the men and orange syrup cake for the women. Mary dressed differently for the two groups. She dressed "down" for the women's group, into jeans, to be one of the group. She chose her clothes for the men's sessions very carefully, aiming for a casual, self-assured, androgynous look.

Mary behaved differently in the two groups. She was much more relaxed as a participant in the women's group. She was continually checking up on her behavior in the men's group. Gendered responses like this between the researcher and participants underscores issues about gender effects on data. A researcher's gender can affect participants' behavior and the nature of the data they provide. In addition, researchers frame their roles and their responsibilities according to the gender of participants.

> Notes from Mary's personal diary. This is heady stuff. I felt the women's data as intense. I feel the men's quite differently—it requires all my concentration to step into their shoes—and then keep them on for any useful length of time. My lessons are to do with empathy and compassion and acceptance. I've had to work hard at them.
> [I] wondered at the difficulty I was having entering into and holding onto the men's ways of making sense of their experiences—I had to face an urge . . . to explain away their "realities" almost dismissively.

Researchers need to be reflexive. That is, we need to reflect on how our behavior as gendered individuals affects our participants' research experiences. Reflection can enhance our awareness of the gender interplay between researcher and participants, and help us manage the effects proactively and responsibly.

Summary

This research made it clear to us that research is a gendered process and that it is important to design gender-friendly research. Gender influences the process from design to recruiting and through analysis and interpretation. It affects all participants, investigators and participant co-researchers, and how they relate to each other. Although books tell us that researcher gender influences participants, no one tells us that participant gender influences researchers. Books tell us to make people comfortable and get them to trust us as researchers, but they do not say how to do that in the recruiting process.

Memory-work needs to be flexible if scholars and memory-work groups are to use it effectively and empathetically. Men and women may respond differently to research topics. Men and women differ in comfort with the memory-work method. Accepting Haug's invitation to use imagination in doing memory-work (Haug et al., 1987; Haug, 1992), we allowed a group of men to adapt its processes to their comfort. Allowing flexibility enabled us to cater to gender-related peculiarities in values. Men and women work the method differently. The women wanted to talk about their personal, individual stories. Although the men told about experiences they had never talked about before, they wanted to distance themselves from their individual stories and construct an abstracted common story, complete in its incorporation of all ideas. Men saw their participation as work and were happy to complete it; they were task oriented. Women saw their group sessions as social time; they became friends through sharing their intimate stories.

Finally, we learned that memory-work could have profound effects on the principal investigator. Mary experienced it. She adapted her behavior to the genders of the people she worked with. In particular, we learned that it requires extraordinary effort to understand and empathize with the opposite gender in research. Researchers must make that extra effort to hear the opposite gender's voice non-dismissively.

Knowing that men and women engage with memory-work in very different ways leads us to expect that every excluded group will differ in how they want to and can do memory-work. Each new group will surely bring idiosyncrasies to the ways they can do the method. Knowing this should prepare researchers to incorporate flexibility deliberately for each new group. Preparing for flexibility is likely easier to say than to do. Researchers will respond differently to different classes, races, literacies, and other ways people differ just as Mary responded differently to different genders. Some groups may even find memory-work processes entirely unsuitable to their values or abilities. This poses important challenges. How can we know how to behave respectfully? What kinds of flexibility might different groups challenge us to provide?

Comments on exclusion

Memory-work can be an excellent process for giving voice to marginalized groups. We believe memory-work contributes significantly to scholarship and to balancing inequalities in many areas. Certain groups in the marketplace are particularly vulnerable, but marketing and consumer researchers have tended to exclude them. They deserve special research attention. For example, the literature has noted we need to better understand excluded groups such as low literates (Wallendorf, 2001), juvenile delinquents (Ozanne, Hill & Wright, 1998), and ethnic minorities (Penaloza, 2000). It is clear that investigators will need to use memory-work imaginatively with special groups. For instance, working with low literate consumers suggests we may need to allow alternatives to writing stories. However, we need to respect how participants cope with what we, but perhaps not they, consider limitations. We need to work with participants to develop ways of working with the method that truly work for them. Further, both they and we must be enabled to comprehend the inequalities in the system(s).

Academic disciplines and paradigmatic perspectives within disciplines have experienced exclusion, too. "People like [that] are intellectual butterflies, flitting from fad to fad. One minute he's a relativist, then he's a Marxist, now he's a postmodernist. What next, a post-postmodernist?" (Smithee, 1997, p. 319). Although a manufactured conversation, the comment attributed to a senior marketing professor is plausible. One of the marketing discipline's leading theorists advocates that we should marginalize certain methods. "As long as mainstream marketing academics believe that advocates of qualitative methods embrace relativism, constructionism and subjectivism, mainstream marketers will, quite appropriately, be unreceptive to qualitative studies" (Hunt, 1994, p. 23). Whole academic disciplines receive inequitable treatment, too. For instance, scholars from other disciplines claim that the marketing discipline and feminist ideologies are inherently incompatible (Catterall, Maclaran & Stevens, 2000; Scott, 2000). This view reflects an anti-market prejudice, which we find repressive and outrageous. Penaloza (2000) cites her experience,

> Articulating the place for feminism in marketing is a complex task. Convincing anyone of their bias is daunting in itself, much less within a discipline like marketing that so prides itself in its objectivity and rigour. Challenges from outside are as pressing as those originating from those within our ranks. . . . I'm very uncomfortable with moralising overtones and the exclusionary tactics exhibited from time to time. Having stepped away from some social roles and worldviews, I am very disappointed to find others imposed upon me in their place. . . . As feminist marketing academics, we will continue to confront challenges from within as well as outside our ranks. While the challenges raised by our internal differences in race/ethnicity, class and sexuality are great, they also afford tremendous opportunities for growth and meaningful connections with others. (p. 40-54)

We argue that consumer research is an extremely important context for memory-work. As academics who do consumer research, we are in positions to create change by helping our students and consumers understand how marketing practice contributes to both marginalization and empowerment and by encouraging them to become activists. Memory-work allows both investigators and participants to understand how we participate in and contribute to inequities in our capitalistic society. Marginalized consumers can become more informed, less exploited, and more autonomous. Furthermore, women are in the marketplace as marketers as well as consumers. Women are more prominent stakeholders than they were in the past. Many small businesses today really do care about consumers and communities. Hence, feminist approaches are entirely relevant in this context.

Memory-work is an ideal way to see how enterprises and consumers of all types co-create value and how they bring different values to marketplace relationships. It may not guarantee transformation, but memory-work can give people the social tools to negotiate their way through the marketing system. Trying to constrain memory-work to certain paradigms or to certain disciplines dilutes its significance while it perpetuates the sort of socially-structured marginalization that it ostensibly aims to emancipate.

References

Bristor, Julia M. & Fischer, Eileen. (1993). Feminist thought: Implications for consumer research. *Journal of Consumer Research, 19*(4), 518-536.

Catterall, Miriam; Maclaran, Pauline & Stevens, Lorna. (2000). Marketing and feminism: An evolving relationship. In Miriam Catterall, Pauline Maclaran, & Lorna Stevens (Eds.), *Marketing and feminism: Current issues and research* (pp. 1-15). London: Routledge.

Catterall, Miriam; Maclaran, Pauline & Stevens, Lorna. (2005). Postmodern paralysis: The critical impasse in feminist perspectives on consumers. *Journal of Marketing Management, 21*(56), 489-504.

Costley, Carolyn; Friend, Lorraine & Babis, Patrycja. (2005). Respect in the marketplace. *Journal of Research for Consumers, 9,* Retrieved February 3, 2007, http://www.jrconsumers.colm/academic_articles/issue_9, 2005?f=5923

Costley, Carolyn; Friend, Lorraine; Meese, Emily; Ebbers, Carl & Wang, Li-Jen. (2007). Happiness, consumption, and being. In Russell Belk & John F. Sherry, Jr. (Eds.), *Research in consumer behavior, 11 (pp. 209-240).* Consumer Culture Theory. Oxford: Elsevier.

Costley, Carolyn; Friend, Lorraine A. & Tsarong, Tenzin T. (2006). Living with respect. *Latin American Advances in Consumer Research, 1,* 139-145.

Crawford, June; Kippax, Susan; Onyx, Jenny; Gault, Una & Benton, Pam. (1992). *Emotion and gender: Constructing meaning from memory.* London: Sage.

Denzin, Norman K. (1989). *Interpretive interactionism.* Newbury Park, CA: Sage.

FitzPatrick, Mary. (2004). *Trust and gender in patient-practitioner relationships.* Unpublished doctoral dissertation. University of Waikato, Hamilton, New Zealand.

FitzPatrick, Mary; Costley, Carolyn & Friend, Lorraine. (2005). On honesty and trust, gods and mortals: Gendered experiences of honesty and trust in patient-practitioner relationships. *Journal of Research for Consumers, 8,* Retrieved February 3. 2007, http://www.jrconsumers.com/academic_articles/issue_8?f=5771

FitzPatrick, Mary; Friend, Lorraine & Costley, Carolyn. (2004). Dissatisfaction and distrust. *Journal of Satisfaction, Dissatisfaction & Complaining Behavior, 17*, 117-129.

Fontana, Andrea & Frey, James H. (2000). The interview: From structured questions to negotiated text. In Norman K. Denzin, & Yvonna S. Lincoln (Eds.), *Handbook of qualitative research,* 2nd ed. (pp. 645-72). London: Sage.

Friend, Lorraine. A. (1997). Memory-*work: Understanding consumer satisfaction and dissatisfaction of clothing retail encounters.* Unpublished doctoral dissertation. University of Otago, Dunedin, New Zealand.

Friend, Lorraine A. (2000). Guilty or not guilty: Experiencing and understanding Sweetie's guilt as dissatisfaction. In J. Schroeder & C. Otnes (Eds.), *Proceedings of the Fifth Conference of Gender, Marketing and Consumer Behavior* (pp. 157-172). Urbana, IL: The University of Illinois Printing Services.

Friend, Lorraine A. & Rummel, Amy. (1995). Memory-work: An alternative approach to investigating consumer satisfaction and dissatisfaction of clothing retail encounters. *Journal of Satisfaction, Dissatisfaction & Complaining Behavior, 8*, 214-222.

Friend, Lorraine A. & Thompson, Shonna M. (2000). Using memory-work to give feminist voice to marketing research. In Miriam Catterall, Pauline Maclaran & Lorna Stevens (Eds.), *Marketing and feminism: Current issues and research* (pp. 94-111). London: Routledge.

Friend, Lorraine A. & Thompson, Shonna M. (2003). Identity, ethnicity and gender: Using narratives to understand their meaning in retail shopping encounters. *Consumption, Markets and Culture, 6*(1), 23-41.

Haug, Frigga. (1987). *Female sexualization: A collective work of memory* (Erica Carter, Trans.). London: Verso. (Original work published 1983).

Haug, Frigga. (1992). *Beyond female masochism: Memory-work and politics* (R. Livingstone, Trans.). London: Verso.

Hirschman, Elizabeth C. (1993). Ideology in consumer research, 1980 and 1990: A Marxist and feminist critique. *Journal of Consumer Research, 19*(4), 537-55.

Hunt, Shelby D. (1994). On rethinking marketing: Our discipline, our practice, our methods. *European Journal of Marketing, 28*(3), 13-25.

Markula, Pirkko & Friend, Lorraine A. (2005). "Remember when. . . :" Memory work as an interpretive methodology for sport management. *Journal of Sport Management, 19*(4), 442-463.

Mick, David G. (2006). 2005 Presidential address: Meaning and mattering through transformative consumer research. *Advances in Consumer Research, 33*, 1-4.

Mick, David G. (2005). Report on the task force on transformative consumer research at the Association for Consumer Research, Retrieved February, 3, 2007, from Association for Consumer Research Web site: http://www.acrwebsite.org.

Oakley, Ann. (1981). Interviewing women: A contradiction in terms. In Helen Roberts (Ed.), *Doing feminist research* (pp. 30-61). London: Routledge & Kegan Paul.

Ozanne, Julie L.; Hill, Ronald P. & Wright, Newell D. (1998). Juvenile delinquents' use of consumption as cultural resistance: Implications for juvenile reform programs and public policy. *Journal of Public Policy & Marketing, 17*(2), 185-196.

Penaloza, Lisa. (1994). Crossing boundaries/crossing lines: A look at the nature of gender boundaries and their impact on marketing research. *International Journal of Research in Marketing, 11*(4), 359-379.

Penaloza, Lisa. (2000). Have we come a long way, baby? Negotiating a more multicultural feminism in the marketing academy in the USA. In Miriam Catterall, Pauline Maclaran & Lorna Stevens (Eds.), *Marketing and feminism: Current issues and research* (pp. 37-56). London: Routledge.

Roper, Johanne. (2000). *Materialism and self in consumption behaviour.* Unpublished master's thesis. University of Waikato, Hamilton, New Zealand.

Rust, Roland T. (2006). From the editor: The maturation of marketing as an academic discipline. *Journal of Marketing, 70*(3), 1-2.

Schroeder, Jonathan E. (2003). Guest editor's Introduction: Consumption, gender and identity. *Consumption, Markets and Culture, 6*(1), 1-4.

Scott, Linda M. (2000). Market feminism: The case for a paradigm shift. In Miriam Catterall, Pauline Maclaran, & Lorna Stevens (Eds.), *Marketing and feminism: Current issues and research* (pp. 16-38). London: Routledge.

Smithee, Alan. (1997). Kotler is dead! *European Journal of Marketing, 31*(3/4), 317-325.

Stern, Barbara B. (1996). Deconstruction strategy and consumer research: Concepts and illustrative exemplar. *Journal of Consumer Research, 23*(2), 136-147.

Vargo, Stephen L.; & Lusch, Robert F. (2004). Evolving to a new dominant logic for marketing. *Journal of Marketing, 68*(1), 1-17.

Wallendorf, Melanie. (2001). Literally literacy. *Journal of Consumer Research, 27*(4), 505-511.

Watson, Jonathan. (2000). *Male bodies: Health, culture and identity.* Buckingham, UK: Open University Press.

Willig, Carla. (2001). Introducing qualitative research in psychology. *Adventures in theory and method.* Philadelphia, PA: Open University Press.

Index

About the Contributors

Carolyn L. Costley is Associate Professor in Marketing at the Waikato Management School in New Zealand. Her consumer research aims to inform responsible marketing practice and benefit consumers. Past research has investigated marketing influences on consumers, ethical issues in the regulation of consumer research, and respect in marketer-consumer relationships.

Bronwyn Davies is a Professor of Education at the University of Western Sydney. She is well known for her work on gender, classroom research and her writing on aspects of poststructuralist theory. More recently she has been working on strategies for writing place, enabling pedagogies and a critique of neoliberalism as it impacts on work.

Margaret S. Ewing is Professor Emerita in Zoology at Oklahoma State University. She received her Ph.D. in zoology from Oklahoma State University. Her scholarly work is primarily in the area of women and biology.

Mary FitzPatrick is Senior Lecturer in Marketing at the Waikato Management School in New Zealand. She used memory-work in her doctoral thesis, which explored trust in patients' relationships with health care practitioners. Her research interests continue to emphasize finding the consumers' voice in their lived relationships with service providers.

Lorraine A. Friend is Associate Professor in Marketing at the Waikato Management School in New Zealand. She teaches in the areas of services marketing, retailing and qualitative research methodology. Her research centers on consumption and social issues, particularly women consumers' shopping and consumption experiences. She was a participant of memory-work collectives that investigated consumer satisfaction in women's retail clothing experiences, and

materialism. She was also a co-researcher in the memory-work collective that
critiqued power in memory-work.

Susanne Gannon is a Senior Lecturer in the School of Education at the University of Western Sydney, Australia. Her diverse research interests include new
methodologies and issues of representation in interdisciplinary qualitative inquiry; feminist interpretations of the body, sexuality and lived experience; feminist poststructural theories; "creative" writing generally and writing pedagogy.
She is coeditor, with Bronwyn Davies, of *Doing collective biography: Investigating the production of subjectivity* (2006, Open University Press/ McGraw
Hill).

Frigga Haug is Professor Emerita in Sociology and Social Psychology, University for Economics and Politics, Hamburg, Germany. A founder of memory-
work research, her early leadership in the field is reflected in the groundbreaking
Female sexualization: A collective work of memory. A member of numerous
editorial boards including a series on Feminist Crime and Fiction, *Das Argument,* and the *Critical Dictionary on Marxism,* for which she is currently Coeditor, her research has ranged from automation and workculture to social science methodology and learning to other areas of women's studies. Her most recent book deals with Rosa Luxemburg's art of politics.

Adrienne E. Hyle is Professor of Educational Leadership at Oklahoma State
University. She received her Ph.D. in higher education and educational administration from Kansas State University. In addition to her research interests in
school and higher education administration, she focuses on gender issues and
organizational change.

Betty Johnston is a teacher and writer on adult numeracy and adult and teacher
education. Her research interests include numeracy practices and social justice
issues, and comparative adult numeracy education, especially in the countries of
the South. Recently retired from her position as Senior Lecturer in adult numeracy in the Faculty of Education at the University of Technology, Sydney,
she now works as a research consultant and is also Director of the New South
Wales Centre of ALNARC (Adult Literacy & Numeracy Australian Research).

Judith S. Kaufman is Associate Professor and Chair of the Department of Curriculum and Teaching at Hofstra University in New York. She received her
Ph.D. in educational psychology and statistics from the State University of New
York at Albany. Her scholarly work is in the areas of cognition, human development, and teacher education.

Glenda Koutroulis is a sociologist and a psychiatric clinical nurse who has a
private practice and also works in the intensive care unit of a private psychiatric
hospital in Melbourne. Excited by questions of epistemology and political and

philosophical debates about method, methodology and clinical practice, Glenda particularly enjoys researching and writing in such a way to further these debates. She appreciates the space memory-work offers to do this, as well as question, challenge and change in a way that in her experience with method(ology), has few counterparts.

Diane Montgomery is Professor of Education Psychology at Oklahoma State University. She received her Ph.D. in education from the University of New Mexico. Her teaching and research interests include creative studies, gifted education, Q methodology, Native American Indian education, and transpersonal psychology

Naomi Norquay is currently an Associate Professor in the Faculty of Education at York University in Toronto, Ontario, Canada. In addition to an ongoing interest in immigration hi/stories, her current research includes exploring white memories of "forgotten" black history in Grey County, Ontario, and a study of beginning teachers' career paths, life history and its methodologies.

Bob Pease is Chair of Social Work at Deakin University in Australia. His main research interests are in the fields of critical masculinity studies and critical social work practice. In the former area, his specific research focus is on men's violence against women, cross-cultural and global perspectives on men and masculinities and post-Vietnam military masculinities. In the later area, he is interested in the application of critical theories to progressive social work practice and profeminist approaches to working with men in the human services. His most recent books are *International Encyclopedia on Men and Masculinities* (co-edited, Routledge, 2007), *Critical Social Work Practice* (co-edited, Allen & Unwin, 2003) and *Men and Gender Relations* (Tertiary Press, 2002).

Karin Widerberg is Professor of Sociology at the Department of Sociology and Human Geography, University of Oslo, Norway. Her research fields include theory of science and methodology, understandings of gender (in general) and time, work and body in a gender perspective, sexual violence and law from a feminist perspective. She is presently involved in the EU-project *Changing Knowledge and Disciplinary Boundaries Through Integrative Research Methods in the Social Sciences and Humanities* and continues to work and write on issues related to the sociality of tiredness and issues related to qualitative methods–in particular memory-work.

LaVergne, TN USA
30 September 2010
199121LV00004B/38/P